Global Conflict and Security since 1945

Editors: **Professor Saki R. Dockrill**, King's College London and **Dr. William Rosenau**, RAND

Palgrave Macmillan's new book series *Global Conflict and Security since 1945* seeks fresh historical perspectives to promote the empirical understanding of global conflict and security issues arising from international law, leadership, politics, multilateral operations, weapons systems and technology, intelligence, civil-military relations and societies. The series welcomes original and innovative approaches to the subject by new and established scholars. Possible topics include terrorism, nationalism, civil wars, the Cold War, military and humanitarian interventions, nation-building, pre-emptive attacks, the role of the United Nations and other non-governmental organisations (NGOs), and the national security and defence policies of major states. Events in the world since September 11th 2001 remind us that differences in ideology, religion and values and beliefs held by a group of societies or people affect the security of ordinary peoples and different societies often without warning. The series is designed to deepen our understanding of the recent past and seeks to make a significant contribution to the debates on conflict and security in the major world capitals.

Advisory Board Members:
Professor Mats Berdal, Chair of Security and Development, King's College London
Ambassador James Dobbins, Director International Security and Defence Policy Center, RAND
Professor Sir Lawrence Freedman, Vice Principal (Research), King's College London
Professor Bruce Hoffman, Georgetown University and former Director of RAND's Washington Office

Titles in the series include:

Vesselin Dimitrov
STALIN'S COLD WAR: SOVIET FOREIGN POLICY, DEMOCRACY AND COMMUNISM IN BULGARIA 1941–48

James Ellison
UNITED STATES, BRITAIN AND THE TRANSATLANTIC CRISIS, 1963–69

Peter Lowe
CONTENDING WITH NATIONALISM AND COMMUNISM: BRITISH POLICY
TOWARDS SOUTH-EAST ASIA, 1945–65

Jon Roper
OVER THIRTY YEARS: THE UNITED STATES AND THE LEGACY OF THE
VIETNAM WAR

T.O. Smith
BRITAIN AND THE ORIGINS OF THE VIETNAM WAR: UK POLICY IN
INDO-CHINA, 1943–1950

Ken Young
WEAPONS SYSTEMS AND THE POLITICS OF INTERDEPENDENCE

Global Conflict and Security since 1945
Series Standing Order ISBN 978–0–230–52123–1 hardcover
(*outside North America only*)

You can receive future titles in this series as they are published by placing a standing order.
Please contact your bookseller or, in case of difficulty, write to us at the address below with
your name and address, the title of the series and the ISBN quoted above.

Customer Services Department, Macmillan Distribution Ltd, Houndmills, Basingstoke,
Hampshire RG21 6XS, England

Britain and the Origins of the Vietnam War

UK Policy in Indo-China, 1943–50

T.O. Smith

First published 2007 by
PALGRAVE MACMILLAN
Houndmills, Basingstoke, Hampshire RG21 6XS and
175 Fifth Avenue, New York, N.Y. 10010
Companies and representatives throughout the world

PALGRAVE MACMILLAN is the global academic imprint of the Palgrave Macmillan division of St. Martin's Press, LLC and of Palgrave Macmillan Ltd. Macmillan® is a registered trademark in the United States, United Kingdom and other countries. Palgrave is a registered trademark in the European Union and other countries.

ISBN 13: 978–0–230–50705–0   hardback
ISBN 10: 0–230–50705–0   hardback

This book is printed on paper suitable for recycling and made from fully managed and sustained forest sources. Logging, pulping and manufacturing processes are expected to conform to the environmental regulations of the country of origin.

A catalogue record for this book is available from the British Library.

Library of Congress Cataloging-in-Publication Data

Smith, T.O.
    Britain and the origins of the Vietnam War : UK policy in Indo-China,
    1943–50 / T.O. Smith
        p. cm.
    Portions of this book were published in an earlier form as "Britain and
        Cambodia September 1945–November 1946 : a reappraisal" in
        Diplomacy and Statecraft 17, no. 1 (March 2006) pp. 73–91.
    ISBN 0–230–50705–0 (alk. paper)
        1. Indochina–Foreign relations–Great Britain. 2. Great Britain–
    Foreign relations–Indochina. 3. Great Britain–Foreign relations–
    Vietnam. 4. Vietnam–Foreign relations–Great Britain. 5. Great Britain–
    Foreign relations–20th century. 6. Vietnam War, 1961–1975–Causes.
    I. Title.

    DS546.5.G74S65 2007
    327.41059709'044–dc22   2007022942

10   9   8   7   6   5   4   3   2   1
16 15 14 13 12 11 10 09 08 07

Transferred to Digital Printing in 2012

For Victor and Joan Smith

'Parents are the pride of their children'.
Proverbs 17:6

Contents

List of Maps

Acknowledgements

I am grateful to John Charmley and Larry Butler for their helpful comments and encouragement during the evolution of this project. Despite fierce competition for their time both indulged me with the opportunity to share ideas and contacts, read various sections of the draft and offered advice. Likewise, I am indebted to many scholars for their previous research in similar fields. However, I am especially thankful to those scholars that took an interest in the work and offered assistance during the early stages of what was then a PhD thesis – Stephen Ashton, Chris Goscha, Rob Holland, Ben Kiernan, Mark Lawrence, David Marr, Thomas Otte, David Roberts, Kevin Ruane, Martin Thomas, Stein Tonnesson and John Young.

To the staff, trustees and individual copyright holders of collections at Birmingham University Library, the British Library, the Centre for the Archives of France Overseas, Durham University Library, the Imperial War Museum, the Liddell Hart Centre for Military Archives, the Middle East Centre Archive Oxford, the Mountbatten Archive, the National Archives Public Record Office and the University of East Anglia Library, I owe a special debt. If I have inadvertently infringed any copyright, I trust that the owner will notify the publisher so that this maybe corrected in any future editions. I would like, also, to thank the University of East Anglia School of History Barney and Mosse funds for financing part of the travel costs to these archives, and Philip Judge for drawing the maps.

Portions of this book were published in an earlier form as 'Britain and Cambodia September 1945–November 1946: A Reappraisal' in *Diplomacy and Statecraft* 17, no.1 (March 2006): pp. 73–91, and are reproduced here by permission of Taylor and Francis Group.

My publisher Michael Strang and his assistant Ruth Ireland have demonstrated aid beyond the call of duty and shown exemplary patience, understanding and support for which I am very grateful.

Finally, I must thank my family who have contributed through their encouragement to this study. I am especially grateful to my parents for their constant love, advice and support. However, without the challenge of my wife, Elizabeth, to return to academia this work would never have been started let alone completed.

T.O. Smith

List of Abbreviations

ALF	Allied Land Force
BDCC	British Defence Co-ordination Committee (Far East)
CCS	Combined Chiefs of Staff
CIA	Central Intelligence Agency
CIGS	Chief of the Imperial General Staff
COS	Chiefs of Staff
DRVN	Democratic Republic of Vietnam
IEFC	International Emergency Food Council
JCS	Joint Chiefs of Staff (US)
JIC	Joint Intelligence Committee
JPS	Joint Planning Staff
JSM	Joint Service Mission (Washington)
MP	Member of Parliament
NATO	North Atlantic Treaty Organisation
NSC	National Security Council (paper)
OSS	Office of Strategic Services
PRC	People's Republic of China
RAF	Royal Air Force
SACSEA	Supreme Allied Commander Southeast Asia
SEAC	Southeast Asia Command
SOE	Special Operations Executive
UN	United Nations
UNRRA	United Nations Relief and Rehabilitation Administration
US	United States

Map 1 Southeast Asia

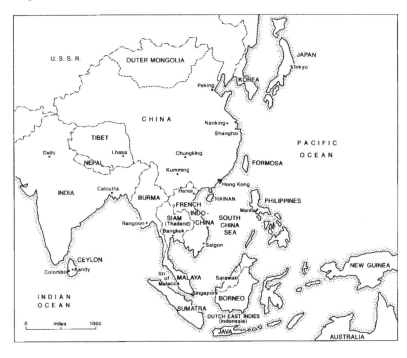

Map 2 French Indo-China

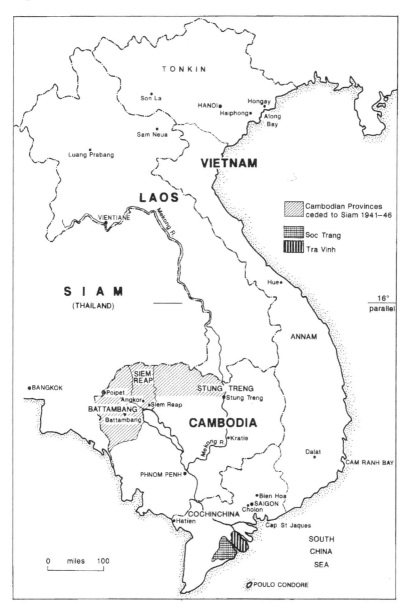

Introduction

No Influence Penetrates Deeper Than Foreign Influence
Vietnamese Proverb[1]

The origins of the Vietnam War are complex. The fact that over 30 years of conflict by the Vietnamese against Japan, France and the US has been overshadowed in the minds of the current generation of Saigon residents by the American war is unsurprising.[2] Most of the literature available has tended to regard the Vietnam War as either primarily a US military involvement in the affairs of a small Asian nation, or at best as one element in the US global power game relating to the containment of the communists. Overt US military assistance to Saigon in 1950, in response to French requests for material assistance, has influenced what has been written and emphasised the situation that President Dwight Eisenhower inherited from President Harry Truman in 1953, rather than what Truman inherited from President Franklin Roosevelt in 1945. This emphasis deflected the difficult question as to precisely when the conflict began yet enabled the concept of a single war from 1946–75 to develop, but with two halves (1946–54 and 1954–75) providing continuity between the French and US periods. The British role in the origins of the war has been obscured and confused by the volume of literature now published on the bi-lateral nature of the US-Vietnamese conflict.

The years 1943–50 were elaborate and dynamic ones for British diplomacy in Southeast Asia. This book builds upon previous scholarship and offers a fresh Anglo-centric study of British policy in Indo-China. It traces Britain's concern for Indo-China through the formative years of the Vietnam War, from Roosevelt's conception of trusteeship to the arrival of American assistance at the outbreak of the Korean

1

War. It establishes that Britain did not unilaterally restore Indo-China to France in 1945 and that Britain pursued active economic, humanitarian, military and political policies towards Indo-China until 1950 when the rigours of the Cold War forced Britain to retire and accept US leadership in the region. French Indo-China 1943–50 is an important case study for British diplomatic history. It reflects the growth of Asian nationalism, Britain's decline as a great power and the ebb and flow of Anglo-US relations. It was a period when, despite Britain's emergence as one of the victorious Allied nations from the Second World War, Britain's strategic and economic needs in the Far East required rapid rethinking as to its role and expectations in the face of a financial Dunkirk.[3] Similarly, Britain was more perceptive to the future global Soviet threat than were the other Western allies; it recognised through its own experiences that only by working with emerging Asian nationalism and ensuring a rise in ordinary people's standard of living could global security be achieved.

British foreign policy towards Vietnam ultimately demonstrates the evolution of Britain's position within world geopolitics following World War Two. It reflects the change of the Anglo-US relationship from equality to dependence. It demonstrates Britain's changing relationship, not only with its own colonies and Dominions, but also with the other European imperial spheres within Southeast Asia. British decolonisation and reliance on the Commonwealth maintained its global status and to a degree independence from the US but at the cost of being subservient to the demands of India and others. It highlights that Britain's relationship with France, particularly its desire to see France restored in Europe to protect European security and stability, enabled the French to place leverage upon Britain and an already Francophile Foreign Office regarding Vietnam. It was a colourful period full of devious characters and eccentric personalities. British foreign policy certainly did not represent a unified coherent approach towards Vietnam. Prime Minister Winston Churchill and Admiral Lord Louis Mountbatten, SACSEA, both pursued independent policies in opposition to both the Foreign Office and the War Cabinet. Later, Special Commissioner Lord Killearn and Commissioner-General Malcolm MacDonald's regional approach to Vietnamese issues was more dynamic and interactive at times than London would have liked. Major-General Douglas Gracey, ALF commander Saigon, has been unfairly vilified for his actions during the Allied liberation, but the true conspirators, through inaction, were the French whose legacy would remain with Vietnam for generations.

This book presents an in-depth examination of British foreign policy towards Vietnam. Its detail reflects: the complex international situation, competing personal agendas, the lack of consistent policies within government departments and between nations, and the relative priority of all issues in relation to the European theatre. When woven together with Britain's Southeast Asian and Indo-Chinese policies an intricate and rich tapestry results.

1
Churchill and Roosevelt, January 1943–July 1945

The origins of Britain's relationship with French Indo-China lay not in London but across the Atlantic with the US President Franklin Roosevelt. He wanted to remove Indo-China from French colonial control and to create a post-war trusteeship that would advance Indo-Chinese independence. Roosevelt did not intend to restore the European balance of power at the end of the war, but to create a new 'international order based on harmony, not on equilibrium'.[1] The Anglo-US Atlantic Charter of 1941 had been produced to calm American fears that it 'was underwriting British war aims', i.e. the return of imperialism. Article three of the charter provided indigenous peoples with the right to determine their own future.[2] Trusteeship was Roosevelt's method of sponsoring indigenous evolution towards independence. However, the Atlantic Charter 'cast the problem of post-war security entirely in Wilsonian terms and contained no geopolitical component at all'.[3] The charter was an attack on the imperial system, fuelled by economic motives.[4] Former President Woodrow Wilson, 1912–20, had advocated values of 'democracy, nationalism and the American way', these were shared by his Assistant Under-Secretary for the Navy, Roosevelt.[5]

Roosevelt's policy of trusteeship for Indo-China demonstrated US commitment to national self-determination as stated in the Atlantic Charter. It was 'a test case for anti-colonialist resolve' by an anti-imperialist who had sardonically remarked to Churchill that 'the British would take land anywhere in the world even if it were only a rock or a sand bar'.[6] Trusteeship occupied a special place in Sino-US relations, because Roosevelt envisaged China as one of the four world policemen predestined to protect post-war peace and security.[7] Britain was not in favour of a US policy that made China a great power and, due to

Britain's own colonial interests, doubted the transparency of Chinese intentions for Southeast Asia especially as a trustee.[8] Roosevelt 'was a juggler' and 'ambiguity was part of Roosevelt's character'. He held Wilsonian ideals but 'hated taking decisions'.[9] Lord Halifax, British Ambassador to the US, noted that 'the President was one of the people who used conversation as others of us use a first draft on paper'.[10] The Foreign Secretary Anthony Eden compared Roosevelt to 'a conjuror, skilfully juggling with balls of dynamite whose nature he failed to understand' but Eden's 'scepticism about the President blinded him to Roosevelt's devious ways of getting things done'.[11] Reciprocally, Roosevelt expressed 'confidence in Mr Churchill, but not in the British Foreign Office'.[12] The US Secretary for War, Henry Stimson, remarked: 'The President is the poorest administrator I have ever worked with' but noted also that he was 'a tough customer'.[13]

An Anglo-US alliance was a crucial facet of Churchill's wartime strategy. He had worked like 'a beaver' and sought to be on 'the most intimate terms' with Roosevelt who, when Churchill was in the US during 1942, visited 'him [Churchill] in his bedroom at any hour' and as Churchill said was 'the only head of state whom he, Winston, has ever received in the nude'. However, Churchill was selective with his work ethic; in dealing with the Lend-Lease Agreement the British Embassy in Washington doubted that he would read the relevant telegrams let alone 'apply his mind to it'. Likewise on the issue of post-hostilities planning, Churchill was 'pretty bored with anything except the actual war'.[14] He wrote to the Cabinet and expressed caution against promises made concerning post-war arrangements that might not be fulfilled when the final victory materialised.[15] Not an advocate of trusteeship or a new world order, he lambasted Eden: 'Nobody cares a damn about the United Nations'.[16]

Churchill's strong anti-trusteeship policy was shared by many in Britain's coalition government. The Labour Home Secretary, Herbert Morrison, ascribed that 'it would be like giving a child of ten a latchkey, a bank account and a shot gun'.[17] Nevertheless Churchill was myopic and forgetful about Britain's Indo-China policy: he refused repeatedly to act in any direction that would result in conflict with Roosevelt and create a crisis in the Anglo-US relationship. Initially 'his instinct was to see Roosevelt's views on Indo-China as an aberration, ... [and] Churchill's instinct was the governing factor in British policy'.[18] However, worried about his place in history, he was eventually galvanised into action following the 9 March 1945 Japanese *coup d'état* in Indo-China. Had the Foreign Office dictated British Indo-China policy from the outset then probably Anglo-US diplomacy and the special relationship would have developed along more confrontational lines. Churchill had to tread carefully; he was the fulcrum of Anglo-US relations, pushed by US anti-imperialism and pulled by Foreign Office support for colonial spheres of influence based upon imperial association; he cut a lonely, isolated and out of touch figure.

Churchill was not aided in his Anglo-US alliance by his tempestuous – and the Foreign Office's more placid – patronage of the Free French leader General Charles de Gaulle. At the Allied Casablanca Conference in January 1943 Roosevelt found de Gaulle arrogant.[19] De Gaulle's 'autocratic temperament and his constant practice of playing off Britain against America' did not endear him to the US or Roosevelt and threatened Anglo-US relations 'through the belief that de Gaulle enjoys full British backing' despite the actuality that he did not 'enjoy the unqualified support' of the government.[20] French capitulation to Germany in Europe and Japan in Asia had not endeared France to Roosevelt.[21] Roosevelt felt that de Gaulle advocated a 'process of infiltration'. He used the example of French membership of the Allied Commission for Italy to complain to Churchill that 'his [de Gaulle's] presence there will, as we know from experience, cause controversy and more trouble with the French Committee'. Reflecting on the constraints of his British ally and the pro-French nature of the Foreign Office, Roosevelt sympathised with Churchill 'I know what problems you have with your own Foreign Office', and lamented 'I wish you and I could run this Italian business. We would not need any help'.[22] Roosevelt continued to remain at odds with de Gaulle. Six months later he wrote to Churchill concerning the arrangements for the supply of supplementary currency to France and castigated 'it seems clear that Prima Donnas do not change their spots'.[23] Roosevelt believed that de Gaulle represented '"acute and unconquerable" nationalism' and that France as a nation no longer had the status of a great power to shape the world – a view shared by his Secretary of State, Cordell Hull, and the State Department.[24] US Indo-China policy served to accelerate Roosevelt's policy of colonial liberation and to punish the French.[25]

Roosevelt's grand scheme for colonial territories was not limited to Indo-China but also included parts of the British Empire, i.e. Hong Kong, and other fanciful directions, i.e. the 'idea of Australia purchasing Timor from Portugal'.[26] Hull would later guarantee to Britain a US 'agreement to respect Portuguese sovereignty in all Portuguese colonies'.[27] But Roosevelt was not embarrassed by previous US guarantees concerning the 'territorial integrity of the 1939 French Empire' made to Vichy France and Generals Giraud and de Gaulle; or a similar statement made after the Japanese attack on Pearl Harbor that guaranteed 'an unqualified undertaking that they would support the return of Indo-China to France in all circumstances'.[28] These pledges had been made on behalf of Roosevelt and he had duly informed Churchill of this US policy.[29] Eden noted the contradictions between US pledges and Roosevelt's trusteeship statements on Indo-China. He briefed Churchill that Roosevelt now made 'little of guarantees about the integrity of the French Empire in general' and therefore had 'little doubt that the French would contrive a "leak" before long'.[30] Indo-China was the political side-show to wartime Allied military policy but Britain needed to develop a coherent policy that would protect its own interests and navigate unforeseen dilemmas.

Trusteeship and French participation in the war in the Far East

On 7 January 1943, at a meeting of the US Joint Chiefs of Staff Roosevelt expressed 'grave doubts' about restoring Indo-China to France, and 'urged the British not to make further promises to restore the French Empire'. Lord Halifax spoke with Hull who was embarrassed at the State Department's exclusion from some of Roosevelt's personal 'predilections'.[31] Churchill despatched Eden to the US for three weeks 'in order to facilitate the establishment of closer relations between the State Department and the Foreign Office'.[32] On 24 March Eden and Halifax met with Sumner Welles, Assistant Secretary of State. Welles elaborated that France should be separated from Indo-China due to 'world interest in the quality and direction of their administration' and he hoped that Britain would be prepared to hand Hong Kong back to China.[33] Two days later Eden and Halifax met Roosevelt at the White House. Roosevelt raised the question of trusteeship for Indo-China; he believed that the actual details concerning trusteeship should be arranged in the 'ironing out of things after the war'. Eden felt that Roosevelt 'was being very hard on the French'.[34] No doubt Roosevelt held that the US, as the major creditor to the European colonial powers, would be able to dictate the form of the new world order.

On his return to Britain, Eden reported to the War Cabinet. He stated that discussions about France were 'of a somewhat varied nature' and that Hull 'clearly hated General de Gaulle'. The US was apparently against the creation of a single French Civil Authority in exile to deal with French issues and preferred to deal with each rival leader,

Generals Giraud or de Gaulle, separately. Eden maintained during his stay in the US that Britain supported the opposite view. Meanwhile a meeting between Eden and the Chinese Ambassador to the US had yielded the assurance that China possessed no territorial ambitions in Siam, Indo-China, Burma or Malaya.[35] This was a significant statement as Britain feared Chinese encroachment in South and Southeast Asia which contained large indigenous Chinese populations.

The Foreign Office believed that the US motivation behind trusteeship and the Atlantic Charter was 'really the old Wilsonian principle of self-determination dressed anew'.[36] Likewise, the Foreign Office was carefully studying events concerning the forthcoming presidential election: 'Roosevelt's attitude is perhaps largely due to his fear that Wilkie next year will mobilise American anti-imperialist sentiment against him'.[37] It predicted that Roosevelt would argue that 'the Atlantic Charter is the document governing the post-war world', but concluded that the 'American conception of the world is not static, and the President might contend that it is for him to interpret and secure the realisation of this as and when appropriate'.[38]

De Gaulle established a committee to consider the Indo-Chinese question for the allies and French participation in its liberation.[39] The French requested representation on the Allied Pacific War Council. In response the State Department cautioned that 'the President may possibly be averse to the idea' and sought Britain's perspective.[40] Churchill decided that the Foreign Office had 'better leave this quiet for a bit. No need to reply for some days'.[41] However, Sir Alexander Cadogan, Permanent Under-Secretary at the Foreign Office, lobbied Churchill for French representation at some Pacific War Council meetings.[42] Churchill remained unmoved: 'No need for action yet'.[43] Cadogan persisted: 'A refusal would confirm the French in their present suspicions that neither we nor the Americans (particularly the latter) wish to see them resume sovereignty over Indo-China. This would add to their sense of frustration and wounded pride'. Considering the US attitude to the restoration of colonies to their former colonial powers Cadogan concluded that 'there is much to be said for the colonial powers sticking together in the Far East'. The French, not content with mere representation on the Pacific War Council, now requested permission to send a military mission to SEAC.[44] Churchill replied that 'this can certainly wait'.[45] When asked three days later if he wanted to mention the French request to Mountbatten, Churchill noted: 'No nothing doing while de Gaulle is master' and instructed Eden: 'We should adopt a negative and dilatory attitude'.[46] The Foreign Office, Dominions Office and Colonial Office all believed that British policy towards French possessions should be made in consultation with the Dominions. They agreed that 'above all, we must avoid a position in which the Dominions side with the US against us'.[47] On 30 November Clement Attlee, Deputy Prime Minister, wrote to Churchill for guidance and clarification as to the Prime Minister's position regarding the future of Indo-China.[48] Churchill answered 'Britain does not pre-judge the question of status of Indo-China any more than that of … British possessions' and summarised his perception of Roosevelt's position that the 'President at the moment contemplates some changes in status of Indo-China but he has not yet formulated any definite proposal'.[49] Briefing the Cabinet on the outcome of the Cairo and Tehran Conferences (November–December 1943) Eden indicated that Indo-China would be 'under some kind of international control'. He noted with interest that the Russian Prime Minister Josef Stalin 'had been highly critical of the French' at the Tehran Conference, declaring that 'the French had not really tried hard in the war and he obviously regarded the state of France as rotten'.[50] Stalin had been particularly shrewd as it was he rather than Roosevelt who had raised the question of Indo-China and 'he played most effectively on the President's … fears of post-war French stability and resentment against General de Gaulle' as well as 'Roosevelt's Wilsonian beliefs in national self determination'.[51] Stalin asserted that he and Roosevelt were 'of the same mind' that 'France should not have all her possessions restored to her'.[52]

De Gaulle continued to develop an Indo-China policy and issued a declaration affirming French sovereignty but sanctioning 'collective development, in the form of a "free and close association between France and the Indo-Chinese peoples"'.[53] Nevertheless, Roosevelt proceeded to concoct his own policy for Indo-China. On 16 December in Washington at a meeting with Chinese, Turkish, Egyptian, Russian, Persian and British diplomats he announced that:

He had been working very hard to prevent Indo-China being restored to France who during the last hundred years had done nothing for the Indo-Chinese people under their care. Latter were still as poor and as uneducated as they had ever been and this state of affairs could not be allowed to continue. He thought that Indo-Chinese who were not yet ready for elective institutions of their own should be placed under some United Nations trusteeship, which would take them toward the stage when they could govern themselves.[54]

Churchill informed Eden that although he had often heard Roosevelt's opinions on Indo-China he had 'never given any assent to them' as they were a matter for 'the end of the war'. Churchill advised that the US could not 'take territory from France forcibly without agreement with France after a French Government has been formed on the basis of the will of the French people'. Again a matter for the conclusion of the war, due to the need for the liberation of France and subsequent elections. Churchill requested from Eden copies of the declarations already made by Roosevelt on 'the integrity of the French Empire'.[55] Eden considered that 'a note of caution' should be raised in Washington. He proposed that Halifax should consult with Hull to ascertain whether Roosevelt's remarks represented 'a concerted White House–State Department policy'. Eden deemed it important for Britain to have a 'definite policy on this matter', especially as the French had established a military mission in Chungking and were keen to develop one in SEAC, both of which could result in French forces being deployed in the Far East.[56] Churchill agreed but still considered that 'questions of territorial transfers should be reserved till the end of the war'.[57] When Halifax spoke to Hull in Washington, Hull 'knew no more about it than I did'. Halifax concluded the 'President's remarks did not represent any settled policy in which [the] State Department has concurred'.[58]

The Foreign Office remained vehemently critical of Roosevelt and US policy which it felt was driven by a combination of a delusion of power and dollar imperialism.

> President Roosevelt is suffering from the same kind of megalomania which characterised the late President Wilson and Mr Lloyd George (the latter to a lesser extent) at the end of the last war and proved the former's undoing. ...
>
> I trust that we shall not allow ourselves to quarrel with the French, without being on very strong grounds, for the benefit of a United States President, who in a year's time, may be merely a historical figure.
>
> If Indo-China is not restored to France on the ground that 'the poor Indo-Chinese' have had no education and no welfare (I have never heard that the Indo-Chinese were anymore unhappy than the share croppers of the Southern United States), the Dutch and ourselves may later on be told that the oil resources of the Netherlands East Indies and Borneo have never been properly developed, nor the rubber resources of Malaya, that the natives are insufficiently

educated according to Washington standards and that these territories must be placed under United Nations trusteeship (perhaps with United States oil and rubber controllers).[59]

The Foreign Office was still sceptical of Chinese motives regarding Indo-China. Likewise, it held that it was unrealistic to prevent France from taking some part in the war in the Far East. The French had 'officers with a knowledge' of Indo-China, which neither Britain nor the US possessed, and could 'provide a substantial number of troops from Africa' in their own ships. In response to a French offer of assistance, it would be difficult to explain to the British public a reply of: '"No, thank you; we prefer to have more of our own soldiers killed"'.[60] The Defence Committee had decided already that it was imperative for a French Mission to be established, as soon as possible, at SEAC to avoid any risk of incidents developing with French troops on the Sino-Indo-China border.[61]

Eden broached the subject of Indo-China again with Churchill on 11 January 1944. Eden had received a report from the British Embassy in Chungking that was fearful of British relations with France and 'post-war collaboration in Western Europe' and concerned about the possibility of a precedent being established which could also be applied to British colonial possessions if Roosevelt succeeded with his designs for Indo-China. The report cautioned that the Chinese would welcome UN trusteeship of Indo-China through which they might be able to extend economic control.[62] Churchill decided that the Foreign Office should pursue the Indo-China issue with the State Department 'and leave till a later stage any direct communications between me and the President'.[63] This was not a shrewd ploy by Churchill to appeal to the State Department. A parallel State Department policy on Indo-China to that of Roosevelt's had not begun to evolve in earnest until spring 1944.[64] Instead it was further evidence of Churchill's desire to avoid the Indo-Chinese issue and thereby a crisis in the Anglo-US relationship.

On 18 January Roosevelt met with Halifax in Washington. Roosevelt appeared not at all embarrassed by his position on Indo-China, jovially retorting that he hoped his ideas would be reported back to the French. In presenting his case for trusteeship Roosevelt confirmed, contrary to Churchill's doubts, that Chinese intentions were that the President Chiang Kai-Shek did not want to acquire Indo-China and that Stalin regarded trusteeship as the best solution. Roosevelt emphasised that he had 'spoken about it 25 times but the

Prime Minister has never said anything'. Did Roosevelt really understand Churchill's position? Churchill desired to maintain Britain as a world power; the Anglo-US relationship was of importance to him, but he showed a lack of interest in post-hostilities planning. If Roosevelt had understood these issues then Churchill's silence should not have been a surprise. Roosevelt denied to Halifax that his previous guarantees about the status and integrity of the French Empire had any bearing on the question of Indo-Chinese trusteeship. Halifax was annoyed with Roosevelt's stance and hoped that he would not hold a 'monologue' with Churchill. When Halifax raised the question of a precedent being established which could be applied to British colonies Roosevelt dismissed the idea and defended the British colonial position, apparently 'we and the Dutch had done a good job but the French were hopeless', Halifax noted. Halifax responded with the need to rehabilitate France as a great power but Roosevelt retorted 'tell Winston I gained or got three votes to his one as we stand today' (China, Russia, and the US versus Britain). Halifax was left with the impression that Roosevelt 'has got this idea in his mind a bit more than is likely to be quite wholesome'.[65] The Foreign Office continued to 'resist strongly any proposal to consult the Chinese but not the French'.[66]

Churchill remained committed to a Europe-first strategy regarding wartime policy and activities.[67] Maberly Dening, Chief Political Adviser to SEAC, questioned the purpose of SEACs role within a solely US Far East strategy in a note to the Foreign Office. 'For the Southeast Asia Command there appears to be no role at all, except to cover General Stilwell's supply route and to employ British forces at the maximum disadvantage to themselves with minimum effect upon the enemy'.[68] The War Cabinet Post-Hostilities Planning Sub-Committee remarked that the actions of the Japanese in seizing Southeast Asia demonstrated the threat to India, Australia, New Zealand and other British possessions in the region of a weak Indo-China. It held that Britain would not be able to meet this threat in the future without the assistance of the US. Roosevelt's position indicated that the US intended participation in the defence of Indo-China, but if the US deprived France of Indo-China the resentment 'would seriously endanger our post-war co-operation' with France and this could result in an 'unfriendly France' hindering British security in other regions. The Committee concluded that US co-operation in the defence of Indo-China should be encouraged and that in order not to offend the French this should be achieved by the establishment of UN bases.[69]

The Foreign Office persisted in its criticism of Roosevelt's opinions on Indo-China: 'this is one of the President's most half baked and unfortunate *obita dicta*'.[70] Eden agreed.[71] On 24 February the War Cabinet approved a memorandum by Eden on the future of Indo-China and French Pacific possessions; this included papers by the Foreign Office and the Post-Hostilities Planning Committee and concluded that Britain 'should aim at continuance of French sovereignty'. Lord Cranborne, the Dominions Secretary, was requested to consult the Dominions in order that an 'Imperial Policy on this matter' could be formulated.[72] However Churchill was cautious of raising the matter with his US ally, preferring not to discuss the Indo-China issue with Roosevelt before the presidential election in case Roosevelt used it to pander to the anti-imperial nature of the US press and electorate. Churchill did not believe the matter to be urgent and considered Roosevelt's opinions 'particular to himself ... chance remarks ... made in conversation'. He held that 'nothing is going to happen about this for quite a long time' and thus the Dominions' Prime Ministers could be consulted when they arrived in Britain in two months.[73] Cranborne pressed Churchill for greater immediate consultation with the Dominions.[74] Churchill agreed but only after he had first approved any telegram to the Prime Ministers, thereby preventing an instant approach. Oliver Stanley, Colonial Secretary, expressed his concern about US hypocrisy over trusteeship and its economic benefits.[75] Eden would later note in September 1944 that the Dominions still had not been consulted about Britain's Indo-China policy, although Australia had told Hull in February that it was in favour of a French return.[76] However, when Roosevelt's digressions concerned the future of the British Empire Churchill offered a forthright defence: 'my irrevocable principle is that no Government of which I am the Head will yield one square inch of British territory or British rights in any quarter of the globe except for greater advantages or moral scruples'.[77]

Mountbatten noted how 'determined' the French were to regain Indo-China. He stressed the importance of accepting a small French mission being established at SEAC lest the French concentrate their efforts on China Theatre headquarters at Chungking instead and thus diminish British influence in the region.[78] Churchill persisted in his inaction, instructing the Foreign Office, 'It will be better to delay. One can always concede'.[79] General Hastings Ismay, Chief of Staff to Churchill in his role as the Minister of Defence, instructed the Foreign Office 'For the time being, therefore, there is nothing that we can do'.[80] Cadogan reflected on Churchill's intransigence, 'I can only infer that the P.M., knowing as I do President Roosevelt – and Admiral Leahy's – sinister intentions regarding Indo-China, is careful not to do anything that might imply our recognition of French input there'.[81] Lord Selborne, responsible for the SOE which would conduct clandestine operations in Indo-China, pressed both Churchill and Eden on the issue of the French mission to SEAC. He highlighted that the delay would damage SOE operations and add to French suspicions of British intentions in view of Roosevelt's opinions.[82] Eden supported the argument but Churchill was not going to be pushed into taking any action. He lambasted Eden:

> It is hard enough to get along in SEAC when we virtually have only the Americans to deal with. The more the French can get their finger into the pie, the more trouble they will make in order to show they are not humiliated in any way by the events through which they have passed. You will have de Gaullist intrigues there just as you now have in Syria and the Lebanon.
>
> Before we could bring the French officially into the Indo-China area, we should have to settle with President Roosevelt. He has been more outspoken to me on that subject than any other colonial matter, and I imagine it is one of his principal war aims to liberate Indo-China from France. Whenever he has raised it, I have repeatedly reminded him of his pledges about the integrity of the French Empire and have reserved our position. Do you really want to go and stir all this up at such a time as this?
>
> I do not like the idea of Mountbatten's command becoming a kind of minor court with many powers having a delegation there. The fact that the Dutch have a section is because we are studying those countries which they own with a view to attack and we certainly have no plans in prospect for liberating Indo-China.
>
> ...
>
> It is erroneous to suppose that one must always be doing something. The greatest service SOE can render us is to select with great discrimination their areas and occasions of intervention.[83]

Nevertheless, on 1 June Mountbatten raised the matter again with the COS. He held that 'it is militarily necessary to obtain the maximum co-operation of the French in pre-occupational work in Indo-China'.[84] The COS raised the issue again with Churchill and enquired if the issue was still to be conceded.[85] Churchill wrote to Major-General Leslie Hollis, War Cabinet Secretariat at the Ministry of Defence: 'Is there any reason why we should not wait and see how we finish up with de Gaulle'?[86] The COS agreed that there was no need to press the issue and informed Mountbatten: 'On the instructions of the Prime Minister a decision is to be deferred for the time being'.[87]

Brendon Bracken, British Minister of Information, remained cynical about Roosevelt's attitude and motives: 'Now that Roosevelt is talking to God he may be even more unreasonable. We have got to tell the gentleman that Europe cannot be wrecked by his Dutch obstinacy'.[88] Reflecting on Roosevelt's relationship with de Gaulle, Churchill sardonically quipped: 'I think it would be a good thing to let the President know the kind of way de Gaulle interprets friendliness. I have now had four years' experience of him, and it is always the same'.[89] However, Bracken believed that Churchill was 'becoming more reasonable about the French', although this did not spare himself, British officials or the French from subsequent Churchillian outbursts.[90] Duff Cooper, British Ambassador to France, so 'irritated the Prime Minister by his extreme Francophilism ... and by his admiration for de Gaulle' that Churchill mocked '"a cat purring at the feet of de Gaulle"' and added that 'he could not recollect ever meeting a decent Frenchman'.[91] Bracken was called a 'lackey of the Foreign Office' and slurred as '"a Foreign Office hack even more ignorant than its normal inhabitants"'.[92]

On 28 July, due to the changed military situation following D-Day and the destruction of Vichy France, the War Cabinet COS Committee reconsidered the question of a French mission being established with SEAC.[93] As the relationship between the French colonists and Japanese in Indo-China began to deteriorate Churchill agreed to a French military mission as well as the French Corps Leger military unit being established at SEAC.[94] The COS placed proposals before the US COS for French participation in the war against Japan.[95] The US COS re-evaluated the issue and consequently agreed with the French request to participate in the war against Japan, except in the area of political warfare which they believed should be limited to the SEAC area.[96] However, Roosevelt ruled that 'approval could not be given to any of these proposals until the President had the opportunity to discuss them with the Prime Minister at their next meeting'.[97] The Foreign Office noted on the issue of SOE work in Indo-China that 'If we were a nation of angels we would still be suspected by some Americans of having sinister motives for anything we did' and regarded the issue as a 'molehill' rather than the 'mountain' the US insisted.[98]

On 14 August, without Churchill, the War Cabinet considered further the issue of the future of Indo-China as this would be one of the topics likely to be discussed between René Massigli, French Ambassador, and Eden during forthcoming talks. The Cabinet affirmed its position of 24 February – the continuance of French sovereignty – and approved Eden's recommendation 'to leave the initiative to M. Massigli on this subject as far as possible'.[99] Ten days later Eden met Massigli at the Foreign Office. Massigli observed that the US attitude towards Indo-China 'had not been cleared up' and that during de Gaulle's recent talks with Roosevelt the President 'had been very vague'. Eden indicated that in the interest of international security Britain was prepared to 'give facilities where others did the same' but would not consider any withdrawals; it was a policy of 'what we have we hold'. He asked Massigli that if Britain undertook a policy of consultation and a joint use of bases as part of an international security process then would France be prepared to do likewise? Massigli personally believed that France would not object to such a policy on the understanding that this did not relinquish sovereignty.[100] John Colville, Churchill's Private Secretary, sent a message to Churchill at the second Quebec Conference (September 1944) to remind him to discuss the French mission to SEAC with Roosevelt.[101] However, despite Churchill's new-found support for such a venture, he strangely 'did not have an opportunity of raising this matter with the President' in Quebec; nor did he raise the matter, following a further reminder, during his visit to Roosevelt's home in New York.[102]

At the same time, Mountbatten held that pre-occupation operations could not begin until questions concerning Indo-China, SEAC and China Theatre boundaries had been resolved.[103] Churchill informed Eden and Ismay that Mountbatten's enquiry should be dealt with by the COS who decided that this could 'remain unsettled a little longer'.[104] Mountbatten considered that Britain was already committed to French participation in the war in the Far East as Britain had accepted a French battleship to be deployed against the Japanese. He believed that if delays concerning the French mission resulted in China Theatre control of Indo-China then this would restrict not only China Theatre operations but also British policy in the Far East.[105] Eden observed: 'This is all very well but <u>PM</u> may take same view as President'.[106] Mountbatten and Eden remained both in contact and in agreement over the participation of the French in the war in the Far East.[107] Eden was embarrassed with Anglo-US inability to satisfy French inquiries.[108] A Foreign Office minute suggested that the continued delay could result in the French mission being established in the China Theatre rather than SEAC, thus diminishing British influence. It requested that Churchill telegram Roosevelt and urge him to make a decision.[109] Eden agreed with both the assessment and the request.[110] In the meantime Britain permitted 'a temporary personal visit' by French General Roger Blaizot to Mountbatten and SEAC.[111]

The French eagerly awaited acceptance of their participation in the war in the Far East but the US COS continued not to respond to British COS proposals. The situation appeared to be locked in a stalemate requiring resolution at a higher level. Churchill finally seemed to want to resolve the dispute. He asked Eden 'had we not better talk this over in Cairo with Mountbatten'? Yet, aware of Roosevelt's likely reaction to the proposals, Churchill appeared reluctant to act. He advised Eden to 'draft a telegram to the President at your leisure'. Churchill would have to approve any draft and did not intend to do so in the near future. He reasoned with Eden that Roosevelt would 'not like the French being let into Indo-China, and we had better keep this particular item till other more urgent matters have been settled' especially as the situation at SEAC 'shows no hope of advance before the beginning of 1946', although he lamely attested 'I am trying to improve this'.[112] Hollis wrote to Churchill advising that the COS recommended that Churchill ask Roosevelt to agree to the French mission and participation in the war in the Far East.[113] Eden agreed with the COS and the next day, with pressure mounting, Churchill made a decision. He instructed Eden to 'proceed as the Chiefs of Staff propose' for the retention of the French mission to SEAC but sought to avoid a conflict with Roosevelt by ruling: 'There is no need for me to telegraph to the President'.[114]

Meanwhile, during September, the French requested to be supplied with an aircraft carrier which they would operate off the coast of Indo-China.[115] Churchill again appeared reluctant to make a decision despite having already made one on the French military mission to SEAC. Due to the 'heavy pressure of work' he directed, three months later in December, that 'it be brought up on a later occasion' as he had 'not yet had time to look at it closely'.[116] The US again sought to avoid any commitment to employ French forces in the Far East. The JSM in Washington maintained that political as well as naval considerations were directing the US response. The British Admiralty believed that it could possibly assist in the refit of French naval vessels. The alternative was for Churchill and Roosevelt to make 'a clear cut decision' but as it proved impossible to supply the French with ships or conduct refits, a decision did not have to be made for the time being.[117] Churchill agreed with the delay and reflected 'I do not expect the French will like it much. If they do not agree, the matter must be settled between the Heads of Government'.[118] The stark warning was that this would involve Roosevelt.

In November rumours circulated in Washington that Mountbatten would have to be recalled due to his bad relations with an unspecified US General.[119] Lt.-General Joseph Stilwell, Mountbatten's deputy at SEAC, the US commander of Chinese armies in Burma and Assam and also Chief of Staff to Chiang Kai-Shek, had had a troubled relationship with Mountbatten. 'Vinegar Joe' Stilwell was a zealous 'enemy of imperialism', and an Anglophobe with an 'equally stark contempt for China'. He had been replaced in October by US Lt.-General Al Wedemeyer who had previously possessed good relations with Mountbatten as his Deputy Chief of Staff. However, Wedemeyer now regarded his role as Chief of Staff to Chiang Kai-Shek to defend Chinese interests even to the detriment of SEAC.[120] By 13 November the Foreign Office determined it was important to resolve the problems that continued between Britain and the US over clandestine operations in Indo-China, French participation in the war in the Far East and the French military mission to SEAC. Nonetheless, before the matter could be brought before Churchill for him to contact Roosevelt it was proposed that Halifax should broach the issue with the State Department and 'urge them to clear it with the President'.[121] Initially this idea had been proposed by Churchill but the Foreign Office was 'dubious ... of achieving the desired result through this channel, since the decision clearly lies with the President'.[122] However, Eden now considered it important at least to try to resolve the matter through Halifax before returning the issue to Churchill.[123] Perhaps this would circumnavigate Churchill's intransigence to discuss Indo-Chinese matters with Roosevelt. The Foreign Office informed the US Ambassador in London

> It would be difficult to deny French participation in the liberation of Indo-China in light of the increasing strength of the French Government in world affairs, and that, unless a policy to be followed toward Indo-China is mutually agreed between our two governments, circumstances may arise at any moment which will place our two governments in a very awkward situation.[124]

At the same time Churchill remained resolute in his defence of the British Empire but appeared to have lost touch with the trusteeship debate. On New Year's Eve he wrote to Eden, 'How does this matter stand? There must be no question of our being hustled or seduced into declarations affecting British sovereignty in any of the Dominions or colonies'. Noting the irony that the US wanted to maintain control over certain Japanese islands post-war for its own security agenda, Churchill blessed the US proposals but maintained '"Hands off the British Empire" is our maxim and it must not be weakened or smirched to please sob-stuff merchants at home or foreigners of any hue'.[125] Eden replied 'we are anxious to persuade the Americans not to go in for half baked international regimes', i.e. trusteeship, 'nor to advocate them for others but to accept colonial responsibilities on the same terms as ourselves'.[126]

Halifax 'repeatedly urged [the] State Department to give ... a reply' to Foreign Office concerns. On 26 December the new US Secretary of State, Edward Stettinius, informed him that 'the question was still on the President's desk'.[127] At the beginning of January 1945 Halifax again broached Foreign Office concerns with Stettinius, who informed Halifax that Roosevelt still thought that any political or military action over Indo-China was premature and that the President intended to raise the issue with Churchill. Halifax protested over the implied delay, citing Mountbatten's urgent military requirements, but Stettinius declined to offer further assistance.[128] Two days later Halifax met with Roosevelt and attempted to resolve the deadlock over SEAC and French clandestine operations in Indo-China. Roosevelt cryptically responded that 'if we felt it important we had better tell Mountbatten to do it and ask no questions. He did not want in any way to appear to be committed to anything that would seem to prejudge [a] political decision about Indo-China [that was] in a sense favourable to [the] restoration [of the] French *status quo ante* which he did not wish to see restored'.[129] Dening believed that as everything was now in place to begin pre-occupation duties in Indo-China it was time to revert solely to Mountbatten's informal Gentleman's Agreement with Chiang Kai-Shek, and to halt further representations to Roosevelt whose intervention could damage SEAC operations.[130] Roosevelt's statement to Halifax placed Britain in an opportune position. Halifax, Mountbatten, the COS and the Foreign Office agreed that 'we should let this particular sleeping dog lie' and Eden pertained that the matter was now solely an issue to be dealt with by the Foreign Office.[131] Stanley, in Washington for discussions on dependent areas, received Roosevelt's continued affirmation of trusteeship for Indo-China.[132]

In the meantime Eden attempted to have France accepted as an attendee at the forthcoming Allied conference at Yalta (February 1945). Writing to Churchill, Eden reminded him that many of France's imperial interests complemented those of Britain. Stating 'we must plan for the future' Eden pressed that it was necessary to have French co-operation; France was a member of the European Advisory Commission, it was due to administer one of the German occupation zones after the war and was to have one permanent Security Council seat at the UN.[133] However, Churchill was not convinced of the need to include France at Yalta: 'we shall have the greatest trouble with de Gaulle, who will be forever intriguing and playing two off against the third'. Churchill doubted that France's rehabilitation was complete and declared that it could not 'masquerade as a great power for the purpose of the war'. Warming to his subject Churchill concluded with a personal outburst against de Gaulle, 'I cannot think of anything more unpleasant and impossible than having this menacing and hostile man in our midst, always trying to make himself a reputation in France by claiming a position far above what France occupies, and making faces at the allies who are doing the work'.[134] Eden pleaded that Churchill's stance could turn France towards Russia for support which would cause problems for British post-war security, but Churchill was unmoved.[135]

Roosevelt, Stalin and Churchill met at the Yalta Conference to discuss the foundations for the post-war world. Returning to the question of trusteeship Churchill vetoed Roosevelt's plans, but he did not pursue the question of further French participation in the war in the Far East as Roosevelt had no military advisers present and thus could not be expected to make a considered decision.[136] Roosevelt was less generous to Churchill during a post-conference press briefing: 'Stalin liked the idea. China liked the idea. The British don't like it. It might bust up their empire', he considered 'it would only make the British mad. Better to keep quiet just now' as Churchill was 'mid-Victorian on all things like that'.[137] Dening remained curious as to French motives about the return of Indo-China, 'do they expect us to bear their cross for them'? From SEAC he concluded 'I am gradually gaining the impression that the French we have are either *mal élèves* or just stupid, or trying to pull a fast one'.[138]

A month later Churchill returned to the question of trusteeship. Reflecting on the scheme of voluntary trusteeship established at Yalta for colonial territories he warned 'I myself oppose such a departure which might well be pressed upon nations like Britain, France,

Holland and Belgium who have had great colonial possessions by the United States, Russia and China who have none'.[139] Churchill appeared to have come full circle. The Foreign Office noted the continued hypocrisy with the US position on trusteeship, 'the Americans have not disdained the use of our territories particularly India and Burma and the considerable resources which those territories have made available for them'.[140] It was sardonically commented that 'The "fundamental principle on which the very existence of the United States rested" was ... in abeyance when the US wrested what is now Southern California, Arizona, New Mexico and Texas from the Mexicans, and when the North forced the Confederate southern states to stay within the Union'.[141] Meanwhile the French Government issued the Brazzaville Declaration to unite the aims of France with the Indo-Chinese Federation as part of a new French Union. It was intended as a progressive statement of direction. The Union would be the basis for French post-war relationships with its Empire; however 'liberty' was only permitted within the Union.[142] In April the Foreign Office replied to Dening's misgivings about French motives. British policy was 'to help her [France] to recover her former strength and influence and to cultivate the closest possible relations with her. We regard a strong and friendly France as an essential factor for our post-war security'.[143] It was important for Britain to defend the interests of all the colonial powers over both trusteeship and voluntary trusteeship lest a precedent be established that would destroy all colonial relationships. However, this represented much more than the future of colonial territories: the stability and security of post-war Western Europe were at stake, also economic regeneration and political harmony would be needed to face the potential threat from Russia. A common European colonial policy could bolster Britain's position as a great power, especially if the Empire and the Dominions in unison alongside the other Western European colonial nations could act as a balance of power against Russia.[144] However, the high policy debate over trusteeship and French participation in the war in the Far East had, for the moment, been eclipsed by a conflict between SEAC and China Theatre command over Allied operations in Indo-China.

Inter-theatre rivalry

Differences between Britain and the US over Indo-China also existed between SEAC and the China Theatre. Officially Indo-China was in the

China Theatre but since the creation of SEAC in 1943 Mountbatten had maintained an operational interest in Indo-China and Siam, as it was through these areas 'that runs the Japanese land and air reinforcement route to Burma and Malaya'.[145] Originally the British COS had intended that the boundaries of SEAC would include Indo-China, Siam and Malaya.[146] However, the first Quebec Conference (August 1943) between Roosevelt and Churchill confirmed both Siam and Indo-China in the China Theatre.[147]

When Mountbatten arrived at SEAC he discovered that 'Anglo-American relations in this theatre were far and away the worst I have ever come across' and he found Stilwell to be 'entirely anti-British'.[148] US personnel within SEAC quipped that it stood really for 'Save England's Asian Colonies'.[149] Mountbatten attempted to end the conflict of personalities both within SEAC and between it and the China Theatre. Mountbatten met Chiang Kai-Shek in Chungking which resulted in a Gentleman's Agreement concerning Indo-China. The Gentleman's Agreement permitted Mountbatten to attack Siam and Indo-China and if successful transfer Siam and Indo-China from China Theatre into SEAC. In the meantime Mountbatten would be allowed to carry out intelligence and other pre-occupational activities.[150] Mountbatten wrote personally and informed Roosevelt of the outcome of the meeting which was confirmed to Roosevelt by US Lt.-General Brehon Sommervell who also had been present and who had helped to broker the agreement.[151] However, Mountbatten's personal letter to Roosevelt merely informed him of a congenial meeting with Chiang Kai-Shek to remove distrust and barriers between the commands but did not specifically mention the Gentleman's Agreement.[152] Similarly, Mountbatten's letters to both Churchill and Sir Alan Brooke, CIGS, concerning the meeting also failed to mention the Gentleman's Agreement.[153] Roosevelt seemed pleased with both SEAC and Mountbatten and expressed confidence in the resolution between the commands, a success that he personally accredited to Mountbatten; but had he, Churchill and Brooke been misled?[154] If Mountbatten had made reference to the agreement and if Sommervell had mentioned it to Roosevelt then could the agreement have been clarified at this stage and the later conflict between the Britain and the US concerning SEAC operations in Indo-China been avoided? The essence of the Gentleman's Agreement was confirmed in a further verbal agreement between Mountbatten and Chiang Kai-Shek in September 1944.[155] However the questions of the theatre boundaries and the Gentleman's Agreement would continue to reverberate in par-

allel with the matter of French participation in the war in the Far East throughout 1944 culminating in the spring of 1945.[156]
On 29 January 1945, Wedemeyer wrote to Mountbatten detailing his plans to co-ordinate and integrate all Anglo-French-US clandestine operations in Indo-China.[157] Halifax was instructed to inform the US General of the Army, George Marshall, of Roosevelt's cryptic approval of Mountbatten's clandestine operations in case Wedemeyer continued to create problems over this matter.[158] Despite the long-standing Gentleman's Agreement between Mountbatten and Chiang Kai-Shek, the senior British liaison officer to China Theatre, Lt.-General Adrian Carton de Wiart, felt that 'only a decision from the Combined Chiefs of Staff will alter his [Wedemeyer's] position'.[159] Despite Chinese reassurances to Britain, Chiang Kai-Shek had imperial ambitions for Tonkin and therefore often 'told Mountbatten one thing and Wedemeyer the other'.[160] The growing disagreement over clandestine operations in Indo-China was complicated further when two British aircraft were shot down by US night fighters over Northern Indo-China having failed to give the US in Kunming 'previous warning' of their operation.[161] Air Vice Marshal Whitworth-Jones accepted responsibility on behalf of SEAC and recommended that the investigation be wound down and 'sealed lips' kept on this tragedy.[162] Wedemeyer wrote again to Mountbatten, on 10 February, in a friendly and gracious tone concerning the growing dispute over clandestine operations in Indo-China, 'You and I are 180 degrees apart with reference to French Indo-China but that requires decisions on a higher level than our own and I am making appropriate representation to clarify and obtain decisions for both of us'.[163] Despite the amicable tone of the letter Wedemeyer had revealed already his political views in Chungking – that he 'has been quite unable to understand why the British Commonwealth holds together, still less why it should do in the future'.[164] French General Jean Boucher de Crevecoeur was less generous in later commenting that Wedemeyer's stance was due to both his German ancestry and his time spent as an exchange student at the Berlin Military Academy.[165] Carton de Wiart reported to Churchill that 'Wedemeyer very much resents any activity on part of SEAC in Indo-China and says they must do nothing there without his permission'. Ominously he predicted 'I feel if [this] situation regards Indo-China is not cleared up very soon it will lead to considerable trouble'.[166] Meanwhile Britain ascertained that the 'Japanese have completed preparations for the occupation' of Indo-China.[167]

The War Cabinet COS Committee reiterated Indo-Chinese importance in post-hostilities planning to British security in Southeast Asia, 'Indo-China is of the greatest importance since it forms the anchor of the chain of bases designed to cover Malaya, Burma and North Borneo and to prevent a serious threat to Australia and India developing ... The security of this alternative chain of bases requires the existence of stable and friendly regimes in Indo-China and Siam and settled conditions in Malaya'. It predicted that Indo-China would be of specific importance if Russia established a presence in Southern China, and that this would require full British, Commonwealth, US and French co-operation in Indo-China's defence.[168]

Eden invited the US Ambassador to China, General Patrick Hurley, to London *en route* from Washington to Chungking and the COS asked for the invitation to be extended to include Wedemeyer so that discussions could take place concerning operations in Indo-China.[169] Wedemeyer declined the invitation.[170] On 1 March Churchill wrote to Eden and Ismay and asked 'What action do we take?' on the Wedemeyer-Mountbatten dispute.[171] Roosevelt had not yet approached Churchill, as Stettinius had indicated in January he would, over political and military matters concerning Indo-China but because of Wedemeyer's attitude, the Foreign Office conjectured, the Indo-China question could not be deferred any longer.[172] Eden replied to Churchill three days later. Accentuating that Wedemeyer and Mountbatten sparring on Indo-China would be a 'constant source of friction between ourselves and the United States', Eden suggested that the only course of action 'likely to produce a decision' was a direct approach from Churchill to Roosevelt. Eden hoped that the President would confirm 'the oral understanding between Chiang Kai-Shek and Mountbatten' and that an exchange of 'intentions, plans and intelligence' could be made between Mountbatten and Wedemeyer in all matters of mutual concern. The Foreign Office asked the COS for its views and Churchill agreed to 'consider an approach to the President' when the Foreign Office paper and the opinions of the COS had been accumulated.[173] If Churchill had intended to use the Foreign Office-COS consultation to delay making a decision, this was swiftly countered as both the Foreign Office paper and the COS views had been prepared during the two days between Churchill's initial enquiry to both Eden and Ismay and Eden's reply to Churchill on 4 March.[174]

On 9 March the Japanese launched a *coup d'état* in Indo-China, overthrowing the Vichy French regime alongside which it had co-existed. The French previously had been directly responsible for the administration of Indo-China but were subject to Japanese supervision and occupation. Most French military resistance was rapidly overcome but a force under General Alessandri attempted to retreat to Son La. The Vietnamese Emperor Bao Dai and Cambodian King Norodom Sihanouk quickly proclaimed independence within Japanese 'Greater East Asia'.[175] Two days later Eden again wrote to Churchill concerning the Mountbatten-Wedemeyer dispute and this time presented him with the Foreign Office and COS papers. Mountbatten's activities in Indo-China were restricted, as proposals put by the British COS to the US COS concerning greater 'French participation in the Far Eastern War, still remained unanswered' due to the 'inaction of President Roosevelt'. Eden doubted if Britain would 'ever get an answer' although ambiguity existed because of Roosevelt's '"off the record"' comments to Halifax concerning his intention 'to turn a blind eye to such activities as Admiral Mountbatten may consider necessary'. However, Wedemeyer insisted that he could not 'agree to activities in Indo-China by Admiral Mountbatten without his prior consent in the absence of instructions from his own higher authorities' because 'Indo-China is in the United States strategic sphere'. Eden acknowledged that, although Wedemeyer's stance was 'technically correct', Wedemeyer 'entirely disregards the oral understanding, of which you [Churchill] are well aware, between Mountbatten and Chiang Kai-Shek'. The COS supported Eden and the Foreign Office desire that 'joint confirmation' by Britain and the US was needed of the Gentleman's Agreement and the appropriate liaison arrangements agreed between Wedemeyer and Mountbatten concerning Indo-China. Similarly the COS agreed that Britain was 'not likely to obtain a satisfactory solution except through your [Churchill's] personal intervention with the President'.[176]

The next day, amidst the growing crisis both in Indo-China and between Mountbatten and Wedemeyer, Churchill decided to act, although not decisively. He requested a brief from Ismay as to the course of events within Indo-China since the start of the war. Churchill appeared unaware as to whether Indo-China was still a Vichy province, or part of de Gaulle's France, or if there were French troops located there. Confusion certainly existed as Indo-China was the only French area not to rally to support de Gaulle following the Allied liberation of France, but considering it was co-habitant with the Japanese this was unsurprising. Churchill concluded: 'I have not followed the affairs in the country for some time'.[177] At the same time Massigli approached Eden concerning the crisis and the possibility of transporting the 600 men of the Corps Leger to the Far East to

assist in French resistance against the Japanese. Eden reported the request to Churchill.[178]
Churchill eventually wrote to Roosevelt five days later and requested that as Wedemeyer was currently in Washington it would seem appropriate to resolve the Mountbatten-Wedemeyer dispute,

> as you [Roosevelt] know he [Mountbatten] has an oral understanding with Chiang Kai-Shek that both he and the Generalissimo shall be free to attack Siam and Indo-China and that the boundaries of the two theatres shall be decided when the time comes in accordance with the progress made by their respective forces. The Generalissimo agreed after Sextant [the Cairo Conference] that this understanding extended to pre-occupational activities.
> ...
> This is a situation from which much harmful friction may spring. Could not you and I clear it up by jointly endorsing the oral understanding which seems a sensible and workable agreement?

Churchill suggested that a mechanism 'for full and frank exchange of intentions, plans and intelligence' be established between Wedemeyer and Mountbatten.[179] Meanwhile limited French resistance to the Japanese inside Indo-China continued and the War Cabinet JIC Sub-Committee suggested that SEAC increase supplies for French forces fighting in Indo-China.[180] In the US, Marshall requested that British Field Marshal Henry Wilson, Head of the JSM in Washington, confer with him over the Mountbatten-Wedemeyer dispute. Wilson held that the CCS never had agreed at the Cairo Conference which theatre Indo-China was to be placed in.[181] He failed to appreciate that despite this disagreement in reality a decision had already been made three months before Cairo at the first Quebec Conference.[182] Nevertheless both the COS and Churchill concurred with the line that Wilson now proposed to take.[183] Ten days after the Japanese overthrow of the French in Indo-China, Churchill appeared to want to take decisive action to assist French forces in Indo-China but instead of raising the matter with Roosevelt he instructed Wilson to convey to the US COS through Marshall that: 'The Prime Minister feels that it would look very bad in history if we were to let the French force in Indo-China be cut to pieces by the Japanese through shortage of ammunition, if there is anything we can to do save them. He hopes therefore that we shall be agreed in not standing on punctilio in this emergency'.[184] Eden agreed.[185] A day later Churchill acted, he instructed Ismay that Mountbatten should take 'emergency action' to assist the French.[186] By coincidence Marshall informed Wilson that US General Claire Chennault had been ordered to fly ammunition to the French forces.[187] Ironically whilst the policy debate raged between London and Washington, US Major-General Robert McClure in the absence of Wedemeyer, and SOE Force 136 had already separately aided the French in Indo-China before Churchill and Marshall's intervention, although by 16 March the US Army Air Force had resumed normal bombing missions and would not supply French forces without permission from Washington.[188]

On 22 March the limited French resistance in Indo-China requested further equipment and the resumption of intervention by the US Air Force. General Alessandri expected that his position at Son La would fall within two days.[189] Five days later, having successfully reinforced and held Son La with additional French units fleeing the Japanese, the French requested finances and medical supplies for the besieged forces.[190] The JSM held that 'it was embarrassing and unfortunate that the Combined Chiefs of Staff should continue to give the French no encouragement'.[191] Britain arranged to send the money and medical supplies requested by the French forces in Indo-China.[192] Chennault protested to Marshall about the lack of co-ordination for operations within Indo-China.[193] Marshall informed Wilson '"Whatever the differences which remained unsettled regarding priority rights in Indo-China operations, it seems to me that Mountbatten's Headquarters should at least notify Chungking of what they are doing or we are riding for a fall out there"'.[194]

Roosevelt, whilst agreeing to full and frank discussions between Wedemeyer and Mountbatten, sought in a telegram Churchill's approval that 'all Anglo-American-Chinese military operations in Indo-China, regardless of their nature be co-ordinated by General Wedemeyer'.[195] Marshall was in agreement with Roosevelt on this but continued to hold that Wedemeyer could not actually control such operations.[196] In Washington Hurley regarded US policy on Indo-China as 'still nebulous' and informed Wilson that Britain could expect more trouble from the 'President and State Department over Hong Kong' and also 'lend lease equipment being used for recovery of colonial territories'.[197] Hurley had been invited to visit London on his return to China.[198] The Foreign Office prepared a brief for the intended visit. The personal analysis of Hurley considered that his 'bark is probably worse than his bite' but identified that he possessed 'crude ideas about our "imperialism"'. Hurley had already informed the Dutch Ambassador in Chungking that the US was 'not going to clear up the mess for the imperialism of Britain and Holland in the Far East' and was suspicious of Anglo-Dutch-French 'collaboration ... to promote their imperial interests' whilst 'keeping the Americans in the dark'.[199] However, the brief assumed that because Hurley had been reported as 'not happy about President Roosevelt's attitude on Indo-China' he would be 'receptive' to the British position.[200] The eventual meeting between Hurley and Churchill proved to be an anti-climax. Churchill noted 'Hurley seemed to wish to keep the conversation to civil banalities' and in his meeting with the COS Hurley limited his discussions to background conditions in Indo-China and would not be drawn on its 'political outlook'.[201]

By 31 March Churchill had still not yet replied to Roosevelt's telegram concerning the Wedemeyer-Mountbatten dispute. Churchill admitted to being 'a little shy of overburdening the President'. He fantasised that the President's telegram 'was obviously not his own' and regarded that the Mountbatten-Wedemeyer dispute should be settled at COS level as he considered Roosevelt to be 'very hard pressed, and I like to keep him as much as possible for the biggest things'.[202] Three days later Churchill appeared to relent. He notified Hollis that he was 'quite prepared to bring this before the President in a day or two'.[203] This was an open statement with no indication that he intended to carry it out. Mountbatten met with Wedemeyer for full and frank discussions and reminded him that both the US COS and Roosevelt had previously approved of the Gentleman's Agreement. Mountbatten showed Wedemeyer two documents which demonstrated this and it was agreed that Wedemeyer could veto only operations that clashed with China Theatre operations.[204] Wedemeyer's subsequent report to Washington also stated that British operations could not be executed until approved by Chiang Kai-Shek.[205]

Churchill at last wrote to Roosevelt on 11 April but by now the dispute appeared to have been resolved. Churchill notified Roosevelt that both Mountbatten and Wedemeyer had reached an understanding concerning SEAC and China Theatre disputes over Indo-China. He proposed that Mountbatten should keep Wedemeyer 'continually informed of all ... operations since forces of China Command will also be operating in the same theatre'. Further disputes would be referred to the CCS. However, Churchill would not subject Mountbatten's operations in Indo-China to Wedemeyer's approval and bluntly warned Roosevelt that 'it would look very bad in history if we failed to support isolated French forces ... or if we excluded the French from participation in our councils as regards Indo-China'.[206] Churchill had boldly aligned British military and political policy over Indo-China with his post-Yalta policy of defending the colonial possessions of European nations. Unfortunately Roosevelt did not have an opportunity to reply as he died the next day.

Roosevelt's death and the ascension of Vice-President Harry Truman to the presidency marked a watershed in US policy and Indo-China in particular. Truman replied to Churchill that Wedemeyer had reported that Mountbatten had agreed to notify Wedemeyer of operations. But Wedemeyer had introduced a new element to the debate that operations could not be actioned until approved by Chiang Kai-Shek, and if SEAC operations could not be integrated with China Theatre plans then Mountbatten would have to withdraw the proposals. Truman approved Wedemeyer's report of the resolution as a 'satisfactory method of solving the problem'. In case of further problems he agreed with Churchill that future disputes should be reported through the respective COS to the CCS and that Wedemeyer had been 'instructed to give the French resistance groups such assistance as is practicable without prejudice to his present or future operations'.[207] Churchill directed Ismay for 'Action this day'.[208] Four days later Ismay informed Churchill that the COS agreed to trial the resolution detailed in Truman's telegram.[209] A day later Churchill replied to Truman that he agreed to trial the proposed resolution.[210] Meanwhile, reflecting a perceived change of political attitudes in the US, Churchill believed that French and Dutch participation in the war against Japan should be discussed by Eden in Washington.[211] Ten days later the COS told Mountbatten that the CCS had agreed that the Corps Leger would be sent to Ceylon as soon as possible.[212]

However, the conflict between Mountbatten and Wedemeyer continued. This concerned Mountbatten flying sorties to aid French resistance groups in Indo-China.[213] Wilson learnt that, in the course of an examination of theatre boundaries, the US COS appeared unlikely to object to Indo-China being included as part of an enlarged SEAC. Despite previous political disputes over Indo-China, Marshall did not know the current direction of White House thinking on this issue.[214] Mountbatten believed that Wedemeyer had 'introduced new factors and interpretations' into the Gentleman's Agreement with Chiang Kai-Shek. Wedemeyer held Indo-China 'of vital importance to the China Theatre' and believed that as Commander-in-Chief to Chiang Kai-Shek he could not agree to the terms of the Gentleman's

Agreement as stated by Mountbatten, especially as the Generalissimo 'desired prior arrangement' of operations as Supreme Allied Commander China Theatre. Wedemeyer attacked Mountbatten's interpretation of the agreement as not being 'in consonance with standard military practice'.[215] Mountbatten replied to Wedemeyer that the dispute needed to be dealt with 'officially'.[216] Wilson confirmed to both the COS and Mountbatten that Wedemeyer could only veto conflicting operations.[217] Marshall cautioned Wilson that Hurley was sending strongly worded anti-British reports to Washington from Chungking, as was Wedemeyer.[218] Marshall remarked to Wilson 'there must be an extraordinary importance to the clandestine operations being carried out ... to justify the possible creation not only of ill will but of a feeling that there is a lack of good faith'. Because of previous correspondence between Churchill and Truman as well as Marshall and Wilson on this dispute, Marshall did not hold that anything further would be gained if the dispute was brought before the CCS.[219] Wilson was surprised with the idea that there was nothing to be gained and concluded that 'there is more in it than meets the eye'.[220] The COS wearily informed Wilson that 'if Wedemeyer acted in the spirit of his directive and if good liaison is established in Chungking, the difficulties would cease' and asked for Marshall to 'advise' Wedemeyer of this.[221]

Meanwhile in India, Britain arranged for the French to use facilities to train French colonial administrators and, in China, the OSS (forerunner of the CIA) organised equipment and training for the Vietminh in return for intelligence reports and the rescue of downed US pilots.[222] The CIGS, Brooke, raised the question of the transfer of Indo-China from China Theatre to SEAC with the COS; they agreed that the SEAC boundaries should be enlarged to include Indo-China.[223] Wedemeyer naturally was opposed to the transfer but the issue was now before the Potsdam Conference (July 1945) and Indo-China was secondary to the Pacific Theatre.[224] In the European victors' arena the ambiguities and distrust appeared to have been mostly forgotten. Truman flattered Mountbatten that both he and the US COS were 'grateful ... for the impartial way' that Mountbatten had managed SEAC and added that 'we in America regard you in exactly the same light as Eisenhower is regarded by the British; that is, we really do appreciate your integrity, and the admirable way which you have run your command'.[225] In a compromise gesture to Chiang Kai-Shek, Truman and the new British Labour Prime Minister, Clement Attlee, divided Indo-China between SEAC and China Theatres at the 16th parallel.[226]

Resolution

The immediate resolution of Britain's conflict with the US over the question of Indo-China lay not within the diplomacy of the Foreign Office or the political acumen of Churchill but in a transformation in the nature of Franco-US relations and the opportunity afforded by a change in President. Although Roosevelt's anti-French and anti-imperial opinions were partially shared by many of his advisers (Hull, Hurley, Stilwell, Wedemeyer, Admiral Leahy Chief of Staff to the President and Chairman of the JCS, and General Donovan Head of the OSS) the positions taken were not appreciated by large elements of the State Department or the armed forces. In February 1943 Roosevelt received a thesis from the State Department Sub-Committee on Security Problems that argued for a strong France as an element in US security policy against a future Soviet threat.[227] Initially Roosevelt had managed to keep the State Department isolated from the Indo-China debate. However, from 1944 onwards, the State Department questioned China's commitment to the Atlantic Charter and as the importance of China in Roosevelt's foreign policy declined so too was his Indo-China policy undermined.[228]

The White House and the State Department each developed different approaches towards Southeast Asia and as a result Roosevelt was more restricted in his policy ramblings.[229] The second Quebec Conference moved the focus of US policy towards a Pacific island-hopping strategy and away from SEAC and China Theatre.[230] In October Roosevelt granted diplomatic recognition to the Provisional French Government. This blunted Roosevelt's policy.[231] France was reconstituted as a European power and the State Department was able to restrict Roosevelt further.[232] On 1 November the State Department lobbied Roosevelt to seek further clarification of the Indo-China policy. Roosevelt decreed that no help was to be given to France over the Indo-China issue.[233] Meanwhile Hull retired and was replaced as Secretary of State by Stettinius; the European Office of the State Department appeared to be in the ascendancy.[234] In January 1945 the Secretaries for State, War and Navy met with Presidential Adviser Harry Hopkins to discuss Roosevelt's Indo-China policy and the damage to Franco-US relations.[235] Hopkins suggested that there needed to be a revision not just of US Indo-China policy but also of the entire US approach towards France. As part of this new approach Hopkins visited Paris and later in the spring a return visit was made by Georges Bidault, the French Foreign Minister, to Washington where he was received by Vice-President Harry Truman. Franco-US relations appeared to be thawing.[236] The Japanese coup of 9 March in Indo-China clarified the Indo-Chinese issue further. As long as the French had collaborated with the Japanese, Roosevelt could indulge in anti-colonialism towards Indo-China.[237] Now, symbolically, Indo-China had lost its association with Vichy France and had become an occupied territory in Southeast Asia with the French seeking to liberate an occupied people in the same vein as the British in Burma, Singapore, Malaya and Hong Kong, and the Dutch in the Netherlands East Indies. De Gaulle did not miss the opportunity to attack the US attitude towards France by claiming in true Machiavellian spirit that an anti-French policy would push France towards Russia.[238] The US State, War and Navy Committee again sought clarification as to US Indo-China policy.[239] The State Department wanted a consistent policy towards Southeast Asia but US policy remained locked in dual camps; although Roosevelt did concede the concept of a conditional French trusteeship for Indo-China.[240] British Admiral-of-the-Fleet James Sommerville informed Mountbatten that talks with Admiral Ernest King, Commander-in-Chief of the US Navy, had revealed that the US COS was not in favour of Roosevelt's policy of keeping the French out of Indo-China.[241] The Secretary of War, Stimson, challenged Roosevelt's control of the trusteeship debate and an OSS report analysing US policy warned against trusteeship 'which may provoke unrest and result in colonial disintegration and may at the same time alienate us from the European states whose help we need to balance Soviet power'.[242]

Roosevelt's untimely death eased the internal US debate between the State Department and the White House. The US Army representative on the State, War and Navy Committee held that a lack of US policy on Indo-China was a 'serious embarrassment to the military' and that Roosevelt's interdiction of their debate must be reviewed.[243] The San Francisco Conference (April–June 1945) provided the opportunity for the external resolution of the Indo-Chinese dispute. Bidault angrily announced to Stettinius that France did not intend to place Indo-China under any form of trusteeship, but Stettinius's amnesia allowed him to reassure Bidault that 'the record is entirely innocent of any official statement of this government questioning, even by implication, French sovereignty over Indo-China'.[244] France's rehabilitation appeared to be complete. Stettinius announced that the fifth permanent seat on the UN Security Council had been accorded to France:

'The United States welcomes this important step in the return of France to her rightful place in world affairs'.[245] Eden found that the new President possessed an 'air of quiet confidence in himself'. Truman informed Eden '"I am here to make decisions, and whether they prove right or wrong I am going to take them"'.[246] John Hickerson, sub Head European Office of the State Department, revealed to the British delegation that the option of voluntary trusteeship (category C) introduced at the Yalta Conference had been 'partly phrased by the State Department in order to permit a climb down from the position that President Roosevelt had taken in conversation as regards Indo-China'. It was made 'clear that the State Department felt that President Roosevelt had gone too far, and that category C was a useful face saver'.[247] The US now required friendship with Britain and France against Russia, in the new post-war world order.[248]

A lost opportunity

Historical debate traditionally has focused analysis upon whether or not the concept of trusteeship died with Roosevelt. Tonnesson has identified that two distinct schools of thought have emerged. Firstly the 'school of lost opportunity' because trusteeship was neither a serious factual policy nor continued after Roosevelt's death. Secondly the 'school of continuation' which argued that as Truman endorsed the French return it marked a continuation of Roosevelt's own revisionism towards the subject.[249] Interwoven into this has been the idea that military necessity and British imperial intransigence destroyed a unique opportunity although it can be argued also that Roosevelt's ill-defined policy delayed a French return thereby creating a lost imperial opportunity.[250]

Roosevelt's concept of trusteeship came in two parts. One, an ideological desire to see independence granted to the colonial peoples, born from the US anti-imperial subconscious. This continued throughout the period 1943–50 and physically manifested itself in the US policy debate towards Indo-China, Indonesia and the Philippines. Two, a practical policy of trusteeship that was in constant revision as Roosevelt engaged in the day to day ebb and flow of power brokering between the Allied powers on both wartime and post-hostility planning. Roosevelt was politically at his most dangerous when the practical and the ideological came together. By maintaining these two streams and not committing himself to a more factual policy Roosevelt created a situation where, after his death, Truman struggled to produce clear directives resulting in some sections of US agencies (China Theatre and the OSS) continued application of Roosevelt's anti-French policy, 'FDR's foreign policy had been so personal to himself that it was doubtful whether Truman or anyone he asked really appreciated what its "general line" had been'.[251] Likewise it is possible that trusteeship symbolically aided the Allied cause; internally in the US, trusteeship could be used to prove that the US was not fighting a colonial war on behalf of Britain and France; externally, trusteeship could produce the hope of freedom from Japanese imperialism and its hollow promise of Asian nationalism. Certainly this argument was not lost on the Vietminh leader Ho Chi Minh.

It was because of Roosevelt's astute political prowess and ability that trusteeship remained in constant revision and unintegrated into any formal policy. Roosevelt was well aware of wartime constraints and complexities both of a physical and a political nature not only within his own administration but also amongst his allies, most notably the British.[252] Roosevelt's frequent outbursts on the subject to the US Joint COS were not just an attack on the British and the French but also an attempt to win the military and political debates about US mandate territories and the future of the Japanese Islands. Fortunately, Roosevelt had the foresight to see that the US would end the war as the only major creditor nation and therefore the major world power. It would be 'an American peace, that belonged to him to dictate its organisation'.[253] Thus he could afford to wait and discuss post-war planning, reconstruction and politics, only involving trusteeship when it was really necessary: this partly explains some of his silence and inactivity. The only eventuality that he had not considered was his death.

However, Britain reacted badly to the trusteeship debate. Roosevelt's fluid revisionism, lack of integration and imprecise policy caused particular discomfort at the Foreign Office: 'The Americans do not wish us to recover our previous position in Asia, confuse this wish in their minds with the principle of self-determination (alias "freedom") and so see in every move to recover lost property a similar desire to enslave native peoples'.[254] The Foreign Office was openly sympathetic to the Free French cause and feared that the French were blatantly being left out of policy and the decision-making process by the US. The French were convinced of US plots and obstruction against them in many areas during the Second World War. Britain rightly suspected that trusteeship for French Indo-China would be only a first step and that Roosevelt would use this precedent to dictate trusteeship to other colonial areas including Hong Kong. Roosevelt had to be careful not to draw the other colonial powers into an alliance with Britain over trusteeship and in Britain Churchill was worried that Indo-China and Foreign Office concern for the French would get in the way of his special relationship with Roosevelt. The silence on this issue by both leaders at various stages of the war helped to cool the pressure on a sensitive area where each others' personal feelings would have created further diplomatic problems and anxiety. Similarly the voluntary trusteeship arrangement agreed at the Yalta Conference was not a victory for the colonial powers in an attempt to derail trusteeship. Roosevelt would have no doubt seen the agreement as merely stalling the inevitable. He could afford to be both pragmatic and magnanimous. The US would finish the war as the major Allied creditor, its power in European reconstruction and the implementation of the UN would leave plenty of room for manoeuvre.[255] Indeed, in what are often quoted as Roosevelt's final words on trusteeship before his death to Charles Taussig, US Adviser on Caribbean Affairs, the President could afford to be verbally generous to the French but he did not abandon his ideology or commitment to colonial peoples: 'independence was the ultimate goal'.[256] Likewise, Churchill was aware of the changes that would have to be made to the geopolitical map after the war. Britain expected and even desired the US to be an active world power, not wanting the US to return to its position of interwar isolation. An active Anglo-US foreign policy could strengthen Britain domestically, economically, within the Empire and mitigate against the fate of rapidly becoming a diminished world power. Foreign Office intransigence lay also in the belief that planning for a post-war world was needed and the logic of European history dictated that a strong France was vital to British security against a threat from Russia or Germany.[257] In addition it was part of a grooming ritual that proved to itself that Britain was still a world power. US naivety failed to recognise that European global economic networks would need to be considered as part of any future debate.[258] The Foreign Office was defending imperial interests against dollar imperialism by supporting the French against the US over Indo-China.

Although by the Potsdam Conference the trusteeship debate for Indo-China was over, Roosevelt left the legacy of independence for colonial peoples permanently enshrined as Article 73 of the UN Charter and on 4 July 1946 the US granted political independence to the Philippines.[259] Trusteeship had never anticipated the growth of Asian nationalism but the war had invigorated it, thereby creating problems for returning colonial powers.[260] Ironically, had Roosevelt lived it has been argued that he would have committed Chinese or US troops to Indo-China, in fact he had requested that an invasion plan be developed.[261] However, he did not live and Britain had realised its goals in the trusteeship debate over Indo-China. The Potsdam Conference was about to throw Britain into greater involvement in the Indo-China issue with the potential boundary change from China Theatre to SEAC and the possibility of Allied liberation duties.

2
Liberation, July 1945–March 1946

The Potsdam Conference charged Britain with ALF duties in Southern French Indo-China. It would be a mistake to blame the British ALF Commander, Major-General Gracey, for the complex nature of the events that unfolded during these duties in Saigon. Britain did not unilaterally restore the French in Indo-China. The ALF inherited not just the anarchic birth pangs of Vietnamese nationalism in Saigon, but also the responsibility in Indo-China south of the 16th parallel for the release of Allied prisoners of war, the surrender and evacuation of Japanese forces, the security of French nationals, law and order, a Cambodian-Siamese border dispute, and a potential famine. The US was also responsible along with Britain for the transportation and equipping of French forces for their return to Indo-China.

Similarly, Britain was limited by the colonial attitude of its French ally. During the Second World War the British Colonial Office debated and investigated policies that after the war would lead to the constitutional reform of British colonies in Southeast Asia. Britain had recognised the need for colonial development and chose to base its policies on collaboration with emergent Asian nationalism, and wanted the other colonial powers in Southeast Asia to follow a similar course. For the French and the Dutch the restoration of their respective empires was more associated with their own national rebirth, and their newly resurrected political systems made the development of a compromise difficult to achieve.[1] French political difficulties included: the instability of frequent changes of governments; the rise of the French Communist Party; the inability of the political left to marry the desire for power with their political convictions; the retirement of President de Gaulle; and a conservative High Commissioner, Admiral Thierry D'Argenlieu, in French Indo-China conducting his own policy removed from the

French political debate. These factors placed pressures on the French Assembly and resulted in a failure to agree on a post-war policy for the French colonies. Britain could not press too hard as the rehabilitation of France was important for the security and stability of Europe.

British policy towards Indo-China also has to be gauged against the domestic situation in Britain. Once Germany had been defeated pressure was exerted on the British Government to rebuild, encourage exports and raise the standard of living. However, Britain had a number of competing priorities; it was committed under Operation Python to the demobilisation of British troops, it had assumed large post-hostility disarmament and peace keeping duties in Europe and Asia which included the distribution of food. In addition Britain was bankrupt, the sudden termination of the Lend-Lease Agreement and its replacement by a post-war reconstruction loan with interest payments of two percent placed additional burdens on a fragile economy and the new Labour Government. It was a period when despite Britain's emergence from the Second World War as one of the victorious Allied nations, its strategic and economic needs in the Far East required a rapid re-assessment of its role and expectations in the face of a financial Dunkirk.[2] Britain's reconstruction crisis and solvency would lead to a dependency on the US and, with other Western economies, a state of permanent submission.[3] Although colonial development could have arguably allowed Britain some leverage, *vis-à-vis* the US, had greater effort been put into it.

Vietnam

The dropping of the atomic bombs upon Japan cut short the Asian war for the British and US military planners. The expectation had been that the war would continue into 1946 as the Allied forces pushed towards Japan. They were not prepared at the Potsdam Conference to begin the task of administering a Japanese surrender and Asian reconstruction. They lacked accurate knowledge of the on-the-ground situation in many of the areas that they were to liberate. In such circumstances it is surprising that Mountbatten returned to Britain for a holiday in the crucial days between the Japanese surrender and the implementation of peacekeeping duties in his now enlarged SEAC.[4]

The Far East Section of the Foreign Office welcomed the change in priorities from Europe to Japan, China and Southeast Asia. The prevailing attitude was that 'Mr Eden, during his regime, neglected the Far

East for Europe and America', although Dening noted in Eden's defence that 'he probably had no choice'.[5] However, the Foreign Office was soon to discover that Eden's replacement as Foreign Secretary, Ernest Bevin, presented them with new problems as he 'read with no great facility and wrote even less'.[6] The Foreign Office was adjusting to Britain's role as the weakest of the great powers and to an emerging new role as the leader of the secondary powers, championing liberalism against totalitarianism in the Far East.[7]

At Potsdam the British COS had hoped that the US COS would agree to the transfer of all of Indo-China to SEAC.[8] However, the SEAC boundaries were expanded to include only areas of French Indo-China south of the 16th parallel. This theatre boundary had been proposed by the US at Potsdam and had been agreed as a compromise solution, between Washington and London, to the problem that had existed throughout the war of whether SEAC or China Theatre had operational responsibility over Indo-China.[9] The French had offered two divisions for operations in the war against Japan and the CCS had agreed that the best place to employ these troops would be in Indo-China. General Marshall asked Mountbatten to accept these two divisions as part of SEAC. Mountbatten welcomed the offer and added opportunely that 'The obvious place to employ them would be in French Indo-China where he would be relieved of the necessity of dealing with a problem which could be satisfactorily only handled by Frenchmen'.[10] The Potsdam Conference was symbolically significant for Indo-China. The division proposed by the US not only divided Indo-China but also Vietnam which was experiencing an indigenous revolution. In Vietnam Britain would be responsible for Southern Annam and Cochinchina. With clear US and British military support for a French return to Indo-China, the key to the return would be how well the French resolved this situation and conducted negotiations with the Chinese Nationalist ALF who were administering the Japanese disarmament and peacekeeping duties in the north.[11]

US General Douglas MacArthur, Supreme Allied Commander Southwest Pacific, held back Mountbatten from landing his ALF forces until he had formally accepted the Japanese military surrender. This was in case Allied troops faced a Japanese backlash when they landed to liberate territories and disarm a proud, and in many cases undefeated military force.[12] The French were eager for the return of Indo-China, and Massigli, the French Ambassador in London, met with Mountbatten to push for a return.[13] However, Mountbatten was to display a cautiousness – especially regarding local nationalists – that would contribute towards the delay of Allied forces.[14] The Chief of Staff to Force 136 had already warned the War Office in the case of Malaya that 'experience has shown, particularly in Greece, that resistance movements must be given clear instructions what to do when their country is liberated. If they receive no such instructions they will inevitably cause trouble, and may attempt to seize power in the principal towns'.[15]

In the meantime the Vietminh began to assume control inside Vietnam. A puppet Vietnamese government had been in control under the guidance of the Japanese since the March *coup d'état*. With a power vacuum developing the Vietminh sought to manipulate the situation and through revolution create an independent Vietnam. A US OSS team had been working with the Vietminh inside Vietnam since 16 July to gather intelligence against the Japanese. Reports from the OSS team stated that the Vietminh was not a communist organisation.[16] This was true in part: the Vietminh was not communist but rather a broad coalition of Vietnamese nationalist parties of whom the Indo-Chinese Communist Party was a significant member. On 6 August the Vietminh declared their intention to disarm the Japanese before the arrival of the allies and receive the allies as the authority in control of the country.[17] The Second National Congress of the Indo-Chinese Communist Party met on 13 August and a state of general insurrection was proclaimed by the Central Committee of the Vietminh to seize power in Hanoi.[18] Events unfolded rapidly in the north. A rally was held on 17 August in Hanoi and on 18 August the Vietminh seized the weapons of the *Garde Indochinoise*. The Vietminh leader Ho Chi Minh, who was also the leader of the Indo-Chinese Communist Party, arrived the following day and took control of Hanoi.[19] The Vietminh spread out from Hanoi and seized further parts of Tonkin, and Emperor Bao Dai abdicated the throne.[20]

The French attempted to begin reoccupation duties and air-dropped Commissioners Pierre Messmer and Jean Cédile into Tonkin and Cochinchina. Both were captured by the Vietminh. The US transported a further OSS team into Hanoi where they were enthusiastically welcomed by Indo-Chinese Communist Party member, Commander of the Vietnamese Liberation Army and Interior Minister Vo Nguyen Giap as a US Mission. Several US Officers met with Ho and due to their own anti-imperial political leanings gave the impression of US support for the Vietminh regime.[21] In an attempt to avoid further embarrassment the Head of the OSS mission Major Archimedes Patti was ordered not to become associated with either side. Jean Sainteny, French Commissioner to Tonkin and Northern Annam, described Patti as 'a rabid anti-colonialist'.[22]

Events came to a head, on 2 September, when the Vietminh declared independence and proclaimed the DRVN. By coincidence on the same day the allies received the formal Japanese surrender and rioting broke out against French nationals in Vietnam.[23] The rioting continued for two days with Japanese forces doing nothing to prevent the situation. This led to claims that the Japanese had aided the Vietminh. Up to three thousand Japanese soldiers deserted within three months of the surrender. Most joined non-Vietminh nationalist groups, although about five hundred joined the Vietminh.[24] Major-General Gracey had to remind the Japanese of Truman's 'Order Number One' to maintain law and order until ALF forces arrived. On 6 September the first British troops arrived in Saigon. Four days later, in London, Bevin wrote on Dening's cable concerning Gracey's entry into Saigon: 'I regard this as an important one to watch'.[25] The power vacuum was caused by three factors: the delay in the Allied occupation; the lack of Japanese determination to maintain control; and the inability of local institutions (the mandarins) to control political affairs. The power vacuum allowed Ho to declare independence and form a government with himself as President and Prime Minister in the region north of the 16th parallel. It demonstrated how he could become the leader of a national resistance struggle against both Japanese and French colonialism. This legitimised the Vietminh struggle in the eyes of the local population, although it would be a mistake to attribute the rise of nationalism solely to a power vacuum.[26]

Meanwhile, de Gaulle was in Washington for talks with Truman. De Gaulle assured the US President that steps would be taken towards the early independence of French Indo-China.[27] This appeared to reflect the more liberal stance that the Provisional French Government had taken since their declaration on Indo-China in March 1945. The State Department 'fully approve[d] of the continuance of French sovereignty'.[28] The Government of India's External Affairs Department contacted the Secretary of State for India in London to solicit clarity regarding Britain's policy for Indo-China. He was asked if it was 'His Majesty's Government policy to facilitate [the] re-establishment of French influence in French Indo-China'.[29] The Secretary of State replied that this was correct.[30] Mountbatten contacted D'Argenlieu and enthusiastically welcomed French forces south of the 16th parallel that had been placed in SEAC. He promised 'to do my best as an Allied Commander to look after French interests'.[31] British peacekeeping operations had solely military boundaries and objectives. Dening warned that Britain would have to be careful in Indo-China lest it be accused of political involvement by the Far East or US.[32] South of the 16th parallel, unlike the north of the country, a patchwork of different Vietnamese nationalist groups had a tentative hold on power in Saigon.[33] None had the resources or skill to unite the different factions in the city, let alone in Cochinchina. The Vietminh south of the 16th parallel had tenuous operational ability and lacked reliable communication with Hanoi, whereas the Cao Dai and Hoa Hao sects possessed large support and quantities of firearms.[34] British peace-keepers, under Gracey, conducted their duties in a power vacuum until the French military could return. Cochinchina had previously possessed special status in the French Empire, closer to that of the metropole. Saigon, with its large French population, represented a difficult powder keg of ambition in September 1945 with Vietnamese nationalism, communism and opportunism competing with a French colonial desire to reassert power. Gracey's military rule prevented the breakdown of law and order, and the anarchy which would have resulted had the colonialists and Vietnamese been left alone. In the north the situation was more clear-cut with Ho's ascendancy in Hanoi and the proclamation of independence.

Following the British arrival in Saigon an uneasy peace initially ensued but after 11 days the Vietminh called a general strike and British and French troops were forced to occupy key buildings. Dening foresaw that there would be local opposition to the return of the French, and demonstrations broke out against British troops on 19 September.[35] Gracey warned the Vietminh of his intention to issue a proclamation to restore law and order. Two days later the proclamation was issued. This banned public demonstrations and meetings, allowed only British and Allied troops to carry arms, instated newspaper censorship and a curfew. British forces operated the public utilities and the Saigon population was fed with help from the Allied forces. A further two days later, French forces began a counter revolution and occupied significant administration buildings in Saigon.[36] Gracey's actions were welcomed by General Philippe Leclerc, the French Commander-in-Chief, who informed the French Minister for War 'that General Gracey had in my opinion taken the best possible measures in the circumstances because if he had shown any weakness the situation might have become critical. As yet no clashes have occurred'.[37] In Gracey's opinion 'no effective civil government exists' and Vietminh claims to the contrary in the circumstances were 'childish'; i.e. 'no legal process exist[ed]'.[38] Mountbatten urgently cabled Gracey that the proclamation was contrary to the orders issued to him; it made him therefore now responsible for all of Indo-China south of the 16th parallel. However, Mountbatten supported Gracey's proclamation as he was 'the man on the spot'.[39] At a meeting with Mountbatten, General William Slim, Commander-in-Chief ALF SEAC and the French Governor-General designate Jean Cédile, Gracey acknowledged that he was restricted to using British troops within the Saigon vicinity but that this did not absolve him from the law and order responsibilities, maintained by Japanese forces acting in accordance with his orders, in the rest of Southern Indo-China. Mountbatten replied that as a result of actions in Greece the British Government did not want British casualties in operations which were not a British responsibility, nor did it want to intervene in the politics of another country; the responsibility was France's 'who must do it with their own troops'.[40]

From Hanoi, Ho telegrammed to the Foreign Ministers Conference in London to inform them of the establishment of the DRVN and appealed for aid to alleviate the famine conditions in the north.[41] Ho then met with US Brigadier-General Gallagher in Hanoi, the OSS team appeared to remain on good relations with the Vietminh. On 24 September Ho issued his second appeal to Truman.[42] This was probably the only appeal to reach the White House, as it had been inserted as a paragraph in an OSS report.[43] Gallagher met with Ho for a second time five days later and the conversation focused on Allied government policy toward the DRVN. Gallagher tried to allay Ho's fear that Vietnam was merely a 'conquered territory' despite knowing that the US had agreed to a return of French sovereignty.[44] As the French continued their coup in the south the DRVN Foreign Minister cabled Attlee to protest against the British role in the coup.[45]

The British were worried about the explosive situation in Saigon. John Lawson, Secretary of State for War, met with Mountbatten, Slim and Gracey to discuss the situation. It was agreed that Gracey's forces would maintain law and order until the French could take over. 'Mr Lawson said it was fundamental of [*sic*] His Majesty's Government not to interfere in the internal affairs of non-British territories and he appreciated that the instructions issued from London made this extremely difficult in French Indo-China; a single slip might well have grave repercussions'. Mountbatten told Lawson that he had received a telegram from Tom Driberg, a Labour MP on a tour of

Southeast Asia, offering his services to the Vietminh southern government to aid reconciliation. Lawson decided that the offer should be welcomed but that no authority should be given to Driberg.[46] Driberg's offer was not well received within SEAC where it was feared that such an advance could be used for propaganda and aggravate an already delicate political situation.[47] It was felt that in his capacity as an MP such action would be viewed with suspicion by the French.[48] Fortunately time was against Driberg. The offer only reached Mountbatten and Lawson on the day that Driberg had to return to Britain. However, Mountbatten had other ideas about the usefulness of Driberg and began a personal correspondence with him. Mountbatten wrote to Driberg following the meeting with Lawson and flattered him that although the offer to aid reconciliation had come too late he had persuaded Lawson to approve of it being accepted. He went on to praise the reasonableness of the Vietminh in agreeing to a cease-fire on 1 October and renewing this on the 3 October. In contrast he wrote 'If only the French will be reasonable and come forward with an imaginative offer, the war in Indo-China can be over. If it is continued through French intransigence, I hope it will be made abundantly clear that it is nothing to do with Southeast Asia [Command]'. Finally, Mountbatten added that if he had been given a 'free hand' in Indo-China and the Netherlands East Indies as he was in Burma, then they both would have been solved. He lamented that it was difficult to leave the political control to other nations when the British were militarily in charge of the situation.[49] Later in their correspondence Mountbatten would use his relationship with Driberg for political purposes. He urged Driberg to raise questions in the House of Commons concerning issues that Mountbatten regarded as unproductive – the size, cost and empire-building at the SACSEA Headquarters in Singapore.[50]

The emphasis to alleviate the situation was now upon Britain and the US to transport French forces rapidly to Indo-China. The JPS in London continued to support the British troop build-up. It insisted that this was to be concentrated in Saigon and that Gracey should leave the rest of the country to the French and only assist where necessary.[51] SEAC began talks with the Vietminh.[52] H.N. Brain, Foreign Office Representative, reiterated to the Vietminh that Britain's position was one of neutrality and that it was not the government's intention to use British forces for political purposes. He stated that 'the United Nations have decided that it will not recognise a change of sovereignty of any territory which has taken place by force during the war'. Brain coaxed that the UN was committed to the development of self-government for colonial peoples.[53] A cease-fire was agreed in Saigon on 2 October. To boost troop numbers Mountbatten used Japanese prisoners of war to keep order.[54] He lobbied London and reminded the government of the impossible situation in Southern Vietnam.[55] He requested additional shipping and troops including the French Ninth Colonial Division.[56] Attlee asked Major-General Hollis for a report on the situation in Indo-China. Hollis reported that on arrival 'Gracey found that the situation was not beyond control but that the Annam Government contributed a direct threat to law and order'.[57] Attlee decided to bring the Indo-Chinese situation and Hollis's report to the Defence Committee for discussion on 5 October.[58] In the meantime, Attlee asked Hollis for further clarification regarding the movement of the French Ninth Colonial Division and what could be done regarding radio broadcasts from Hanoi. Hollis replied that, according to the COS, to accelerate the French division would either mean that Britain had to accept a delay of three months in the return of the 12,000 Indian troops due to leave the Mediterranean in October, or a similar delay of the drafts of 6000 British troops from Britain to India. In addition, there would be a delay of about a month for any shipping sent to Saigon to return to India and continue Operation Python demobilisation duties. Regarding Hanoi radio, Wedemeyer took action on Mountbatten's request to prevent unhelpful broadcasts from Hanoi.[59]

In Whitehall, the Defence Committee debated the need to accelerate movements of French troops to Indo-China due to the imposition that this would place upon Operation Python and other shipping requirements. The CIGS, Brooke, in response to a question by Attlee, thought that it was too early to foretell the direction of events in Indo-China: 'He recommended that the situation was not at present sufficiently serious to pay the expense involved in speeding up the arrival of the extra French division by one month only'. However Oliver Harvey, Assistant Under-Secretary at the Foreign Office, said that the Foreign Office was anxious to speed up the arrival of the French division and return law and order to the French but that France had not raised the prospect of acceleration. The Prime Minister sided with Brooke. Attlee concluded that the situation did not warrant a change to the schedule of French troop movements to Indo-China, therefore condemning Gracey to a further period of uncertainty regarding the role of the ALF.[60] The JPS felt that Britain would legally remain responsible for law and order but that British commitments should be limited to a minimum and thereafter handed over to the French. The Foreign Office held that if Mountbatten announced that Britain had only military objectives in Indo-China then this might encourage revolutionary activities. The JPS agreed. The Foreign Office suggested that an announcement should be made along the lines that Mountbatten would not tolerate activities that threatened the implementation of tasks or security. Again the JPS concurred.[61] The COS supported the Foreign Office recommendation, anxious to avoid negative French reaction to events due to the need for their support in wider security issues.[62] Bevin believed that Mountbatten's statement was important in defining Britain's role in Indo-China, but that it was difficult to defend the differences between the British role in the Dutch East Indies and French Indo-China.[63]

Whilst the British Government deliberated the delicate situation in which it found itself, the Vietminh made it clear in a broadcast where it believed the current uncertainty in the south stemmed from.

The British delegation is entirely responsible for the bloodshed in Vietnam which heralds a third world war. The cowardly French Imperialists could not start trouble within Vietnam without the support of the British delegation.

...

We officially bring to the notice of the world the bloodshed which is about to occur in our land. A deadly war is about to begin on our land and it will only be due to the British delegation which has oppressed us, favoured the French traitors and thought only of her interests in the Far East.[64]

The British Civil Affairs Agreement with France was signed in London on 9 October. This gave France administration of Indo-China below the 16th parallel.[65] John Sterndale Bennett, Head of the Far Eastern Department at the Foreign Office, questioned SEAC ability to deal with the political and economic problems throughout Southeast Asia.[66] Mountbatten took personal charge of the situation in Indo-China and met with Gracey and Leclerc at Rangoon to formulate a policy for the difficult circumstances on the ground.[67] A day later the Vietminh broke its cease-fire agreement. The British were caught again between the aspirations of the French and the Vietminh. Slim questioned the directives from the JPS to Gracey as being unworkable and the situation was poised to deteriorate even further.[68] Mountbatten passed to the British Government Vietminh demands for the immediate restoration of the Vietminh authority in Saigon, the rearming of the Annamites and the disarming of the French. Mountbatten urged Gracey to avoid claims of the numbers of Annamese killed or 'giving the world the impression that we are threatening to use all weapons of war at our disposal. ... That is one way to lose the sympathy of public opinion in Europe and America'. Likewise, Mountbatten reminded Gracey that he was not allowed to authorise any handouts or interviews to the press.[69] Mountbatten and Slim urged the Cabinet to accelerate the arrival of the French Ninth Colonial Division.[70] A further report from the Vietminh in Saigon to Britain stated that 'France by her selfish policy has lost her rights in French Indo-China and in [the] Pacific generally. [The] Vietminh has proved the right and ability of [the] people of Indo-China to rule themselves'.[71] Truman complicated the political climate by claims in his Navy Day Address that all people prepared for self-government should be permitted to choose their own form of government.[72]

On 24 October Bevin responded to a question in the House of Commons with a statement on the situation in Indo-China. This was a mixture of 'half truths and untruths: it was a louche statement of lies'.[73] Bevin's statement was a bland synopsis of events since August. The Foreign Secretary's oratory side-stepped the gravity of the situation in the south and it reiterated Attlee's desire not to become 'involved in the administration or the political affairs of non-British territories'. He concealed the political situation from the House by claiming that the 'liberal attitude' of the French Government was 'reflected in the very conciliatory manner in which the local French representatives have dealt with the Annamite leaders'. Bevin discharged the Government's responsibility by concluding that 'every effort is being made to expedite the movement of French troops to Saigon'.[74] Bevin's performance was symbolic of the Labour Government's policy towards Indo-China, it was a minor concern in an era when Britain was still unsure where its economic and political post-war role lay.

Only when Gracey's responsibilities are viewed in the light of the complex situation in Indo-China and the restraints imposed upon him by a difficult international situation, faced with limited British resources, can it be understood how misrepresented his actions have been. Gracey has been vehemently attacked and blamed for the Vietnamese loss of life.[75] Yet the wider dimensions of the burden facing Gracey in September and October 1945 and the unworkable nature of the directives that Gracey received from the JPS in London conspired against him.[76] The nature of the JPS directives was unsurprising considering Bevin's parliamentary performance and the government's disorientation as to relevant post-war strategy and priorities. Attlee already had confused SEAC by denying a statement by Lawson that British troops were being used to support French interests.[77] Gracey worked within British military rules, the Hague convention and international law.[78] He was praised by Leclerc for his actions but this did not mean that Gracey approved of the French coup or their methods. Promises made to Gracey by the French to use a minimum of force during the coup had proved false.[79] Gracey was deeply troubled by the morality of French operations. In a letter to Slim, Gracey described Leclerc's operations against the Vietminh as being pursued 'with much unnecessary brutality'. He noted that: 'The French troops are leaving a pretty good trail of destruction behind them, which will result in such resentment that it will become progressively more difficult for them to implement their new policy, and, I am convinced, will result in guerrilla warfare, increased sabotage and arson as soon as we leave the country'. Gracey was troubled by the attitude of the French, the resentment that they were building, and the future of the political process towards self-government. The Japanese troops were also troubled by the actions of the French and requested that all orders to their forces be given by British rather than French officers as they found it 'increasingly difficult to carry out the orders resulting from their [French] schemeless plans'. Gracey agreed with the Japanese assessment, writing that: 'The last is, alas, so true about the implementation of their plans'.[80] However, Mountbatten was willing to play a double game with the French. He was eager to assure D'Argenlieu that SEAC forces were honoured to serve in close co-operation with the French but pressed Gracey that any unsavoury jobs of military necessity should be left to the French.[81]

In October the US withdrew participation in SEAC and terminated the OSS mission to Hanoi, although four additional US missions remained in Hanoi.[82] The US was wary of imperial entanglement and was also readjusting its priorities in a post-war world. Fifty thousand US troops were sent to China to oversee peace-keeping duties between the communists and the nationalists in the Chinese Civil War.[83] Ho appealed to Stalin, Attlee, Truman and de Gaulle, warning of French attacks against DRVN.[84] By November Ho, aware of the changing US priorities and of Western suspicion of communism, dissolved the Indo-Chinese Communist Party, which went underground.[85] The Vietminh could now be seen as a broad non-communist nationalist coalition fighting for independence. This provoked the question that was later to haunt both US and British policy makers as to whether the Vietminh were nationalist, Titoist or Stalinist. Ho still continued to lobby the US for diplomatic recognition.[86] In December the US withdrew all of its personnel from the DRVN.[87] US disassociation was interpreted as covert support for colonialism.[88]

Meanwhile the British in Saigon learnt that a Russian mission of seven members was expected to arrive in Hanoi.[89] Colonel Walker-Chapman, on a trip to Indo-China, visited Hanoi in December where he found the Vietminh to be communist and Ho a 'friend' and 'disciple' of Lenin. Walker-Chapman held two interviews with Ho in which Ho stated that as a last resort the Vietminh could retire to guerrilla warfare against the French. Walker-Chapman compared the zeal displayed by Ho's youth movement to that of the Hitler Youth. Whilst Walker-Chapman was in Hanoi a signal was received at the British Mission to arrest Indian Nationalists based in Hanoi. The Chinese loaned the British one platoon of military police and on 23 December General Chatterjee, Premier of the Indian National Movement of Liberation, and seven officers were arrested.[90]

As British operations began to be reduced and replaced by the French, Mountbatten was pleased to be informed by Gracey that British officers were no longer commanding Japanese forces. Lord Halifax reported from Washington that US public opinion had been incensed at the use of Japanese troops by SEAC and Mountbatten feared a Western public opinion backlash and political repercussions.[91] Asian public opinion was already strained. In Ceylon and India there was strong support for Pan-Asian nationalism. The Secretary of State for the Colonies advised the Governor of Ceylon to issue a statement in support of the evolution of self-government but told him that Mountbatten 'had to use force to meet violence by the extremists'.[92] Nevertheless, the State Council in Ceylon unanimously passed a motion in support of the struggle of the peoples of Indonesia and Indo-China.[93]

Mountbatten informed Gracey that he would tell the CIGS, Brooke, how skilfully and tactfully Gracey had handled the situation in Indo-China.[94] Mountbatten received the formal surrender and disarmament of Japanese forces in Indo-China and was given a gift of a Samurai sword. He sent the Samurai sword as a present to Attlee on behalf of SEAC and used the opportunity to protest to the Prime Minister regarding the problems that SEAC had experienced in Indo-China. Mountbatten cryptically wrote that the problems were 'not made any easier by the extraordinary attitude of some of the leading Allied personalities'.[95] Attlee replied thanking Mountbatten for the gift on behalf of the forces in SEAC but sagely did not mention anything regarding Mountbatten's accusatory outburst.[96] By contrast Mountbatten in his continued correspondence with Driberg boasted 'I am rather proud of French Indo-China since I think I have succeeded in carrying out the British commitment with more success than any of the prophets forecast'.[97]

On Christmas Day Britain began to withdraw its forces from Indo-China, and on New Year's Day 1946 Mountbatten and D'Argenlieu issued a joint declaration of French responsibility for law and order south of the 16th parallel.[98] The French, grateful at SEAC's success in Southern Indo-China, expressed the desire to award military decorations to the British forces. Brain's replacement as British Consul-General in Saigon, E.W. Meiklereid, warned that the political implication of the awards would be that Britain was receiving them for putting the French back into Indo-China.[99] At SEAC headquarters Gibson wrote to Mountbatten's secretary that 'Suspicion of our hypocrisy and possible dishonesty in this matter would be intensified by the acceptance of purely military decorations on the accomplishment of what has been stated to be purely pacific tasks here'.[100] Jawaharlal Nehru in an address to the Indian Congress compared British action in Indo-China to Nazi intervention in Spain.[101] The Governor-General in New Delhi contacted the Secretary of State for India and expressed that whilst from a military point of view he did not object to the awards, from a political point of view he considered the decorations an embarrassment especially as the Indian National Assembly had just passed a motion protesting at the continued employment of Indian troops in Indo-China. He advised that not to accept the awards could be construed as a snub by the French and therefore felt that awards should be restricted to acts of bravery and presented after the end of March when most of the British forces would have been withdrawn for over two months.[102] The British Government, eager to avoid political embarrassment over the issue, replied that 'the King's Regulations do not permit our forces to accept decorations for actions taken after the official date of the armistice'. Mountbatten reluctantly informed D'Argenlieu.[103]

In the meantime a row had erupted between Mountbatten and Dening. Mountbatten reported this to Whitehall. When Dening saw the telegram Mountbatten had sent he was so incensed that he wrote directly to Bevin to complain about Mountbatten's 'mixture of fiction and malice'. He protested that Mountbatten had ineptly orchestrated political policy within SEAC. In the Netherlands East Indies, Dening asserted that Mountbatten's 'open advocacy of the Indonesian cause' and 'his harmful utterances against the Dutch' were responsible for the complicated situation in which SEAC found itself – SEAC liberation forces were caught up in violence between the returning Dutch colonial regime and the aspirations of the Indonesian nationalists that had used the sudden power vacuum at the end of World War Two to proclaim independence. Although Dening acknowledged to Bevin that he could not now remain as Mountbatten's Political Adviser, the Dutch Lt.-Governor-General, Dr Van Mook, had asked that he stay until the British Ambassador arrived and therefore not leave Dutch SEAC issues in the hands of Mountbatten. Comparing the roles of Foreign Office staff and the military personnel at SEAC Dening informed Bevin 'I am not, however, satisfied to leave my staff at the tender mercies of the Supreme Allied Commander and his headquarters which has now attained a standard of inefficiency which makes it a by-word'. On Indo-China, Dening said that Mountbatten had 'consistently ignored' Brain, his Foreign Office Representative, for the last 18 months. Dening commented that his experience in the last two and a half years had led him to conclude that Mountbatten was only impressed by superior rank. Dening pushed for an early decision on the appointment of a special commissioner whose rank would be above that of an ambassador so that Foreign Office policy would not be hindered. Finally, Dening stated that Mountbatten had never taken him on any journey outside SEAC where political questions had been involved, except for the Cairo Conference which he attended at the request of the British Representative in the China Theatre, General Carton de Wiart. Dening complained that he was even unable to brief Mountbatten prior to such meetings as he often did not learn of the circumstances until after the event.[104] Bevin, aware that the political situation would be resolved by the forthcoming appointment of a special commissioner, side-stepped the conflict and asked Dening to settle his differences with Mountbatten amicably.[105]

Ho did not give up in the face of an imminent French return to the south. China was still responsible for ALF duties in the north and the Chinese were content to work alongside the Vietminh. The DRVN provided China with a political counterbalance to the French in a complex triangular relationship in which China never recognised the DRVN.[106] On 6 January 1946 the DRVN held elections in the north for a national assembly, to add democratic legitimacy to its cause.[107] Meiklereid observed that the election was 'purely a political move principally for external consumption', probably to impress the US, and that it was backed by the Chinese.[108] Chinese encroachment into Southeast Asia had been a fear of the Foreign Office despite Chiang Kai-Shek's pledge in August 1945 that China had no territorial designs on Indo-China.[109] China might have had no territorial ambitions but it could still possibly regard Indo-China and Southeast Asia as an area of political intrigue and influence. Again Ho cabled the US for support and recognition.[110] Meanwhile, the size of the expected Russian mission to Hanoi doubled. Britain learnt that fourteen rooms in the Metropole Hotel plus a large villa had been now allocated for their purposes.[111] However, the British ALF handed over the guarding of the Japanese to the French, and Gracey departed Indo-China on 28 January.[112] Remaining British ALF tasks were performed by a British Interservice Mission, and on 5 February Leclerc declared at a press conference that Cochinchina and Southern Vietnam had been completely pacified.[113]

The US had not completely abandoned Ho and sent a special fact-finding mission to see him in Hanoi between 14–24 February, but US priorities continued to change.[114] Policy makers were coming to terms with a possible Soviet threat. George Kennan telegrammed to Washington from Moscow a dispatch on US policy towards Russian nationalism since World War Two. Kennan asserted that there was no permanent resolution possible with Russia and that this therefore left no choice for the US but to build up British and US forces.[115] The Greek civil war that began in May vindicated this choice and as a consequence the US and the British supported the monarchists against the communists. The US and Russia also clashed over the presence of Russian troops in Iran.[116] Churchill highlighted the growing world divisions with his prophetic iron curtain speech delivered at Fulton in Missouri.[117]

Although Ho had succeeded in directing nationalist aspirations in Hanoi and maintained the government of the DRVN, his position was still not yet secure. There were various factions in Vietnamese nationalism and Ho did not have all of the popular support of all of them. When it was reported that Ho was in negotiation with the French, demonstrations took place in Hanoi against Ho's leadership.[118] As the demonstrations continued it emerged that opposition to Ho in the north was principally by the Vietnam Quoc Dan Dong nationalist party; one demonstration even called for the return of the ex-Emperor Bao Dai as President.[119]

In the meantime a Sino-Indo-Chinese Relations Agreement was signed between France and China. In the agreement the Chinese

Nationalist Government agreed to hand back Northern Vietnam to the French in exchange for the termination of French extra-territorial privileges in China.[120] Similarly, French Indo-China was removed from SEAC. Ho concluded initial negotiations with the French, and the Ho-Sainteny Agreement was signed between the French and the Vietnamese, although D'Argenlieu announced that this did not apply to Cochinchina as this was a separate state.[121] In the agreement France recognised the Vietnamese republic as a free state with its own government, parliament, army and finances but as part of the Indo-Chinese Federation within the French Union. The Union of Tonkin, Annam and Cochinchina would be discussed at a later date. The Vietnamese would receive the French army peacefully. Foreign relations and future status would be discussed at a future conference.[122] In Laos French Forces reoccupied the capital Vientiane and defeated the Lao Issara nationalists. On 16 March a large French naval and military force arrived in Hanoi.[123] Indo-China was no longer in SEAC and therefore the operation was entirely French. Mountbatten and SEAC were not involved and they were only given the relevant information by the French in late February.[124] Ho, desperate to preserve Vietnamese nationalism and the DRVN, sought diplomatic recognition from Britain.[125] Whilst the British Government considered its response the Northern Indo-Chinese press accused France of bad faith and reported that Ho's political position was under pressure from extremists.[126] Britain resisted the pressure and declined to accord recognition due to the ongoing nature of Franco-Vietnamese negotiations.[127] The French were duly informed of the Vietnamese request and the British response.[128] Meanwhile the US opened a consulate in Saigon and sought to improve relations with French Indo-China.[129] The US Consul Charles Reed acknowledged 'the general unpopularity of Americans in French Indo-China who are blamed for being responsible for the situation in North[ern] French Indo-China by insisting [at the Potsdam Conference] in making the Chinese responsible for the disposal of the Japanese in that area'.[130]

Cambodia

In direct contrast to the violent situation that had developed in the British ALF administered areas of Southern Annam and Cochinchina, the British ALF in Cambodia were easily able to assimilate power from the Japanese and remove the Cambodian Nationalist Prime Minister Son Ngoc Thanh. As had happened in the rest of French Indo-China the

Japanese had overthrown the French in the coup of 9 March 1945. On 13 March, in response to the Japanese, the Cambodian King Norodom Sihanouk declared Cambodian independence, co-operation with the Japanese and annulment of all Franco-Cambodian agreements. The independence proclaimed by Sihanouk was in reality relative and largely symbolic. The Japanese remained in control of Cambodia replacing the French as the colonial power. However, under the guidance of the Japanese, Cambodian nationalism had the opportunity to evolve.[131] In May, Thanh, former adviser to the Cambodia nationalist newspaper *Nagara vatta*, was brought back from exile in Japan and made Foreign Minister.[132] Thanh, not content with the direction of Sihanouk's regime or of Sihanouk's preparations to resist the return of the French and safeguard Cambodia's independence, became Prime Minister after the failed anti-royalist coup of 9–10 August.[133]

Thanh's leadership was dynamic but short-lived. Its failure had little to do with the arrival of the British in Phnom Penh but more with Thanh's inability to carry the support of the Cambodian elite, even members of his own cabinet, for his policies. Thanh sought to maintain Cambodian independence and prevent the return of the French. Therefore, on 2 September, in an attempt to gain Vietnamese support, he recognised the government of the DRVN and permitted it to establish a mission in Phnom Penh.[134] Thanh's government contacted the DRVN several times in September 1945 and accepted proposals for talks to co-ordinate resistance to the French. A Cambodian delegate was dispatched for the talks but negotiations stalled at the Cambodian precondition for the return of the historically lost Travinh and Soc Trang provinces.[135] Thanh's association with Asian nationalism was not limited to the Japanese or the DRVN; he also sent emissaries to seek Chinese and Siamese aid.[136] Thanh tried to reinforce his own position and legitimacy by organising a nationalist demonstration of 30,000 in support of his policies in Phnom Penh. A referendum was held in which there were 'allegedly 541,470 votes in favour of independence' and only 'two' against.[137] Desperate to preserve independence Thanh organised his own armed militia, the Green Shirts, to fight the French. Demonstrating where real authority lay, though, the Japanese selected Thioum Muong to lead the militia.[138] The militia was created on 31 July whilst Thanh was still Foreign Minister and by September numbered 800 troops armed and in uniform, paid for by exploiting Cambodia's forests.[139]

Meanwhile, with the dangerous situation and limited British resources in Saigon, Gracey cabled Mountbatten on 25 September that 'Cambodia has no strong militant anti-French element at the moment and appears passive'.[140] With the continuing problems in Vietnam in mind, three days later Gracey again raised the issue of Cambodia at a meeting with Mountbatten. Gracey, worried that British intervention in Cambodia would have similar consequences as in Vietnam, suggested that the best way to handle the situation in Cambodia was to 'condone the past actions of the P.M. [Thanh] and to enlist his support; in fact to treat him in the same manner that we had dealt with Aung San in Burma' – to work with the nationalist movement. Mountbatten agreed with this political solution. It was decided that Cédile would settle the situation in Phnom Penh with Thanh and that French troops would take over from the Japanese, thereby sparing Gracey's limited resources from involvement in Cambodia.[141] However, the plan was not put into action. At a meeting later on the same day with Lawson, Mountbatten was told that the British Government did not want 'to interfere in the internal affairs of non-British territories'. Lawson empathised 'that the instructions issued from London made this extremely difficult in French Indo-China'.[142] The French were now responsible for Thanh. British forces would have to go to Phnom Penh solely to perform Japanese surrender duties whilst maintaining a difficult position of neutrality neither to endorse Thanh nor to turn him over to the French. However, it transpired that it would be the Cambodian elite and members of Thanh's own cabinet that would decide his immediate fate.

Thanh, in seeking to ally himself and Cambodian independence with the DRVN in order to prevent the return of the French, had unwittingly alienated himself from the rest of the Cambodian population. The Vietnamese like the Siamese to the west had been Cambodia's traditional enemy. Cambodia had long feared colonisation by one or other of its more powerful Southeast Asian neighbours and at various stages in its history had been subject to programmes of Siamese and Vietnamese incursion. By associating Cambodian nationalism with the DRVN Thanh had ignored the basic logic of Cambodian history; the fear of Vietnam seeking to influence a weak Cambodia could not be ignored by the Cambodian elite. Thanh's overtures to the DRVN caused dissent in his own cabinet with the Defence Minister Khim Tit, Minister for National Education Nhek Tioulong and Minister for the Interior Sum Hieng unprepared to support him. Additional reasons for this discord were: notably, a fear in elite circles at the growing power of Thanh; the traditionally conservative nature of Cambodian society and support for the monarch; fear of republican ideas disseminating from the Vietnamese; that the French would be best placed to recover the provinces in the west lost to Siam in the war of 1941; that Cambodia suffered from a lack of technically educated and professional nationals; and that the withdrawal of the French would leave a dearth of talent.[143] Likewise, Thanh's leadership and nationalism did not have the same religious appeal to unify the masses as did Sihanouk's divine monarchical status.

Therefore, Khim Tit flew to Saigon for discussions with the British and the French concerning Cambodia, and to request the return of the French.[144] On 9 October British Headquarters staff of the ALF Phnom Penh, under the command of Lt.-Colonel E.D. Murray, arrived in the city and assumed command of all Allied forces in Cambodia; senior Japanese officers were flown to Saigon under arrest.[145] Murray's orders were: to maintain law and order in Phnom Penh; to safeguard Allied nationals; to ensure the stability of the Cambodian government; to disarm the Annamite police in Phnom Penh; and to prevent Annamite arms from being smuggled into Phnom Penh. Murray's forces consisted of one platoon of the first Battalion Gurkha Rifles, two companies of light French Commandos, released Allied prisoners of war, the Japanese 55th Division, Japanese Air Force and police stationed in Cambodia as well as the Cambodian police.[146] The two French companies under Lt.-Colonel Houard had followed Murray to Phnom Penh to arrest Thanh but strangely failed to do so.[147]

The French failure to arrest Thanh complicated Murray's position, yet Murray worked alongside Thanh and his government until General Leclerc flew to Phnom Penh to arrest Thanh himself. On 10 October Murray called upon Khim Tit, who had returned to Phnom Penh and brokered arrangements for the ALF.[148] Two days in conference at ALF Headquarters Khim Tit and Lt.-Colonel Houard arranged for the Annamite element in the railway workers to be removed.[149] An hour later, Murray visited Thanh to discuss the disarmament of the Annamite police.[150] Thanh confirmed to Murray that all the Annamites were disarmed and explained that the aim of all Cambodia was to achieve self-government.[151] The following day Thanh attended ALF Headquarters in Phnom Penh for a conference with Murray and his staff. Thanh asked Murray to define a clause in his orders to 'ensure the stability of the Cambodian Government'. Murray cryptically replied that he (Murray) had no civilian authority, 'it meant ensuring that the lawful Govt [sic] of Cambodia was not interfered with, by subversive influences or force'. No one asked for a definition of 'lawful', but Murray's tone in the rest of the conference implied civilian government rested with Thanh and his ministers. Thanh assured the British of the full co-operation of the Cambodian Government and made arrangements for Murray to visit Sihanouk on the 18th, following a four-day pilgrimage by the king. Later that evening Khim Tit dined with Murray and strengthened his position; events of the following day were to sharply contrast with the mutual co-operation of the previous few days. Firstly, by order of Khim Tit, Japanese guards were placed on the railways and in the railway workshops to prevent Annamite workers stealing tools or committing sabotage. Secondly, Murray flew to Saigon for urgent talks with Gracey concerning Cambodia and the arrest of Thanh.[152]

The British had been forced to work with Thanh due to the incompetence of the French in failing to arrest him. The French were keen to remove Thanh and the British Government eager to leave such domestic considerations to the French; this compromised the British position in Phnom Penh. If Murray successfully worked with Thanh it would strengthen Thanh's position and naturally upset the French, who regarded him as a Japanese collaborator rather than a Cambodian nationalist. Yet Thanh's co-operation with the DRVN and lack of support from senior ministers in his cabinet could prove problematic. Murray could ill afford to let the situation deteriorate into unrest similar to that which the British were trying to cope with in Saigon. In such circumstances, the Annamite population in Phnom Penh could prove to be a haven not just for Cambodian nationalism but also as a base for Annamite reprisals against the British for actions in Southern Vietnam. Both Murray and Gracey needed to clarify the situation. It was Murray's opinion that Thanh should be arrested as soon as possible to avoid a descent into chaos.[153] The next day Leclerc flew to Phnom Penh and Thanh was invited to the British Headquarters, handed over to Leclerc and escorted to Saigon.[154] The Cambodian police and the *sûreté* were placed under Murray's control, anti-French agents were arrested in Phnom Penh and a new government was formed under the new Prime Minister Prince Monireth.[155] Three Cambodian chiefs and two officers of the Green Shirts were arrested later that evening.[156]

The situation in Phnom Penh was still not stable. The backlash to Thanh's arrest began on 16 October. Railway workers went on strike and the Japanese were forced to operate the trains to keep them running. Thanh's Green Shirts were still armed and in Phnom Penh, but the timely return of Sihanouk from his pilgrimage was greeted by large crowds and this stalled any action. Mountbatten later claimed it imperative in preserving Sihanouk's neutrality that Thanh was arrested whilst the king was absent from Phnom Penh.[157] The next day the Green Shirts were disarmed by the Japanese. The British held a conference with the Cambodian police and the national guard chiefs; a further ten Annamite agents were arrested. On 18 October Murray met with Sihanouk and this with the intervention of Khim Tit in the railway workers strike ended the opposition to the arrest of Thanh. By 22 October French troops were carrying out exercises in Cambodia, and a day later Cambodian French status was officially restored by Sihanouk.[158] The remnant of Thanh's nationalist supporters and allies fled to Siam and Cochinchina, some to continue the struggle as the Free Cambodia Party, others to join the Indochinese Communist Party, the Vietminh and the Khmer Issarak.[159]

With the security situation in Phnom Penh satisfactorily resolved, Murray was promoted to Brigadier and began to organise food convoys between Phnom Penh and Saigon in order to relieve the food crisis caused by the Vietminh blockade of Saigon.[160] Reconnaissance to other parts of Cambodia found the 'country quiet and the inhabitants friendly to the French'.[161] There were further incidents with Annamites, who were driven out of Hatien on the Vietnamese-Cambodian border by Lt.-Colonel Wenham with the aid of 300 Japanese on 20 November, but security in Cambodia had improved to the extent that, on 25 November, Murray began the formal surrender proceedings of General Sakumay and the Japanese 55th Division Headquarters in Phnom Penh.[162] By 19 December a British unit to investigate Japanese war criminals had arrived in Phnom Penh and 8372 Japanese had been disarmed and evacuated.[163]

The Cambodian-Siamese border dispute

SEAC's involvement in Cambodian issues was not limited to the problem of Thanh or the administration of the Japanese surrender. SEAC also had to contend with the problem of the Siamese-Cambodian border dispute. In 1940, following the defeat of the French in Europe, Siam had raised the issue of the return to Siam of Cambodia's western provinces, Battambang, Siem Reap and Stung Treng which had been lost by Siam centuries before. In January 1941 Siamese troops invaded Cambodia and defeated the French. The French counter-attacked against the Siamese navy, destroying over half of it without loss. The Japanese intervened to stop the fighting and imposed a settlement, whereby the French were forced to cede the Cambodian territories to Siam.[164] Cambodian and

French national pride had been damaged over the border dispute and in 1945 both nations wanted to avenge this defeat, retrieve the lost provinces and secure the return of a sacred religious icon, the Emerald Buddha, which had been taken by the Siamese.[165] De Gaulle denounced any arbitration on the matter, declared that Cambodia remained part of French Indo-China and that France 'considers herself to be at war with Siam'. The British War Office feared that whilst Southeast Asia was under SEAC France would try to occupy the lost provinces in Cambodia before the conclusion of any political settlement. It gravely noted that: 'The view of the United States Government is that the future of Cambodia should be decided by a plebiscite or by world organisation machinery. ... His Majesty's Government supports France. Thus there will be a head on collision with the United States Government if SEAC supports by force the re-entry of French colonial administrators into this province'.[166]

In reality, Truman and his administration were struggling to come to terms with the complexities of building a lasting world peace. The negotiations with the Russians, the Allied occupation of Japan, the disarmament of Japanese forces and European reconstruction all meant that former President Roosevelt's ideals of trusteeship and self-determination for colonial people had been quietly dropped from the US policy debate some months previously. Bidault visited the French Embassy in Washington and indicated to Sir John Balfour, British Minister in Washington, that 'he was satisfied with the American attitude toward the question'. Balfour made his own enquiries on the matter to the State Department: 'The State Department replied that, as is well known, they do not recognise any territorial changes which have been made under duress during the war. They have mentioned to the French Embassy however that there might be a case for re-examining Indo-China Siam pre-war boundary in this area'.[167] The Foreign Office sensed that the French had a real opportunity to improve relations in Southeast Asia, if they could seize the initiative and offer some kind of gesture to the Siamese. It was noted that the French were generally perceived badly, and 'once the Japanese have left Siam, will soon be undisputedly the best-hated foreign nation'. It was suggested, by A.C.S. Adams, that the US would be able to profit from the goodwill established during de Gaulle's recent visit to the US to propose that the French should submit the frontier question to arbitration at an early date.[168] However, caution was advised. The Foreign Office preferred to leave the arbitration to the US to follow up. It maintained that now was not the time to extract an undertaking from the French on the issue.[169]

Dening was asked to inform Siam that Britain did not recognise changes of territory obtained under the duress of war and that Siam and France would have to settle this issue separately.[170] Similarly, Mountbatten was instructed to assume that all French Indo-Chinese territory in Siam would only revert to Cambodia after a political settlement had been reached between Siam and France. If the French attempted to take the territory by force of arms, Mountbatten was to refer to London for instructions and not to assume that he would have to intervene and establish an Allied military government in the area.[171] Planning staff at SEAC Headquarters had already prepared a plan to 'institute martial law in Siam and French Indo-China with or without reference to the Siamese or French authorities'.[172]

On 26 September Dening met with the French negotiator Pierre Clarac and Siam's Prince Viwat in an attempt to resolve the dispute. Dening predicted that the issue would pose some difficulty as the Siamese were unprepared to negotiate, believing that they had the support of the US on this matter.[173] But the US did not advocate the Siamese claims and the State Department encouraged the British-led negotiations to seek an early re-examination of the Indo-China Siamese border.[174] Britain was eager for the dispute to be resolved as Siam had been identified as a possible key area of post-war strategic co-operation for the defence of Malaya, Burma, India, Indo-China and the security of the Indian Ocean and Southwest Pacific areas.[175]

D'Argenlieu wanted the two provinces returned as soon as possible to Cambodia and sent French observers to Battambang without British or Siamese approval. Mountbatten, eager to avoid a diplomatic incident, told D'Argenlieu to attach his observers to Lt.-General Geoffrey Evans's staff located there as part of SEAC's ALF Siamese obligations. Mountbatten also turned down a request from D'Argenlieu to transfer Battambang from Evans's to Gracey's command, therefore, symbolically avoiding uniting the lost provinces with Cambodia and edging them out from Siamese control.[176] The French issued instructions to their observers in Battambang along broad but controversial lines:

a – Keep the spirit of France present in the province despite any active propaganda by Siamese officials.

b – Show that France does not renounce its claim to Battambang province but on the contrary to emphasise the rightful claims of Cambodia.

c – Keep the High Commissioner accurately informed of the political developments and of Siamese intrigues in the province.

d – Maintain contact with the representatives of the Allied forces in Siam whose authority extends to Battambang province and adopt an attitude in keeping with your role of recognised observers who may require the assistance of the British authorities.[177]

Evans discussed with Gracey and the British Consul-General in Bangkok, Hugh Bird, the directives given to the French observers and recommended that clauses 'a' and 'b' be removed from the directive as these might have given the observers too wide a scope of activities and could lead to further serious incidents. Evans could not spare troops from the Seventh Division for operations in the disputed territories after 10 January 1946, leaving behind only two officers as the Allied representatives in Battambang. He cabled to Major-General Harold Pyman, Chief of the General Staff ALF SEAC, asking him to confirm that

a – You do not require me to station any troops that area as consider we might become involved unnecessarily [*sic*].
b – We reserve right to withdraw French observers if they exceed their directif [*sic*].
c – Commandant Cretin [a French army officer acting as an observer] to be withdrawn from duty disputed area as he is already unpopular and will not improve relations [*sic*].[178]

The French agreed to limit the activities of their observers and to the removal of Cretin. However, the French insisted that they could not withdraw all their personnel by 23 December, as had been requested, and informed the British that ALF Siam had already agreed that two French observers should remain in Battambang to prevent a Siamese moral victory.[179] Sensing that the French were pushing their boundaries over the issue of observers Gracey cabled Evans for his views. Gracey had been informed that the French would press for six observers to work in the disputed territories including one at Evans's headquarters.[180] Evans replied with a stark warning 'unless SACSEA permission already obtained grateful if you prevent this as serious risk of Siamese detaining aircraft and bodies'.[181]

On 11 December, the First Secretary of the French Embassy in London visited the Foreign Office to discuss the dispute. The Foreign Office agreed to try to move the negotiations along, and for the French to exchange diplomatic letters with Siam.[182] Dening was instructed to reiterate to the Siamese Government that Britain did not recognise the territory seizures of 1941. The US was in agreement with the British stance.[183] Meanwhile, to avoid further incidents or complications, Mountbatten was warned of the dangers of the French being allowed to make radio broadcasts in Siamese to Siam and ordered to prevent such broadcasts.[184] Mountbatten was unable to prevent the broadcasts from Saigon, but texts of the broadcasts were shown to the British. The local Foreign Office and Far Eastern Publicity Representatives felt the propaganda to be useful and advised non-intervention unless the broadcasts were embarrassing to Mountbatten because this would insinuate a lack of British influence.[185] The COS was content with Mountbatten's broadcasting arrangements, 'provided that the French accept guidance as you suggest'.[186] This proved to be a grave error of judgement. The British Political Adviser and Far Eastern Publicity Representatives in Bangkok reported that the Siamese press were reacting in a hostile manner to the French broadcasts. SEAC tried to persuade the French of the need to abandon the broadcasts. Clarac in a compromise move agreed that no further reference would be made in broadcasts to the disputed territories until negotiations had been completed.[187]

However, the Siamese appeared unmotivated to settle the dispute quickly. A report by the British JIC concluded that the French regarded Siamese inactivity as provocative.[188] Yet at times both sides could be intractable. It took Dening and Meiklereid two weeks working behind the scenes to persuade D'Argenlieu to agree to send an emissary to meet the Siamese in Singapore to discuss the dispute, although 'six weeks have elapsed and the Siamese have given no outward sign whatsoever that they intend to do anything about it'. Dening warned that if Siamese intransigence continued then this might push D'Argenlieu into more drastic measures. He concluded: 'I am afraid that I can think of nothing I could say or do to improve the position'.[189] Clarac now feared that D'Argenlieu wanted to pursue a more aggressive radio broadcast policy with the ultimate goal of seizing the disputed territories with troops. He asked if the British Government could bring further pressure to bear upon Siam to begin the talks in Singapore with the French.[190]

The Foreign Office sent a telegram to Bangkok on 9 March 1946 that the British Government demanded a stable and peaceful Southeast Asia and urged Siam to open negotiations with the French at once. It reiterated its previous statements by declaring that the British Government did not recognise the 1941 frontier and that Siam must therefore restore the pre-war *status quo*.[191] Siam's response was that it wished to negotiate with the French and resume normal diplomatic relations in return for French rectification of the border.[192] Meiklereid held further discussions with Clarac who promised to interpret Paris instructions liberally in order to meet the Siamese request.[193] Later Clarac confirmed that France was prepared to undertake frontier adjustments.[194] However, D'Argenlieu was less convinced about Clarac's liberal brief and telegraphed Paris for further clarification, thereby delaying a French response.[195] Meiklereid warned that the situation remained complicated as France was technically still at war with Siam.[196]

Geoffrey Thompson, British Minister in Bangkok, met with the Siamese Foreign Minister to discuss the Siamese intransigence. Thompson feared that the dispute could escalate. He had obtained evidence that certain Siamese elements were supplying arms to factions in Laos and that the increased French impatience with the Siamese could affect Siam's entry into the UN, with France as a permanent Security Council member vetoing Siam's application. Thompson urged the Foreign Minister to transfer the disputed territories: 'I said that if the Siamese would courageously grasp this nettle I thought it very likely that the French would be disposed to negotiate agreeable frontier rectifications'. However, the Siamese Foreign Minister wanted to change the existing arrangements and send a delegation to Saigon and not Singapore. He requested that the British Government assist in brokering a resolution to the dispute.[197] With British activities in SEAC reducing in French Indo-China, the Foreign Office agreed with Siam and recommended switching the Franco-Siamese meeting to Saigon in an attempt to extricate itself from the prolonged dispute. London stressed that it would like to see the border question settled as soon as possible, and normal relations resumed between French Indo-China and Siam, but Britain could not become involved in a dispute which was now solely French and Siamese.[198]

Rice and relief

As in the rest of Southeast Asia the British ALF in Indo-China was charged with maintaining law and order; part of this inevitably involved dealing with the problem of supplying food and emergency supplies to the civilian population. In Indo-China famine had already broken out in the north during the last months of the Japanese occupation. Problems at the end of the war included civil unrest, Japanese stockpiling of resources, the lack of an administrative structure, a dearth of shipping and locomotives, and a breakdown in the rail and irrigation systems. These problems were caused by natural erosion and drought, Allied wartime bombing and indigenous attacks. It created a volatile situation where continued unrest and the lack of a bureaucratic structure could result in the famine spreading to the rest of Indo-China. Famine politically united the masses in a common cause. Traditionally the Mekong and Red River deltas of French Indo-China were vast rice growing areas. Rice was exported to other parts of the French Empire as well as the metropole, Hong Kong, India and Singapore. Therefore problems with rice production in Indo-China had grave consequences for other British-administered areas that, like French Indo-China, experienced food shortages at the end of the war. This was part of a global food shortage, especially of rice.

On 28 August 1945 the rice situation was further complicated when Chiang Kai-Shek, who was facing his own transport difficulties and aware of the problems in the north of Vietnam, requested the purchase of 5000 tons from Mountbatten in Saigon in order to feed troops involved in maintaining the Japanese surrender.[199] Mountbatten replied that he was unable to supply the rice required as he was not in control of the commodity. He arranged for the matter to be taken up with the UN International Food Control.[200] Britain had no realistic method of assessing the size of the rice situation prior to Gracey's troops arriving in French Indo-China in September. Nevertheless, to prevent rice inflation and the activities of the black market, the Cabinet proposed to co-ordinate rice prices from London in the three main producing areas in Southeast Asia – Siam, Indo-China and Burma.[201] The Ministry of Production consulted with the War Office and the Board of Trade to try to establish a minimum relief programme to French Indo-China.[202] A programme was established in September to prevent disease and unrest but France was encouraged to use procurement to prevent reliance upon Britain's limited resources.[203] Mistakes were made in the assessment of Indo-China's requirements. For example it was reported 'that there are in French Indo-China considerable quantities of rice and rubber available for export', but Britain was prepared to offer and orchestrate what relief it could.[204] Meanwhile, the French procured from the US 15,000 tons of relief supplies of flour, condensed milk, iron and steel, paper, cement and chemicals. These were loaded onto two ships in San Francisco. One vessel was supposed to go to Southern Indo-China and the other to the north, but due to complications in the French relationships with the Chinese liberating authorities both vessels were sent to the south.[205] The French assured

Britain that a further five ships had been earmarked in the US for service to Indo-China and that 60,000 tons of supplies would be shipped from the US to French Indo-China by the end of the year.[206] Administrative responsibility of the British forces for food supplies and relief eased when on 9 October the British and French Governments agreed that administration and judicial issues in Indo-China should now be passed back to the French.[207] Although British officials were aware of the continued food shortages, British attempts to alleviate the situation became increasingly ineffective and observational with the French restored to administrative control. Meanwhile the interallied Combined Food Board allocated the export of 66,936 tons of rice from French Indo-China for the immediate relief of the Dutch in Netherlands East Indies. The War Office, keen to extricate itself from a difficult political situation, held that Britain could not establish a rice unit in French Indo-China and that the Dutch Government should deal direct with France in this matter. Mountbatten telegrammed Saigon that the 'political situation may make export of rice by French authorities difficult'.[208] The British did attempt to fly food into Northern Indo-China to relieve Tourane using six Japanese aircraft; but unfortunately the Chinese impounded the aeroplanes.[209]

When the French resumed administrative control they were keen to restore their prestige as an independent great power able to maintain its own affairs. However, the need for relief both in SEAC and French Indo-China continued to escalate. On 25 October Meiklereid reported that in Northern French Indo-China under Chinese control food and medicine levels for Europeans were adequate but that prices were rapidly increasing. The Vietnamese in DRVN administered areas were not so fortunate. There was disquiet because of the imposition of a poll tax despite the continued famine. Food levels in the north were reaching critical levels due to further floods. The French authorities in Saigon, needing coal for the power station, loaded 2000 tons of rice onto a ship in Saigon to exchange for coal when it reached Haiphong.[210] Gracey sent Major Hambrey Tracey to be the British Military Liaison Representative in Hanoi with the task of supervising the distribution of the rice from the south and the loading of the coal.[211]

Administration of relief in Southern Vietnam was also hampered by continued civil unrest. In order to resist the return of the French the Annamese had organised a food blockade around Saigon and Cholon. This political action did not aid British relief activities in the area. However, with the security situation in Phnom Penh satisfactorily resolved, Brigadier Murray organised a food convoy between Saigon, Cholon and Phnom Penh in order to relieve the food crisis there. Cambodia was now identified as an essential source for supplying fresh food to Saigon and Cholon to break the Annamese food blockade in Cochinchina.[212]

In November a British Cabinet sub-committee on the Far East received a note regarding French Indo-China. It stated that the UNRRA Chungking had on 28 September contacted the UNRRA Washington and reported the dire conditions in Northern Indo-China. The note concluded that 'This zone falls outside Southeast Asia Command and is not, therefore, a matter for British action. The Committee may, however, like to bear these conditions in mind when considering the relief requirements of French Indo-China'.[213]

British officials in Saigon issued a report in December to the Foreign Office on the rice situation in Indo-China. If half the Japanese rice proved inedible then the shortfall would be in the region of 35,000 tons. The report highlighted that due to the current security problems farmers had been unable to bring rice to market since June and that even if it were possible to harvest the new crop, security and transport issues could prevent it from reaching the market. The French Economic Counsellor in Indo-China had reserved 200,000 tons of the new crop to address the famine conditions in the north, as a priority. The French production problems would affect not just French Indo-China but all of Southeast Asia and other areas. Only 61,000 tons of rice had been exported from French Indo-China up to the end of August 1945, compared with 500,000 tons in 1944 and 922,000 tons in 1943.[214] Despite D'Argenlieu's insistence that it was not possible to find any rice for export Mountbatten pressured him to find some.[215] To aid the French it was decided to carry out a photographic aerial survey of rice crops to estimate the probable harvest yield in 1946.[216] Conditions in the north continued to deteriorate. In a visit by Colonel Walker-Chapman to Hanoi he observed that the Annamites were reluctant to sell food to the French and that the black market was increasing. With coal production at 100 tons per day, and the availability of Japanese prisoners of war as labour, the Chinese believed that it was possible to export coal from Hongay to Southern French Indo-China in return for rice.[217] However, due to a shortage of shipping this proved unrealistic.

By January 1946 the food situation in Cochinchina appeared to have stabilised and market prices decreased.[218] At a staff meeting with Gracey in Saigon an enquiry was made concerning the prospect of exporting rice from French Indo-China. Meiklereid answered that due to transport problems, the needs of the north and a reduction in the size of the crops, there would be no exportable rice. He advised that further food needed in SEAC must be acquired from within the rest of SEAC and that an application to the UNRRA had been made.[219] Meanwhile the British learnt that under pressure from his advisers D'Argenlieu had appealed through Paris to the UNRRA for assistance in the shipping and loading facilities for rice and medical equipment at Tonkin. Dening observed that the French were suspicious of the UNRRA due to the implied presence of US economic observers but 'felt constrained to formulate [an] appeal to safeguard themselves against world criticism when famine conditions [in] Tongking [*sic*] became known'.[220] The UNRRA visited Saigon to discuss displaced persons and the economic situation in French Indo-China. Meiklereid reiterated the difficulties the French faced over the rice situation to the Foreign Office and further warned 'Unless very drastic and immediate measures are taken, the death-roll in the Tonkin from famine is likely to be measured in millions rather than in thousands'.[221]

In the north, although the Chinese ALF was supposed to remain neutral to the political situation, they chose to work alongside the DRVN administrators rather than the French mission.[222] Meiklereid warned the Foreign Office that the Chinese were not taking any action regarding law and order and recommended the intervention of the great powers to prevent 'disorder, anarchy, ruin and famine'. Otherwise the results he again predicted would be that 'the Annamites will die by the hundreds and thousands and due to unrepaired dykes floods will bring devastation'. Meiklereid concluded that with the Japanese disarmed the Chinese were no longer useful and that the French were capable of relieving French Indo-China.[223] SEAC had requested 164,000 tons of wheat supplies for Southeast Asia for the first six months of 1946 but the allocation proposed at the Washington meeting was only 127,000 tons.[224] With the British role in French Indo-China coming to a conclusion Mountbatten proposed to leave British interests in the hands of a Foreign Office political adviser and the Consul-General in Saigon, along with a British Interservice Mission (comprising of two battalions plus administration troops). They would, in between other duties, inform Mountbatten of French plans to rehabilitate the rice industry and export rice.[225] This token gesture by Mountbatten revealed the extent of his effectiveness concerning the famine conditions in French Indo-China. Mountbatten had previously had little influence over D'Argenlieu concerning rice distribution and now had none. The serious rice shortage in the north persisted, there remained a lack of shipping and the French maintained no confidence in the Chinese being able to distribute shipped rice. The 1945–46 harvest forecast for Southeast Asia was poor due to 'undersowing by farmers for lack of inducement in price and consumer goods'.[226] A further half-hearted proposal was put forward by SEAC. In order to address the coal shortage in SEAC Britain could lend a ship to aid in the transportation of rice from Southern French Indo-China to the north in exchange for coal.[227] Mountbatten's delusion was confirmed when he sent a telegram to the COS at the end of his responsibility for French Indo-China in which he reported that the British position in French Indo-China had never been better and that there was the possibility of 'cashing in on the goodwill of both the authorities and civil population' for British trade whilst there was also 'an excellent opportunity for consolidating British prestige'. He predicted that the only area of conflict was the continued freeze of French Indo-Chinese funds, particularly by India, and optimistically predicted that by June there would be the possibility of both rice and coal being available for export.[228] Mountbatten's telegram was acknowledged by both the COS and the Foreign Office but neither further pursued Mountbatten's suggested benefits for Britain.[229]

Despite the situation in French Indo-China being both grave and outside their control the British Government optimistically predicted that for the rice calendar year 1946 the surplus of exportable rice from French Indo-China would be 100,000 metric tons.[230] In February the Minister of Food revised his previous predictions by adding stringent parameters. Based on the 'latest information' on the 'disturbed state of the country' he noted that even if it were possible to harvest, collect and transport rice in Indo-China 'it would be unsafe to rely on the export of more than 100,000 tons from French Indo-China in 1946'.[231] Two days later in a move to co-ordinate the problems of rice supply in Southeast Asia as a region the Cabinet agreed that a special commissioner 'should be instructed to initiate and supervise a vigorous campaign for increasing the supply of rice from Southeast Asia'. Bevin was invited to make the appropriate arrangements and the appointment of Lord Killearn as Special Commission Southeast Asia was announced to the House of Commons on 21 February.[232]

Military aid

SEAC was able only to place a dangerously small amount of resources and troop numbers into its ALF duties for French Indo-China. Britain's limited resources were highlighted by the need to use Japanese prisoners of war to assist in carrying out liberation duties.[233] Limited shipping resources meant that the supply of British and French troops to French Indo-China was competing with transport required for Operation Python to demobilise British and colonial troops.[234] The French Navy was able to use its ship in the region, the *Richelieu,* to transport troops, although its capacity was limited.[235] Mountbatten, anxious to avoid involving British troops in further clashes in Southern Vietnam, requested additional shipping and troops including the French Ninth Colonial Division.[236] The Ninth Colonial Division was 'organised on American war establishment and war equipment tables' and was therefore 'fully armed, clothed and equipped in accordance with the standard establishment of a United States Army Infantry Division'.[237] It would be impossible to maintain such a force with US material unless the US withdrew its ruling that no American equipment was to be issued to French forces in SEAC.[238] Mountbatten hoped that Leclerc would be able to take over in Indo-China on 2 October 1945, when the French would have 2425 troops in Southern Vietnam or at the latest by 20 October when a further 2150 had been scheduled to arrive.[239] Mountbatten had planned to use a SEAC brigade in Indo-China to relieve the Australian ALF in Borneo by 31 October.[240] The British Government was also aware of the bad publicity that the use of Indian troops in French Indo-China could have with Indian public opinion.[241] It was important for the government to withdraw Indian troops as soon as possible to avoid Indian nationalist claims of Britain using Indian troops to suppress Asian nationalism on behalf of a white French colony.[242] The British Commander-in-Chief in India believed that he could not even agree to the movement or staging of French troops through India *en route* to Indo-China.[243] Britain therefore sought to alleviate the situation by discussing the shipping of troops to Indo-China with the US.[244]

Bevin was desperate that any available US warships be used to speed up troop deployments to the Dutch East Indies and French Indo-China.[245] Fearing further British involvement in Indo-China Slim reported that no French forces of any real value were yet available. British forces were maintaining essential services and preventing the massacre of French civilians but he warned that if there was a full scale uprising then the British forces would be unable to cope. He stated that the situation was very dangerous, that the British were very unpopular with the Vietnamese and therefore needed to leave as soon as possible.[246] Eight ships were provided by the US to transport the 7700 troops planned to leave France for Indo-China in October and an additional 14,000 from Marseilles on 23 October.[247]

Nevertheless, by November Mountbatten was again pressing the War Office for the French to relieve him of the burden of Indo-China 'owing to the very delicate situation in Netherlands East Indies and the big calls it is likely to make on my resources, more than ever necessary to shift the burden of French Indo-China onto French shoulders with all possible speed'.[248] With increased French troop numbers, Leclerc asked Britain to supply one squadron of RAF Spitfires to be flown by French pilots. Leclerc felt that his operations were disadvantaged by not being able to use British air support for French troops and by not having suitable French aircraft available. Mountbatten accepted Leclerc's request and advised the COS that one squadron of Spitfire Mark IV's and spares could be turned over to the French with the financial aspect of the arrangement left to the British and French Governments to settle.[249]

The French had frequently asked the British and the US for transport for troop movements and equipment for their forces. The US were well aware of French requests to the British and requests from SEAC to London, as much of the correspondence was copied to the JSM in Washington; thus implicating a legitimate British expectation of US involvement pertaining to French requests. Similarly, the British were aware of US sensitivities concerning the use of their equipment under SEAC control. The First Sea Lord, in reply to a French request to supply landing craft to their forces in French Indo-China, had responded that as most of the stock attached to SEAC was of US lend-lease origin the British navy would be only able to supply two craft. If the French got the approval of the US to use American craft then he would be able to supply more.[250] The US was willing to supply equipment to the French in Indo-China especially if the French were prepared to purchase such equipment. In December 1945, 279 vehicles purchased by the French from the US were in Calcutta awaiting shipment for Saigon.[251]

The British were wary of merely handing over lend-lease material to the French without US approval, and in order to avoid any political problems, stated that in the first instance 'British substitutes should be used where possible'.[252] Yet Britain could not avoid the lend-lease issue. In trying to supply equipment for the French Third Colonial Division the War Office had intended that no lend-lease material was to be used.[253] Only 900 vehicles of British origin were available to transfer from the 20th Indian Division but a further 1300 vehicles were available to transfer which were of US lend-lease origin.[254] Major F.H.

Weaver, dealing with the problem, cabled Mountbatten and requested that 'you obtain permission of the Americans' for the lend-lease equipment transfer.[255] Weaver then cabled the US to seek agreement for the transfer of the lend-lease vehicles, the quantity of which had now reduced to approximately 800.[256] Britain also provided training teams for the French for the equipment supplied. However, these proved to be under-used by the French who had a tendency to 'rush equipment up country before it has been put in working order'.[257]

SEAC was prepared to continue to assist in the maintenance of French forces 'until such time as the French no longer require[d] such assistance'. But after 15 February 1946 all such supplies would have to be paid for.[258] It was agreed, in talks with French representatives in London, that Britain would maintain French forces in Indo-China until 31 March 1946. Thereafter Britain would provide for the provision of 3,300,000 pacific rations but beyond that provision SEAC would have no responsibility for French forces.[259] However, French forces in Indo-China, although accepting responsibility for guarding the remaining Japanese prisoners of war, would not accept any financial obligations until the situation had been clarified by Paris.[260]

In the meantime, the question of the Indian response to the situation in French Indo-China was again brought to the fore. It was difficult to move French or Dutch supplies from Europe to French Indo-China or the Netherlands East Indies without using bunkering and watering facilities in India. The British could not use Ceylon for fear of a port strike and labour unrest. Singapore was too far for many vessels and possessed only limited stocks due to SEAC duties. The Commander of the Indian Expeditionary Force had already agreed to accept two or three French vessels a month but labour strikes were threatened. The Viceroy of India, Field Marshal Archibald Wavell, therefore agreed to accept ships flying British or US flags carrying French forces provided that no more than two or three harboured together at any one time for a maximum of two or three days. No French troops would be allowed to land and their presence was to be concealed. No provisions were made available. The operation was to be top secret because if the details were leaked out labour strikes would preclude any further ships using Indian harbours.[261]

In January 1946 the US became keen to disassociate itself from the formulation of military policy in the Netherlands East Indies and French Indo-China but remained interested in Siam.[262] Despite the US disassociation it insisted that Southern Indo-China was to remain within SEAC until all the Japanese prisoners of war in all of SEAC were evacuated. In recognition of the changing circumstances in French Indo-China, the US was prepared for such tasks to be delegated to the French.[263] Brooke believed that as the US did not want to hand command over from SEAC in Indo-China 'the Americans wished to have it both ways' and he recommended that Mountbatten relinquish command for Indo-China as soon as possible 'lest any further occurrences started there'.[264] The COS was unable to agree with the US proposal to keep French Indo-China within SEAC and offered the compromise that Mountbatten would keep the responsibility for the Japanese through Leclerc.[265] Brooke was eager for the question of responsibility for French Indo-China to be settled rapidly by the JSM as French operations were starting in Southern Vietnam (which led to French troops landing in the north) that could have grave implications for Mountbatten and SEAC should they still be responsible for Southern Indo-China.[266] The US agreed to the British compromise solution and both Britain and the US were able to disassociate themselves from French military actions in Indo-China.[267]

The co-ordination of British policy

Potsdam in 1945 split Vietnam as Geneva later would in 1954. Both conferences prevented Vietnamese Nationalism from uniting the country. On the ground Britain had to avoid an anarchic power vacuum but in terms of high policy Britain and the US never questioned French sovereignty or the legitimacy of the nationalist movements. The British role in Indo-China, although limited, was larger than the spotlight upon Saigon has suggested. It evolved from ALF duties in Cambodia and Southern Vietnam to incorporate the Cambodian-Siamese border dispute, humanitarian relief and rehabilitation, and jointly with the US of transporting and rearming the French military. Thus the British did not unilaterally restore the French in Indo-China.

Similarly, Britain was coming to terms with a new dependency upon the US. Had Britain's comprehension of its economic and political role in the world been different, Attlee would still have been limited by economic circumstances. However, his personal commitment to the Python program or ignorance of Asian nationalism could have been different. The post-hostilities watershed was not without its failings of judgement or missed opportunities. Pre-war colonialism could not return. The Labour Government certainly compounded SEAC's problems in Indo-China with unworkable directives, restrictive policy and a commitment to the restoration of France in Europe. There were always going to be higher government priorities in the immediate post-war period, but a transparent Indo-China policy would have had to emerge from a Foreign Office whose wartime support for the restoration of France continued into the post-war period.

By the spring of 1946 the Labour Government had deduced that not only were British policies toward Indo-China and the Dutch East Indies erratic and ill-managed by SEAC, but that British economic stability and colonial policies required delicate co-ordination. Britain needed to develop policies on the Cambodian-Siamese dispute, humanitarian relief and rehabilitation, reconciliation with the aspirations of Asian nationalism, the furtive spectres of the Chinese nationalists and communists and latent communist influence within the indigenous Southeast Asian populations. Therefore the Labour Government sought to co-ordinate British policy with the appointment of Lord Killearn as the Special Commissioner Southeast Asia.

3
Lord Killearn, March 1946–May 1948

In the spring of 1946 Britain made a co-ordinated effort to manage its policy towards Indo-China. British interests in Indo-China were summarised in a Cabinet paper on the Far East as 'strategic', 'political' and 'economic'. Strategically, Indo-China was regarded as an important base that controlled the South China Sea and the approaches to Singapore. Politically, the conflict between the French and the Vietnamese could have 'disturbing reactions in British territories'; similarly, 'whatever government is finally established in Indo-China would inherit causes of friction with China and Siam in which we might become involved'. Economically, the 'French intention of an "open door" policy in Indo-China might offer new openings to British trade'. However, in conclusion the paper cautioned that although France would regain Indo-China 'her position is likely to be precarious unless she can win over the leading Annamites to acceptance of her political and economic advance'.[1]

The appointment of Killearn as Special Commissioner for Southeast Asia acted as the focal point for the alignment of British concerns for Indo-China alongside regional responsibilities. The main area of this debate was the export of Indo-Chinese rice in a continued effort to alleviate regional famine conditions. However, the growth of the international spectre of communism would entangle this process. Britain believed in raising living standards in 'poorer countries', but the move from political dialogue to guerrilla warfare in Indo-China threatened this policy.[2] Similarly, the military conflict in Indo-China threatened the availability of exportable rice, bringing an economic and humanitarian crisis to the British colonies of Hong Kong, Malaya, and Singapore. Britain was directly concerned with the stability of the region – the decolonisation of Burma and India meant that Britain had to reconcile itself with the aspirations of Asian nationalism. The Cambodian-Siamese border dispute remained unresolved, and the large indigenous Chinese communities in Southeast Asia continued to be an area of tension that escalated with the growing likelihood of communist success in the Chinese Civil War. Bevin was not indulging in flattery when he described Killearn's appointment as 'the biggest job of your life my dear boy'.[3]

Vietnam

Following the March 1946 Ho-Sainteny Agreement, negotiations continued between the French and the Vietminh. The Foreign Office remained optimistic that the settlement was reasonable and that a 'progressive and liberal policy is successfully being pursued'.[4] The French approached Britain and 'in view of the pending negotiations with Viet Nam' asked the Foreign Office to disclose the diplomatic apparatus used by India in 'relations with foreign powers'.[5] D'Argenlieu, however, regarded the agreement 'as the equivalent of Munich'.[6] Unfortunately, he 'didn't understand the nature of the problem in Tonkin' and 'refused to visit Hanoi'. As the negotiations progressed D'Argenlieu met Ho for the first time on a battleship in Along Bay.[7] The situation appeared delicately balanced, Meiklereid informally visited Ho who expressed concern that the French desired to encourage separatism in Cochinchina.[8] Reed cautioned the US Secretary of State, James Byrnes, with the hope that neither side would do anything to jeopardise the negotiations.[9] In a note to the French Ambassador in Washington, Byrnes officially approved of the reversion of Indo-China to the French, although he 'ignored the fact that the French had already signed an agreement recognising Viet Nam as a free state'.[10]

The timid optimism of March was replaced by anxiety in April. The Dalat Conference was fraught with disagreement between the French and Vietminh over the unity of Vietnam and the future of Cochinchina.[11] Leclerc gloomily concluded that 'France is no longer in a position to control by arms an entity of 24 million people, amongst whom xenophobia and perhaps even nationalism have taken root'.[12] Undeterred by the impasse with the Vietminh, D'Argenlieu pressed ahead with his policy of separation for Cochinchina and created an autonomous republic with its own provisional government.[13] Between 6 July–10 September the Fontainbleau Conference attempted to revive the negotiations between France and DRVN, but again no agreement was reached on substantive issues. Whilst Fontainbleau was taking place D'Argenlieu continued to develop an Indo-Chinese solution independent of, and in opposition to, the Vietminh. A second Dalat Conference was held between Annam, Cambodia, Laos, France, and the Montagnard hill tribes but not the Vietminh.[14] The British feared the bi-polar direction that negotiations appeared to have taken and Killearn advocated 'close contact and liaison with French Indo-China'.[15] Lt.-Commander Simpson-Jones, British Naval Intelligence in Hanoi, regularly met with Ho three times a week for about an hour and a half to gather information on the developing situation.[16] The French needed a reliable moderate Annamese with whom to negotiate and who would also present exemplary credentials as a nationalist to the masses. Meiklereid indicated that the 'general feeling' was that the new Cochinchina government had been established by the French 'purely as a "puppet" government'.[17] Simpson-Jones warned about the consequences of eliminating Ho.[18]

The DRVN continued to advocate a placatory policy towards the situation in the north and Vietminh troops in Hanoi were disarmed to prevent any trouble between the French and Vietminh troops.[19] Killearn noted the food situation in Indo-China at his monthly liaison conference as 'encouraging' and British Rear-Admiral Archer visited Saigon between 10–15 August for a 'flying the flag' morale visit.[20] Nevertheless, France pressed on with an uncoordinated policy. On 27 August France signed a Modus Vivendi with Laos making it a unified state within the French Union. A similar agreement was signed with Ho on 14 September. Mr Narn, a secretary to Ho, visited Britain and left the Foreign Office with the impression that 'so long as he [Ho] is in charge he will exercise moderating influence'.[21] Meiklereid added that the Modus Vivendi seemed to have strengthened Ho's position 'and there appears little danger of him being ousted by extremists'.[22]

In Paris, Ho sought to alleviate the deadlock by appealing direct to the US. He contacted the US Embassy and requested American intervention in the dispute. The following day at the embassy Ho asked for US 'enterprise' and 'capital' in return for a lease on the strategic naval base at Cam Ranh Bay.[23] Ho's advances went unheeded. US policy had continued to evolve in response to its role as a global power and as a counterbalance to Russia. Ho and the Vietminh were now regarded with suspicion because of their communist background. Under-Secretary of State Dean Acheson contacted Saigon in October and complained of the communist style in the design of the

DRVN flag.[24] Paradoxically the French remained suspicious of the US whose approach to world affairs was regarded as 'too "light-hearted"'.[25] Nevertheless, the US Moffat mission to Indo-China in December was warned by Acheson of Ho's status as an international agent of communism.[26] Before visiting Southeast Asia Abbot Low Moffat, Head of the State Department Southeast Asia Division, visited his opposite Richard Allen in the Foreign Office in London for Anglo-US talks on Indo-China. Moffat feared that D'Argenlieu and Clarac were too 'reactionary and imperialistic' and that they would 'drive' the Indo-Chinese towards communism. Allen asked Meiklereid for his assessment on and the accuracy of the US views.[27] Meiklereid replied that Moffat's analysis was 'unduly pessimistic'.[28] In Hanoi Moffat met with Ho and representatives of the DRVN. He urged for a peaceful settlement and affirmed US support for the Ho-Sainteny Agreement and the Franco-Vietnamese Modus Vivendi. Moffat's report, however, concluded that US interests rested with French dominance of Indo-China.[29] He then went on to Singapore anxious to enlist Killearn's support for his own 'proposal of joint Anglo-American good offices with the French in F.I.C. [French Indo-China]'. Killearn remained non-committal but Moffat, who Killearn noted was under the influence of alcohol, vehemently complained 'that the normal attitude of the Foreign Office, and particularly of Dening and Allen, was inclined to be over cautious and lacking in appreciation of the issues at stake and imagination generally'.[30]

In contrast to the French and the US, the British were more open to Ho. Britain viewed Ho as a moderating influence within the DRVN, and although the Foreign Office was wary of his communist background, he was regarded as the more acceptable face of the Vietminh. Britain reasoned that nationalism was ultimately stronger than communism. From 1–6 October Meiklereid visited Hanoi and spent a couple of days with the less moderate Defence Minister Giap. Giap was exercised with the French ill faith over Cochinchina.[31] Soviet interest in Indo-China had strengthened with the arrival of a Russian mission in Saigon to repatriate 320 Russians who had been serving in the French Foreign Legion.[32] In November Meiklereid dined with D'Argenlieu in Phnom Penh. D'Argenlieu raised the spectre of communist influence in Southeast Asia and 'its effect on the French relations with the Viet Nam Government'. By doing so D'Argenlieu had labelled Ho a communist. Meiklereid still regarded Ho as a moderate, keeping the extremists in the DRVN in check; he predicted that should Ho be 'ousted the possibility of any form of lasting agreement will become increasingly precarious'.[33] However, Meiklereid thought that a French agreement with DRVN was now impossible.[34] As tension on the ground mounted, the Chinese Embassy in London proposed Anglo-Chinese negotiations to avoid a conflict.[35] The Foreign Office discussed the question with the US Embassy but concluded that no 'useful purpose would be served by intervening'. Allen noted 'as the Chinese must be aware, the French are notoriously sensitive to intervention from outside in their affairs, and such intervention is liable to produce prejudicial and unsatisfactory results'.[36] Nevertheless a week later, after the Vietminh uprising in the north, the Chinese again broached the prospect of Anglo-Chinese representations to stop the conflict. The view from the Foreign Office was that it was 'not ... wise to intervene at the moment'.[37] A similar approach to the State Department a week later was also rejected.[38]

Meiklereid failed to observe that the Vietminh had not been idle while negotiations with the French remained unresolved. By December the Vietminh had consolidated their position in the north by eliminating, both politically and militarily, the two other nationalist parties, the Vietnam Quoc Dan Dong and the Dong Minh Hoi.[39] On 19 December the DRVN proclaimed general uprisings in Northern Vietnam. These uprisings proved to be a debacle and the Vietminh were forced to retreat from Hanoi and other towns in Tonkin. The strategy for 1945–46 had been to use security and militia units for the seizure of Hanoi and other main towns and to achieve administrative control of the provinces. This strategy had failed because there were inadequate military forces to counter French actions. This led to a greater willingness to adopt the 'Maoist' strategy of using guerrilla forces to control the countryside first and then move into the towns. The French were in the military ascendancy. Would this be the opportunity to pressure Ho into a settlement? It seemed not. French strategy had changed. They had now identified a possible indigenous political alternative to Ho, 'the reinstallation of the Emperor Bao Dai'.[40]

The US offered to assist the French over the crisis. Acheson proposed that France raise the conflict in the UN, with the US assisting France to adjudicate issues.[41] John Carter Vincent, Director of the Office of Far Eastern Affairs for the State Department, sent a memorandum to Acheson stating that France lacked the strength to recapture Indo-China. The government in Paris was weak and divided; it lacked public support. Vincent believed that the guerrilla war could go on indefinitely, and US uneasiness about the communist nature of the Vietminh persisted.[42] France rejected the US offer.[43] The US Division of

Southeast Asian Affairs felt that the 'US was being put in an increasingly difficult position by the French'. On 7 January 1947 Moffat, in Bangkok, reported to Washington that he regarded that the Soviets were not yet directly active in Southeast Asia. In revision of his December report he predicted, due to French actions, that the only solution in Vietnam was independence.[44] He concluded that the only alternative was 'a gigantic armed colonial camp'.[45]

Britain was preoccupied with the establishment of machinery for Burmese independence.[46] Dening, promoted to Assistant Under-Secretary of State at the Foreign Office, expressed his 'uneasiness' about the consequences of the Indo-China crisis on Burma. He warned of

> repercussions in India and Burma ... and awkward questions in Parliament and we shall be torn between the obvious need to maintain close friendship with France in Europe and the equal necessity in our weak economic and military position in S.E. Asia, to avoid taking sides in a racial conflict against the nationalist movements of that area.
> In the meantime there is nothing we can do.[47]

Allen went to Indo-China on a six day mission to discuss the situation in the north with D'Argenlieu. The High Commissioner appeared to revoke the legitimacy of the Ho-Sainteny Agreement: he admitted that 'the French had only signed the March 1946 Agreement with Viet Nam under pressure from the Chinese'.[48] It transpired that the French authorities would 'resume negotiations as soon as the current military phase is over but not (repeat not) with Ho Chi Minh'.[49] D'Argenlieu attempted to isolate the DRVN and asked all foreign consuls to cease contact with the Vietminh.[50] Although Britain agreed to D'Argenlieu's request, communication was kept open with the DRVN as the British Consul in Hanoi, Arthur Trevor-Wilson, continued to meet with the Vietminh along with the Red Cross to negotiate for the release of hostages.[51] Bevin informed Attlee 'the outcome of the Indo-China situation is difficult to foresee but we are unlikely to be able to influence it'.[52]

The US Ambassador in London was asked for the British assessment of the situation.[53] The new Secretary of State, General Marshall, agreed with Britain's position. In a statement to the US Embassy in Paris, Marshall accepted French sovereignty in Indo-China but was critical of the French colonial outlook. He expressed concern at the communist nature of the DRVN but concluded 'frankly we have no solution of [the] problem to suggest'.[54] However US global policy had entered a new phase. On 5 March Acheson noted it would be important to study regions of the world where technical and military assistance might be required.[55] Seven days later the President announced the 'Truman Doctrine'. This was 'the political embodiment of containment', 'to support free peoples who are resisting attempted subjugation by armed forces or outside pressures'.[56] Military and economic assistance was offered to Greece and Turkey, although in order to placate Congress Acheson explained to the Foreign Relations Committee that this did not set a precedent for intervention elsewhere and that all future requests would be assessed individually.[57]

The Foreign Office remained worried about the situation in Indo-China. It was concerned that France was losing control and saw no prospect for a settlement.[58] From Singapore Killearn cautioned

> it is not always easy to say where nationalism ends and communism begins, and if we are trying to back the one and not the other, we may sometimes find that we are backing a horse from the wrong stable. The fact is that these are restless days, and whatever labels one attaches to the various movements, they all spring much from the same soil and much the same seeds.[59]

The removal of D'Argenlieu prompted Foreign Office speculation that the appointment of a new High Commissioner might lead to a resumption in negotiations with Ho.[60] Trevor-Wilson suggested that by the autumn of 1946 Ho had remained in Paris too long, thereby allowing Giap and the extremists to plot a more radical course of action.[61] The French arrest of Ho's representative in Paris and his extradition to Indo-China to face trial hardly indicated a lowering of tensions for a resumption of Franco-DRVN negotiations.[62]

In May, ironically, Paul Coste Floret, French Minister for War, stated that 'there is no military problem anymore in Indo-China ... the success of French arms is complete'.[63] Both the Laotian and Cambodian constitutions were promulgated. D'Argenlieu had been replaced as High Commissioner by Emile Bollaert but Reed noted that Bollaert had no confidence in Ho or DRVN negotiations and that it was impossible to identify anyone else to negotiate with.[64] In Hanoi Trevor-Wilson continued to meet with the DRVN Foreign Minister to discuss humanitarian issues.[65] The State Department issued guidance to US diplomats:

> Key [to] our position is our awareness that in respect [of] developments affecting [the] position [of] Western democratic powers in

Southern Asia, we [are] essentially in [the] same boat as [the] French, [and] also as [the] British and Dutch. We cannot conceive setbacks to [the] long-range French interests [of] France which would not also be setbacks [of] our own.[66]

Indo-China was being measured in terms of US-French relations and Washington's desire for France to be restored as an important link in European security.[67]

During the second half of 1947 US concern about the international threat of communism began to escalate. Russia had become increasingly isolated and the big three co-operation of the Second World War had broken down.[68] This was to develop into the 1950s under the crude assertion that the US was protecting the free world against a conspiracy from Moscow and later Peking. In July US Lt.-General Chamberlain published a paper 'Positive US Action Required to Restore "Normal" Conditions in Southeast Asia'.[69] The State Department began to consider the scenario of a Vietminh controlled government for Vietnam and asked its Consuls in Saigon and Hanoi to consider its implications.[70] Guillaton, the French Indo-China Economic Adviser, arrived in Singapore for talks with Killearn and relayed the deterioration of the past couple of months. Unfortunately Guillaton saw no hope of the situation changing. He believed that 'D'Argenlieu had been mistakenly hard' and that 'some sort of arrangement must sooner or later be made with the inhabitants'.[71] Killearn cautioned the Foreign Office that the Vietminh were communist-inspired nationalists and that in October 1946 Colonel Dubrovin had led a mission from Russia to Indo-China.[72]

Sensing the change in the international political climate, Ho again held an olive branch aloft. The DRVN Cabinet reshuffle that he enacted appeared to eliminate some of the more extreme members and positioned himself 'midway between the Mao of the Long March and Gandhi at the spinning wheel'.[73] Analysis at the Foreign Office was divided, 'It has always been a moot point how far Ho Chi Minh himself is actually working to the Kremlin line'.[74] The State Department was equally confused. The US Embassy in London approached the Foreign Office for their interpretation of 'Ho Chi Minh and communism in French Indo-China'.[75] The Foreign Office Minister Hector McNeil met with Kennan of the State Department. The US was 'embarrassed by the failure of the French ... to come to an understanding with the nationalist movements in ... Indo-China'. If the Bao Dai solution was a success and Indo-China was 'threatened by a communist China' the crisis could be taken to the UN where Kennan stated 'Indo-China could count upon full American support'. However, the US was suspicious of French motives for advocating support for Bao Dai. 'The Americans wanted to be quite sure that the French really meant to play the same game, and not if Bao Dai was successful, to attempt to restore complete colonial French rule through Bao Dai. The Americans could support Indo-China but they could not support French colonialism'. McNeil was left with the impression that the 'Americans expect the United Kingdom to take the lead in this region'.[76] The French Representative on the UN Security Council was instructed to veto the Council's intervention in Indonesia, for fear of a precedent being established that could in the future challenge their authority in Indo-China.[77]

In contrast to Stalin's policy of 1945–47 that concentrated on the West, Soviet attention began to focus on the nationalist struggles of indigenous colonial people. E.M. Zhukov wrote in *Pravda* that 'only Leninism offers a solution of the national colonial problem'.[78] In September the political confrontation increased when in a speech to launch the Communist Information Bureau Andrei Zhdanov expounded the two camp thesis. This assumed a new post-war alignment of political forces into the 'imperialist anti-democratic camp' and the 'anti-imperialist democratic camp'. Vietnam was associated with the second camp led by Russia which advocated the need for a continuing world revolution.[79] The US Army Staff Plans and Operations Division paper 'Current Situation in Indo-China' predicted that a communist victory in China would strengthen the Vietminh and bring them under the influence of a communist China.[80] Ironically, in the same month the DRVN began to purchase arms from the Chinese communists.[81]

By the close of 1947 France appeared to have established a two tier Indo-Chinese policy. Both Cambodia and Laos had evolved constitutionally within the French Union and had held national assembly elections, but Vietnam remained an anathema to the French.[82] The First Along Bay Agreement between France and Bao Dai was an attempt to allow Tonkin and Annam independence within the Union under the same terms as Cambodia and Laos. Cochinchina continued to maintain a separate status.[83] In Bao Dai the possibility of an indigenous nationalist alternative to Ho had whetted the French appetite. On the international stage the Zhukov thesis was published in Russia which applied the two camp thesis to Asia. State Department and Foreign Office policy papers appeared united in suggesting that the DRVN would be a communist state.[84] The Foreign Office advised the British delegation to the UN that if the crisis in Vietnam was brought before the Security Council 'we should claim that the Franco-Vietnam impasse is a domestic matter under Article 2(7) of the Charter'. The Foreign Office expected 'the French to use their veto to good purpose'.[85] However, contrary to expectation, India failed to raise the Vietnam crisis in the UN. India had anticipated France using its veto but doubted whether the DRVN exercised *de facto* authority in Indo-China. India was also preoccupied with the UN consideration of the India-Pakistan dispute over Kashmir.[86]

In January 1948 Bevin cautioned the Cabinet that the Soviets aimed 'to turn Asiatic peoples against the Western democracies and to pose as the champion of oppressed colonial peoples'.[87] The DRVN began to establish guerrilla bases in the Chinese border areas and later in areas not reoccupied by the French. On the international stage the World Federation of Democratic Youth Conference in Calcutta discussed concerted communist plans for Asia. In Europe a pro-Soviet government took over in Czechoslovakia. Against the rising international tension Ho demonstrated a deft understanding of *realpolitik* with a show of openness and goodwill by inviting US observers to his camp; the US considered sending a Chinese agent.[88] British activity appeared to be limited to observation and a 'flying the flag' gesture of support for the French. The British Commander-in-Chief of the Pacific fleet visited Saigon in his flagship accompanied by three destroyers and one sloop.[89]

Meanwhile Bao Dai appeared to undermine the faith that the French had placed in him as an amiable alternative to Ho. Bollaert attempted to conclude an agreement with Bao Dai who suddenly embarked for a tour of Europe. Philippe Baudet, Chief of the Asia-Oceania Section of the French Foreign Ministry visited London and complained to Dening that 'Bao Dai is a poor tool for the French to use; unfortunately, he [Baudet] said, they have no other'.[90] Perhaps Bao Dai sensed that he was negotiating from a position of strength or of a fear not to be seen as a puppet and an object of popular scorn. The European tour appeared to represent an opportunity to wring further concessions from the French that would strengthen his nationalist credentials. In London he challenged the separation of Cochinchina from Annam and Tonkin with a declaration for the 'unity and independence of the Viet-Nam countries, within the French "community"'. He called for the new state of Vietnam to be accorded a constitution similar in status to that of a British Dominion.[91] Applying further pressure to the French he admitted 'that at present he has no real *locus standi* and does not represent officially anyone but himself'.[92] Bao Dai seemed to be advocating the need for a constituent assembly to legitimise his position. The French, however, 'appear[ed] to be in no hurry' to resolve the issue.[93] Killearn visited Saigon where he was briefed by the new Consul-General Frank Gibbs as to the 'extraordinary situation [of siege] which prevails' every night with 'opposition' mortar and rifle fire which Killearn noted sardonically as being 'all extremely jolly'. In conversation with Bollaert, Killearn discovered that the High Commissioner did not think highly of Bao Dai but that 'there was no one else to back'. In conclusion 'Bollaert made no bones about it that the situation with which the French are faced is excessively difficult, and he added wryly that it was made none the easier by the repeated intervention of politicians from Paris'.[94] Killearn cautioned Bevin that the French inclination was 'to lump together under the term "communists" all those – whether communists, nationalists, or merely bad hats – who actively oppose colonial rule'. He judged

that if you suppress a nationalist severely enough you will find him tending towards communism because it is the communists who have consistently supported nationalist movements in dependent territories. And it is also true that once a nationalist movement is outlawed or driven underground it is usually the communists who gain control owing to their great experience and efficiency in clandestine organisations.[95]

In March the international tension continued to escalate. The Brussels Treaty was signed advocating European co-operation in the face of the feared Soviet threat. Burma, having achieved independence from Britain in January, experienced communist uprisings. The US Congress approved $4 billion funds for Marshall Aid. Butterworth, at the State Department, invited H.A. Graves of the British Embassy in Washington to discuss the Foreign Office assessment of the Indo-China situation.[96] R.C. Mackworth Young advised: 'If Ho Chi Minh gains the upper hand it will be a great triumph for communism throughout S.E. Asia. I therefore suggest it would be best to paint the picture as black as possible to the Americans'.[97] Meanwhile the Vietminh regained the territory that they had lost to the French in the autumn of 1947.[98] Chinese Communist Party Radio North Shensi hailed the heroic fighting of the Vietminh and implied their support.[99] From Singapore, P.S. Scrivener observed the futility of the situation and 'the persistence ... of the French in cracking their heads against a sort of military brick wall'.[100]

The Cambodian-Siamese border dispute

Any optimism in managing to untangle Britain from the Cambodian-Siamese border dispute soon proved to be unfounded. The Siamese political situation remained delicate. One government had just fallen and the endurance of its successor could be undermined by any loss of prestige in negotiations with Indo-China. The export of Siamese rice was important to the stability of the region. Political instability could threaten such exports and affect the famine conditions in British territories and the region.[101]

On 1 May, Killearn had separate talks with the new Siamese Prime Minister and Foreign Minister during a trip to Bangkok to discuss the disputed provinces. The Prime Minister, Dr Pridi Banomyong, was frustrated that the delegates he had sent to Saigon had returned without making an agreement with the French. In a moment of historical revisionism, he expressed his grievance that the French had forgotten the complacency of the Vichy regime that had allowed Siam to be 'overrun' by the Japanese. Pridi pressed Killearn that the Siamese were being most amicable in the negotiations. He went on to suggest three solutions to the current impasse: referral to the UN, a plebiscite, or Siamese purchase of the provinces. Not surprisingly, these suggestions had already been rejected by Paris. However, the Siamese were eager for some kind of solution that would preserve Siamese prestige and avoid any implication of submitting to France. Killearn empathised with Pridi and reiterated the British Government's preference for a return to the pre-war frontier: 'It was pretty clear to me that what the little man was fishing for was that we should come in as honest broker and think out a formula acceptable to both sides'.[102] The situation remained unresolved.

Border incidents between Cambodia and Siam continued to plague the political situation. Pridi protested to the British Minister in Bangkok that on the 24 and 26 May large numbers of French troops had crossed the Mekong and engaged Siamese forces.[103] French Captain Leschuiton arrived in Singapore from Saigon and along with two other officials called on Killearn. They used the meeting to emphasise France's legitimate stance regarding the dispute. Killearn professed ignorance of the situation, as he was still awaiting the report, but believed Siam to be passing the matter to the UN. The French delegation reiterated that the incidents were of 'a small police matter' and that the Siamese had little real control in the disputed areas. The tone of the encounter troubled Killearn and he noted in his diary with suspicion: 'there was nothing really novel in all of this but I thought it as well to record it as one never knows what one may be quoted as having said'.[104] The Siamese Government instructed its representative in Washington to report the encroachments to the Secretary General of the UN, along with an earlier report of French bombardment.[105] Meanwhile, the French Ambassador in London, Massigli, protested to the British Government that France had used 'exemplary patience' towards Siam. He requested that both the British and US governments make representations in Bangkok about the dispute.[106] However, the British Government considered that the French attacks had damaged the credibility of France's cause, but reflected that faults existed on both sides. To prevent escalation, British and US observers were sent to the French side of the border to monitor the situation. US and British ministers in Bangkok urged Siam to cede the disputed provinces.[107] Britain cautioned Siam that France was now likely to block its application to join the UN.[108]

On 9 August, the State Department informed the British Embassy in Washington that the US had reached an understanding with the French concerning the disputed provinces and would now try to secure a settlement with the Siamese. The US even professed a willingness to be accepted as interim administrator of the provinces in order to achieve an acceptable solution to the dispute. Washington urged the Siamese to accept the US-brokered French proposals that: damage payments from Siam to France would be arbitrated by the International Court; the US would be accepted as an interim administrator with Cambodian, Laotian, French and Siamese local help; that, if Siam agreed to the first two proposals, then France would end the state of war and not block Siamese entry into the UN; finally, Siam would withdraw its complaint over the dispute to the Security Council.[109]

On 12 August, the French representatives to the regional liaison meeting at Singapore, Clarac, Guillaton and Gaudin, dined with Killearn and Meiklereid. Clarac, eager to give the French version of events, raised the question of the Siamese dispute. He believed that there was some prospect of the issue being settled in bi-lateral discussions at the UN.[110] Three days later Clarac called upon Killearn and expressed his concern at the US pre-occupation with Siam, nationalism in China and Southeast Asia. Killearn deduced that Clarac feared US interest would not leave France 'a free hand in French Indo-China'. Clarac revised his opinion from their previous meeting and now felt that the Siamese dispute had been neglected by Paris and that the dispute would be better resolved 'off stage', away from the UN. Killearn agreed with Clarac's sentiments and shared the Siamese request for a way out of the dispute which would not damage their prestige. He emphasised to Clarac the grave implications of the dispute regionally and that it could prejudice the export of rice from Siam. Clarac concurred and noted that the disputed territories were 'the richest [rice] provinces of French Indo-China'.[111]

Confidential discussions began in Washington on 27 August between France and Siam. The French were only prepared to negotiate minor border changes, but the Siamese delegation wanted greater territorial concessions. The French delegation suspended the negotiations in order to consult with Paris.[112] In the meantime, on 9–10 August, 500 Cambodian and Vietnamese rebels, allegedly accompanied by small numbers of Siamese, attacked Siem Reap and took up positions in Angkor Wat, a twelfth century temple and the symbol of Cambodian statehood and society. French paratroopers were deployed and a fierce battle ensued.[113] Following the incident the French Government withdrew from negotiations and 'asked the US Government to regard their good offices as suspended'.[114] British intelligence in Bangkok reported that the French were prepared to resort to force to retrieve the provinces.[115] D'Argenlieu requested that all observers in the disputed provinces be withdrawn to Bangkok.[116]

As the situation deteriorated, Thompson warned the Foreign Office that the French appeared willing to play the British and the US against each other because of their misplaced idea of Anglo-US rivalry in Siam. He suggested that French co-operation with Britain could be more advantageous to the French, as military action might prove to be unproductive in Washington. Thompson urged the Foreign Office to ask the Consul-General in Saigon to speak to Clarac in an effort to relieve the situation.[117] Meiklereid met with Clarac on 2 September and emphasised that there was no Anglo-US rivalry over Siam. He relieved the tension in London stating that 'there are no indications here that France are still contemplating having recourse to arms over the dispute'.[118] In October, the Cabinet considered a report from Siam. Although the report indicated that the general information from Siam was good, as the dispute now rested with the UN, it warned that 'in some quarters' there was unease that the French could attack during the forthcoming dry season. The report concluded that, given the poor state of the Siamese forces, it was feared that the French would use the opportunity to gain additional territory.[119] Reluctant to become involved, the government continued to view the dispute from a distance with unease.

In November, negotiations began again in an attempt to resolve the dispute. The French, in an effort to relieve the tension, requested that British observers remained on the disputed border even after the remainder of ALF troops had been withdrawn from Siam.[120] The British COS had no objection to the proposal, but the Foreign Office reflected that, if time permitted, observers should be withdrawn and only used to monitor the situation if an actual transfer of territory took place.[121] SEAC decided to withdraw the British observers as their safety could not be guaranteed, and their withdrawal would not have any negative military implications. SEAC advised that any proposed return for a territorial transfer would have to be decided upon at a later date.[122] The COS agreed with SEAC and informed the Foreign Office.[123] It was arranged that British staff in the disputed provinces would be withdrawn from Battambang on 18 November. However, although the British observers were removed, British plans were superseded by the completion of successful negotiations between Siam and Indo-China. On 17 November, a Franco-Siamese treaty was signed regarding the return of the disputed provinces and the French requested international observers to monitor the territory transfer. The US agreed to send some officers as observers and planned to have them arrive in Battambang on 24 November.[124] Mountbatten was ordered to send British officers urgently as observers despite no escort guard being available. British officers were dispatched, and monitored the transfer of the provinces.[125]

Rice, relief and regionalism

During 1946–48 Britain was moving towards the decolonisation of India and Burma; any unrest in Indo-China could have repercussions for this policy. The Government of India regarded Southeast Asia as an area that could purchase Indian manufactured goods, also as a supplier of raw materials (iron ore, coal and rubber) and rice to feed the growing Indian population.[126] In particular, Killearn and the British Viceroy in India, Field Marshal Viscount Wavell, were concerned at the lack of rice exports from Indo-China. Similarly, control of the supply of rice was used as a strategy by the Vietminh to bring pressure upon the French and other colonial nations to resolve the 'nationalist' struggle in Indo-China. Killearn was worried not just by the regional economic effects of the conflict in Indo-China but also by the growth of US purchasing power and economic imperialism within traditional European colonial spheres. The US would later press for Indo-Chinese and other

Southeast Asian raw materials to be used in the reconstruction of Japan.[127] This was something that would upset traditional economic relationships, as the European nations required the raw materials to finance their own post-war reconstruction; they also needed to market their manufactured goods in Southeast Asia. In addition Killearn was concerned with the regional growth of nationalism and communism, although it was British Government policy to leave the responsibility for local disputes to the individual European nations concerned.[128] British co-ordination of colonial policy and defence rested with the Governor-General Malcolm MacDonald. Finally, Killearn warned the Foreign Office of the potential danger that faced Southeast Asia from its large indigenous Chinese population who formed the only real middle and mercantile class in a number of the colonies, and had tight kinship ties, community and identity.[129] This group could become politically aware, restless and disruptive either with its own nationalist ambitions or, as the communist victory in China became more likely, part of Chinese communist state-sponsored indigenous world revolution.

The food situation in Southeast Asia remained perilous throughout 1946. Killearn in Singapore assumed SEAC's responsibility for the distribution and shipment of rice, food production and procurement, allocation and distribution of coal, currency and financial matters, imports and exports.[130] Although Killearn had no actual authority over non-British territories his role involved regional liaison and consultation about regional problems.[131] At the March Food Conference in Singapore the food shortages were regarded with the 'gravest anxiety'; the gravity of the world-wide deficit was estimated at 3 million tons for 1946.[132] In London at a Cabinet World Food Supply Meeting Lord Nathan, the Under-Secretary of State for the War Office, predicted that no exportable rice surplus would be available from Indo-China for 1946 thereby increasing food supply problems. He hoped that it would be possible for experts to visit Indo-China and encourage similar steps to those taken by Burma and Siam to improve food production.[133] All the British territories in Southeast Asia remained short of food supplies; it was calculated that Burma, Hong Kong, Malaya, and North Borneo required a minimum of 156,000 tons of rice and wheat, but only 136,000 tons could be allocated.[134] No exports from Indo-China appeared forthcoming and the French were asking for the loan of ten tugs and 50 three-ton lorries in order to facilitate any possibility of their allocated export of 100,000 tons of rice to other areas.[135] A British expert was employed by the French Government to survey the rice milling situation in Indo-China, and Britain was already exporting spare parts and machinery to restore this production capacity.[136] The March Food Conference considered sending consumer goods to Indo-China to encourage old rice stocks to be put on the market for export but Lt.-Colonel Kirkwood, SACSEA Interservice Mission Representative to French Indo-China, did not consider this a relevant strategy.[137] He believed that the political difficulties of the French were not appreciated by the conference.[138] The unrest meant that it was not possible for the French to survey conditions in the interior, and therefore no accurate statistics could be produced.[139] Kirkwood stressed that the famine situation in Northern Indo-China continued, with April and May predicted as the danger months. Rice could not be exported from the south to the north until June, but in contrast to the equipment needed for international rice export 'the French were not asking for any help'.[140] The conference concluded that due to the political situations in Siam and Indo-China it would be unjustified even to offer the assistance of an aerial survey.[141] Meanwhile French demands for transportation assistance increased to 12 tugs and 350 vehicles.[142] Curiously Meiklereid, in a visit to Northern Indo-China, failed to observe any of the pessimistic famine reports that the French had issued and noted that the locals had indicated increased production of rice, maize and potatoes.[143] The Economic Intelligence Section at SACSEA headquarters suggested that the goodwill achieved by Britain with the French during the reoccupation should be used to secure 'an open door' trade treaty with Indo-China granting Britain 'most favoured nation status'.[144] However, the British delegate at preliminary International Trade Organisation talks in Paris concluded that the French 'would not lightly abandon their "imperial preference"'.[145]

At the close of the April Food Conference Killearn met in Singapore with Mountbatten, the British Colonial Governors, the Consul-General in Saigon and a representative of the British Legation in Siam for an informal review of foreign policy and other matters. Killearn outlined the importance of Southeast Asia and discussed the need of 'carrying the Dutch, the French, and Siamese along with us ... and hope of, general collaboration with the United States'. The discussion also touched on China and the traditional fear of the large indigenous Chinese populations in the region, who through 'Chinese law and tradition remain Chinese nationals'.[146] Killearn invited representatives from Indo-China, the Netherlands East Indies and Siam to a May technical conference of nutritionists and medical personnel in Singapore.[147] He lobbied also for a greater area of Indo-China to be put under food cultivation.[148] Therefore, the situation in May appeared to be in remission, especially as Indo-China had tentatively offered 16,000 tons of rice for the current quarter, of which over 5000 tons had already been promised and reserved.[149] At the April Food Conference Guillaton offered a further 50,000 tons for the second half of 1946.[150] However, any optimism that an Indo-Chinese contribution to the regional or world food shortages would be forthcoming soon evaporated. The Cabinet noted that the provisional allocation from Indo-China for July of 10,000 tons was 'conjectural' and 'that the prospects are deteriorating'.[151] It was observed that the situation was further complicated by the French who had 'not yet agreed to the principle of pooling rice for distribution to the territories under IEFC procedure on the grounds that their first responsibility is toward their own territories'. Both Killearn and the US were concerned with the disparity in rice prices that had arisen. The price from Burma was £28 per ton, Indo-China £31 per ton and Siam £12.14 per ton, and it was feared that Siam would stockpile rice to inflate its price closer to parity with Burma and Indo-China.[152] Killearn met informally with French Admiral Aboyneau who agreed 'the need of some form of mutual consolidation and get-together'.[153]

The British Consul-General in Saigon was unable to confirm the availability of the 10,000 tons of rice already promised by the French.[154] The French withdrew their representatives from the July liaison officers meeting, Meiklereid felt that this was because they were unhappy over the allocation figures and did not want to have to commit themselves at the meeting.[155] To assist with rice exports from Indo-China five tugs were transferred from New Delhi.[156] Due to the uncertainty of Indo-Chinese supplies Killearn advised the Foreign Office that Indo-China could not be considered as part of the Southeast Asia pool for 'pro-rata entitlement'.[157] Killearn consulted the Australian Representative in Singapore, Massey, who approved the idea for a regional international committee at Singapore to discuss mutual problems.[158] However, D'Argenlieu prevented any further French presence at liaison meetings, insisting that no instructions had been issued from Paris.[159] Whilst Killearn sought permission from London to arrange exports directly from Indo-China to Hong Kong and other Southeast Asia areas without referring such negotiations to London or Washington under existing food control procedures, British officials continued to meet with French officials to discuss other issues such as the export of coal from Indo-China.[160]

The situation continued to deteriorate. In August, Malaya rice stocks were exhausted. Reports from Indo-China indicated that the French were prepared to export 65,000 tons instead of the 20,000 tons already planned under the IEFC, but with no firm promise for the fourth quarter the rice situation continued to be perilous.[161] The death of the Siamese King in July and the Good Offices Committee Netherlands East Indies decision not to export from Java occurred at the same time as the French attitude began to harden and 'their apparent ignorance or disagreement with the machinery of the International Emergency Food Council resulted in drying up of rice from French Indo-China'. Hong Kong had been without rice for two weeks and Ceylon was without flour.[162] In a renewed effort to exact co-ordination Killearn contacted D'Argenlieu, and the High Commissioner agreed to send Clarac and Guillaton to the monthly Food Liaison Officers Conference at Singapore. In conversation with Clarac, Killearn expressed a desire to expand economic collaboration from food to include nutrition and public health, and he encouraged 'regional collaboration and consultation'.[163] D'Argenlieu referred the proposal to Paris.[164] Killearn believed that the concept of regional collaboration went further than food and other humanitarian issues. He hoped to attract eventually Siam, Indo-China and the Netherlands East Indies 'into collaboration with Britain in defence matters'.[165] Killearn desired that Clarac and Guillaton would prove more amiable than previous French officials, whom he described as 'stubborn'.[166] Nevertheless, he maintained doubts about the quality of the French officials. In September Killearn was disappointed with the arrival of Dimitrescu from French Indo-China to further discuss rice issues: 'he seemed an unimpressive petty official with little authority in him'.[167]

Despite the supply problems and the contradictory grand gestures of large scale rice exports, Indo-China only managed to export 5000 tons to India in September.[168] Michael Wright, from Killearn's staff, visited Saigon, and the French asked for the return of frozen Indo-Chinese war credits in Malaya and Hong Kong, 2000 tons of bunker coal and 1200 tons of flour. In return D'Argenlieu promised to supply 8000 tons of rice. Wright pressed D'Argenlieu over the grave rice situation in Southeast Asia: 'I told him shortage had now reached a point where labour troubles and civil unrest were in the offing at the very moment when political problems were so delicate themselves'. D'Argenlieu offered to talk such matters over with his economic experts and then have further discussions. He noted 'the impact of the famine on the political situation' and concluded that 'communism was after all the greatest danger and failure to improve material conditions would play straight into the hands of the communists'.[169] At the same time British fears of Chinese subversion were expedited by the influx of Chinese immigrants, containing some communist party members, into Laos *en route* to Malaya and Siam.[170] Indo-China remained unable to supply the 10,000 tons of rice planned for October, and already the third quarter exports looked doubtful apart from the initial quantity being loaded for release.[171] A general strike in Burma heightened Southeast Asia rice supply and famine fears for Killearn in Singapore.[172] The subsequent supply of 11,000 tons of rice from Indo-China to Malaya in October was therefore regarded as something of a windfall.[173] In an attempt to aid further shipments of rice a sub-committee of the Food Liaison Conference was set up in Colombo with all the nations represented.[174] D'Argenlieu praised the 'continued comprehensive collaboration with British authorities in India, Hong Kong and Singapore with particular reference to Lord Killearn on the international regional plane'.[175] Meiklereid dined with D'Argenlieu in November in Phnom Penh. D'Argenlieu expressed interest in how Britain was coping with similar problems in Burma and Malaya. He pressed for co-operation against the common enemy, communism. Meiklereid replied that Britain was alive to the threat and that both Killearn and Wright had already emphasised the advantages of co-operation to D'Argenlieu, in working and planning on a regional level as circumstances permitted.[176]

Despite their unproductive track record the French proposed to export 200,000 tons of rice from Indo-China, of which 100,000 tons would be available in January or February 1947.[177] But again the French promises proved hollow, as the political situation in Indo-China continued to hamper the export of rice. In January 1947 Meiklereid reported that the situation in Cochinchina had deteriorated further, as an attempt by the Vietnamese to surround Saigon had led to a decline in food supplies.[178] Bevin advised Attlee of the political situation in Burma, Indo-China and Siam from where it was hoped to produce three quarters of the total world supplies of rice during the first half of 1947.[179] The economic outlook for Indo-China remained dire. The retail price of rice had doubled over the course of 1946 and trebled between February 1946 and February 1948.[180] Prices in Phnom Penh increased by 58% in 1947 but receded marginally at the beginning of 1948.[181] Rubber production in 1947 reached 38,000 tons – 60% of the 1938 total; coal mined was 250,000 tons – 11% of the 1938 total; and cement produced was 40,000 tons – 15% of the 1938 total. Therefore, the balance of trade deficit increased from 154 million Piastres for January–June 1947 to 350 million Piastres for

July–December and 434 million Piastres for January–June 1948. Indo-China imported 39,000 tons of goods at 214 million Piastres from January to June 1948. The pre-war average was 40,000 tons but exports from Indo-China were only 44,000 tons, compared with a pre-war average of 322,000 tons. The main imports were from France 50%, US 20%, and China 20%; the main exports were to France 30%, the French Union 17% and importantly, for Britain, Hong Kong and Singapore 11% each.[182]

The French thought that they had done their best to provide food for Southeast Asia; now they decided that the situation in French colonies on the West African coast was more desperate.[183] Moffat visited Killearn in Singapore and agreed about the need to construct 'some sort of regional arrangement in Southeast Asia'.[184] In the first seven weeks of 1947 Hong Kong received only 7700 tons instead of the planned 21,000 tons and prices increased rapidly. It continued to be a poor year for rice exports from Indo-China and the total exported tonnage decreased by 54,983 tons from 1946.[185] Meiklereid reported that an aerial survey of the two provinces returned to Indo-China from Siam indicated a dearth of rice acreage sown. It was predicted that 'normal' levels of production could not be attained before 1951.[186] This must have been a grave disappointment for Killearn who nevertheless continued to try to work with and aid Indo-China. The French Consul-General in Singapore, Guibant, proposed that Killearn approach Indo-China to assist with the problem of coal shortages.[187] Between 23 April and 8 May, Haywood of Killearn's staff travelled to Indo-China to discuss coal policy with Guillaton.[188] However, as with the issue of rice, the question of coal proved complicated due to a coke shortage in Indo-China. Killearn again demonstrated his patience and generosity by making emergency arrangements for the export of 75 tons of coke from 'very limited Singapore stocks', and 100 tons from Calcutta to 'prevent a complete stoppage of industry in French Indo-China'. Yet when the Malaya smelting industry was faced with a severe shortage of anthracite, due to the failure of Indo-China to export any supplies, Malaya was forced to source stock from the US.[189]

The Indian Council for World Affairs organised an inter-Asian relations conference for the last week in March and first week of April to discuss national freedom movements and post-colonial development.[190] Dr H.V. Evatt, Australian Minister for External Affairs, had already pressed for 'a sort of Southeast Asia Commission'.[191] Wright proposed to Dening to expand Anglo-French collaboration on technical issues, social welfare, food, exchange of experts, items of common interest and relations between Indo-China and Malaya. But Wright cautioned that it was important not to give the 'impression of a policy of "Southeast Asia for Europeans". So long as there is no agreement between the French and the Asiatics in Indo-China we must put each foot down warily'.[192] In the meantime Killearn forewarned that the communist nature of the DRVN leaders was of concern to British territories and that Britain should avoid being seen as supporting a French imperial policy 'which we ourselves have renounced elsewhere'.[193] Dening was not forthcoming with a reply. He was cautious of the proposal due to the nervousness of British territories regarding actions which could be viewed by nationalists as politically significant. He therefore suggested that co-operation should remain at the current level unless the French were able to achieve a political settlement. As the French previously had approached Britain on this issue Dening advised: 'I think we must aim at maintaining the cordiality without committing ourselves to anything specific'.[194] The Foreign Office pressed the Colonial Office for all the British colonial territories in Southeast Asia to harmonise their policies towards their various Chinese communities.[195] Killearn was left to reflect upon his relationship with the French, 'there is something very attractive about nice French people. When they are bad they are horrid, but when they are really nice they are superlatively so, and so intelligent'.[196]

Military aid

A proportion of the equipment that was used by the French in Indo-China had been supplied by Britain, thus the resupply of this equipment and other military issues in Indo-China continued to concern the British. The Interservice Mission attached to the British Consulate had been temporarily responsible for various transfer duties when Indo-China had left SEAC, and Britain had intended to maintain a staging post in Saigon for use on the main air traffic routes to Hong Kong and Japan.[197] It was intended to replace the Interservice Mission by a small interservice body attached to the Consul-General's staff.[198] In the meantime, a number of Indian transportation units remained in Saigon to assist the French with dock operations and maintenance. These units were withdrawn during April 1946, and in May it was agreed that the Interservice Mission would be scaled down with the removal of RAF staff and the disbanding of the air section, although a RAF staging post remained at Saigon, operated by 330 RAF personnel.[199]

During June Britain supplied two hospital ships to evacuate French women and children from Saigon; in July the French requested more hospital evacuation ships from Britain. Lt.-Commander Williams noted that in the two ships already supplied, the percentage of actual sick had been very low and that there were only five stretcher cases in total.[200] Killearn advised D'Argenlieu that Britain was unable to supply further ships and suggested that he should approach the US.[201] Meanwhile, Dr Thinh of the Cochinchina Government asked Meiklereid if Britain could assist in the supply of 500 rifles for each of the republic's 20 provinces as the French were experiencing supply problems. Meiklereid dodged the issue by referring Thinh to D'Argenlieu, via whom the request would have to come.[202]

As French military operations in Indo-China progressed, France became increasingly concerned about resupply issues. The French had purchased aircraft from the RAF but were worried about the transfer of US lend-lease materials such as the propellers on the purchased aircraft.[203] The British Ambassador in Washington, Lord Inverchapel, raised the matter with the State Department. The US explained that it would oppose the transfer of lend-lease material to Indo-China but not the sale of war material to the French Government in Paris. Inverchapel advised that the French should forget the lend-lease issue and that the aircraft should be transferred.[204] In January 1947 the Governor of Burma, Sir Hubert Rance, expressed concern at potential political repercussions of the transit of French aircraft there *en route* to Indo-China.[205] The British Air Ministry, anxious to be accorded an agreement to over-fly French territories to reinforce Hong Kong from Singapore, urged Air Headquarters Burma to ensure a speedy transit of French aircraft.[206] The governments of Burma and India took a similar position, allowing five military aircraft each way per month.[207]

In the meantime, the French asked the British headquarters of its Southeast Asian Land Force in Singapore for large supplies of weapons and ammunition. Killearn warned that if Britain supplied Indo-China from Singapore some of the supplies would have to be sourced from India. In order to avoid political repercussions he requested that supplies be provided from Europe rather than Singapore and cautioned that 'compliance by me with this request might well land us in extremely deep waters'.[208] In Paris the British Ambassador, Cooper, understood Killearn's predicament but stressed the risks attached to the French not being able to restore control in Indo-China as soon as possible.[209] Later Cooper briefed the Foreign Office that the French were becoming increasingly sensitive to suggestions in Burma of the raising of nationalist volunteers to help fight the French in Indo-China and of a dock strike in Singapore against the loading of supplies for Indo-China.[210] Suspicion had already led the French Government to complain to the British Embassy in Paris of British and US arms being smuggled to the Vietminh in commercial ships flying Panamanian and British flags.[211] The British investigated these charges but no conclusive evidence of these shipments could be produced, although limited arms smuggling was occurring between Siam and Cambodia.[212] A paper prepared by Dening on Southeast Asia warned that British co-operation with Indo-China depended on the French resolution of the conflict: 'We must not appear to be ganging up with Western powers against Eastern peoples striving for independence'. Instead, the paper advised that co-operation was to be encouraged between 'independent or soon to be independent Eastern peoples and Western powers who by their past experience are best able to give them help'.[213] Bevin met with Dening, Wright, Pierson Dixon (Bevin's Principal Private Secretary) and Sir Orme Sargent (Permanent Under-Secretary Foreign Office) to discuss Southeast Asia. Bevin agreed that an approach should be made to the US to request their attendance at Defence Committee meetings in Singapore.[214]

Bevin briefed the Cabinet about Killearn's concerns regarding the supply of munitions to Indo-China from Singapore. It was feared that if this was not agreed, this refusal along with other requests that previously had been denied might push France towards the Soviets. The Ministry of Defence strongly supported the need to restore the French in Indo-China. But Attlee opposed the munitions shipments from Singapore and the meeting concluded with an agreement that Britain would supply only munitions from Britain to metropolitan France and that the French would be responsible for their distribution.[215] Bevin was asked in the House of Commons what British arms, equipment and aeroplanes had been supplied to Indo-China in the past six months. Bevin replied that during the last war Britain had aided the armed forces of its allies with military equipment including the French forces in metropolitan France. He concluded that 'when British forces in French Indo-China were replaced by French forces, a certain amount of war material was handed over to them in order to complete their equipment'.[216] The next day the French also asked Britain to supply aviation and motor spirit to Indo-China. Britain had already agreed to supply 4000 tons of aviation and 28,000 tons of motor spirit between January and April 1947. The French were asking for the same rate of delivery from May to December. The Foreign Office considered this new request against Attlee's munitions ruling. Gordon Whitteridge felt that 'we would rather not have been asked this question' but argued that 'fuel like food and water, should be available in the normal way of commerce to all nations with whom we have normal friendly relations'. In avoiding a moral dilemma he concluded that 'its eventual use is of no concern to the supplier'.[217]

A month later the Reuters news agency reported from Paris that, over the last 16 months, Britain had supplied £17,500,000 of military equipment direct to Indo-China to aid the French against the Vietminh. The report stated that a new Franco-British agreement worth £1,726,000 had been made to equip an airborne division and 'contract purchase' 92 warships. Thompson, in Bangkok, concluded that this was French propaganda designed to give the appearance that Britain was supporting the French against the Vietminh in Indo-China. He warned that 'this will do us great harm'.[218] However, a certain element of the report was true as on 22 March the French Assembly approved military credits to purchase from Britain the equipment for one airborne division in Indo-China.[219] The question of British military aid to the French in Indo-China was raised again in the House of Commons. Due to the Cabinet's conclusion on 19 February, McNeil replied that 'No aid specifically designed for Indo-China has been given to the French armed forces'.[220] The French intended the equipment for Indo-China but Britain was supplying France not Indo-China; the eventual use was being ignored.

In July the JPS outlined proposals for the terms of reference of the new BDCC Far East, under MacDonald. This revitalised the British Defence Committee Southeast Asia to include enhanced terms of reference similar to the Commanders-in-Chief Committee Far East, and both China and Indo-China were included within its remit.[221] Meanwhile in May, the India Office wrote to the War Office worried about the sale of surplus military lorries and tractors to Indo-China. They were alarmed about the possibility of a reaction from the Indian population which could provoke dock strikes.[222] The Foreign Office was livid at not being consulted on the problem by the India Office and informed both government departments that they should suspend any further action until the Foreign Office had consulted Paris and formulated a view.[223] Upon considering the situation, the Foreign Office evaded responsibility for the supply issues and the potential crisis. Allen instructed the French Ambassador in London that, unless they could arrange the appropriate transfer directly with the Government of India and provide the shipping needed for transportation, no tractors or lorries could be sent to Indo-China.[224] The Foreign Office also noted that, in contrast to the investigations in January and February when limited arms smuggling had continued between Siam and Cambodia, large-scale smuggling was now occurring between China and Saigon. US arms that had been supplied to the Chinese Nationalist Army were being bought by Chinese merchants and being smuggled into Saigon through Hong Kong. The arms were loaded onto legal cargo vessels in Hong Kong and transferred onto Vietnamese junks outside Indo-Chinese territorial waters.[225] In September the DRVN began to purchase arms from the Chinese communists.[226]

The rebranding of British policy

Indo-China had been removed from SEAC in March 1946, but British policy remained concerned with the developing situation there. Strategically, politically and economically Indo-China was important to Britain. The Franco-DRVN dispute could directly threaten British territories and affect Britain's position in the region during a period of a 'controlled' re-definition of Britain's post-war responsibilities. The Labour Government's appointment of Killearn demonstrated the degree of co-ordination envisaged in Southeast Asia. Parallel to Britain's regional responsibilities Killearn would direct specific British Indo-Chinese policy regarding the Cambodian-Siamese border dispute, rice supply, relief and aspects of regional collaboration. Similarly both Britain and the US maintained close co-ordination regarding their Indo-Chinese policies in response to both the local and growing macro nature of the conflict. Both were directly concerned with the growth of Asian nationalism and communism, although the US appeared more zealous than Britain in its suspicion of Ho's communist ideology.

Despite the often intransigent French, Killearn succeeded in aligning British concern for Indo-China alongside Britain's regional responsibilities. In December 1947, however, the British presence in Indo-China was reduced. Air Vice Marshal Whitworth-Jones visited Saigon 11–13 December prior to the dissolution of the RAF staging post at Saigon.[227] This was symbolic of a change in British policy in Southeast Asia. Britain had been bankrupt since the end of the Second World War and was now restrained by the growing dollar gap with the US. To control expenditure, a meeting of the Treasury in April 1947 had proposed to merge the offices and functions of the Special Commissioner and Governor-General in Singapore. The merger date was set for 2nd March 1948 when Killearn's initial term of office finished; MacDonald would assume Killearn's regional duties. Bevin had agreed to the proposal.[228] In the meantime Killearn's staff and operations were to be scaled down.[229] Attlee agreed with the merging of the positions and Bevin wrote to Killearn explaining the need for the changes.[230] Killearn was devastated and upset at the amalgamation of the offices.[231] It left British policy to be co-ordinated by the newly entitled Commissioner-General MacDonald. The subtle rebranding of British co-ordination in Southeast Asia moved Indo-China from Killearn, a senior Foreign Office official, to MacDonald, a Labour politician. MacDonald would now have to co-ordinate British Indo-Chinese policy regarding the recognition of Bao Dai, the continuing rice supply shortages and the growing spectre of Chinese communism.

4
The Winds of Change,
May 1948–January 1950

The new post of Commissioner-General took effect in March 1948. However, MacDonald did not begin to enact British policy until May when he returned from his holiday in Canada. There was thus no formal handover or briefing by Killearn, who had retired to Britain. In London, Foreign Office officials were 'seriously concerned' about Indo-China and asked Dening to discuss the matter with MacDonald, who would be passing through, 'particularly as the French are obviously losing grip and we see no real prospects of a settlement'.[1]

MacDonald inherited many of the macro Southeast Asian and micro Indo-Chinese problems that had occupied Killearn. MacDonald was preoccupied with the political status of Ho, the recognition of Bao Dai, support for the French, the growth of Soviet and Chinese communist influence, and the indigenous Chinese populations. Similarly, he was concerned with rice supply and export to alleviate world food shortages, the need to raise living standards as a weapon to fight communism, Southeast Asia as a market for manufactured goods, the growth of regional co-operation, and the possibility of aid. The parallel questions of the communist threat to Southeast Asia and Indo-China, and the recognition of Bao Dai were to dominate this period. MacDonald was to operate, however, in a different political climate to Killearn. Killearn had enjoyed a degree of autonomy in managing his brief but MacDonald experienced greater interest and direction from Attlee, Bevin and others. This translated into an unclear and ill-defined Indo-China policy where the preferences of a 'wait and see' strategy and consultations with the US prevailed.

Anglo-US relations remained the pivot of British foreign policy, i.e. Marshall Aid and the creation of NATO. France was interwoven into this relationship both economically and militarily, as an ally of both

Britain and the US against the communist threat in Western Europe. France would use the possibility of a French withdrawal from Indo-China to convince the US that 'a non-communist Indo-China was vital to Western – and specifically American – interests' of drawing a line to contain communism in Southeast Asia.[2] However, Britain had to wait for the US to develop a clearly defined policy for Southeast Asia.[3] Historically, Britain had appreciated flexible alliances and was suspicious of the single-focused French Indo-Chinese policy.[4] It needed to appease and maintain the Commonwealth to strengthen Britain as a third great power alongside the US and Russia.[5] The Indian dimension therefore developed as an important aspect in British foreign policy considerations especially regarding its neutrality in Indo-Chinese affairs.[6] Attlee feared that any approach to the Indian Prime Minister, Nehru, about Indo-China would result in charges of a colonial conspiracy; Bevin was concerned that, because of Pan-Asian nationalism, Nehru might decide to support Ho.[7]

MacDonald's return to Singapore coincided with an escalation in international tension. In June the Malaya Emergency began with anti-British violence building up towards an armed struggle. In the Philippines Taruc declared himself a communist and resumed the struggle against the government. In Europe the Berlin blockade commenced and Yugoslavia defected from the Soviet camp.[8] Tito's defection brought further debate to the Franco-DRVN conflict. Could Ho be a non-aligned communist similar to Tito or something more useful to the West? 'The question to be asked, however, is whether America might have found in Ho not merely a second Tito but a new species of political animal; one who could transmute Marxism into true Internationalism. We shall never know. The chance was lost'.[9]

Indo-China

Following the identification of Bao Dai as an indigenous nationalist alternative to Ho, the French continued to pursue an uncoordinated and non-transparent policy towards Indo-China, in particular to the growing crisis in Vietnam. In Saigon Gibbs noted that 'there is no hope of peace in Indo-China unless the Vietminh are appeased'. Mackworth Young at the Foreign Office was, however, critical of such an assessment, 'Don't we know what the appeasement of communists means'?[10] Harvey, now British Ambassador to France, informed the Foreign Office that the French would be holding a meeting in Along Bay to ratify Vietnamese independence within the French Union. Before this meeting a new Provisional Government was established under the presidency of General Xuan. The implications of such a treaty seemed unclear as negotiations were ongoing and the problem of Cochinchina's independent status remained. Harvey concluded that 'what is not at all clear is the extent to which this commits the French Government to the principle of the unity of the three *Kys* [Tonkin, Annam, Cochinchina]'.[11] Bao Dai indicated that he was unwilling to return to power at this juncture. Gibbs believed that the Provisional Government would 'be short lived' and that the 'prospects of a satisfactory settlement are still remote'.[12] On the other hand Ho was clear in his course of action, 'Our independence is like gold and precious stones shut up in a safe. To get them out we must find the key. We have found the key to our independence. And it is to strike hard at the enemy'.[13]

On 5 June Bollaert, Bao Dai and General Xuan met in Along Bay and a protocol between the French and the new Provisional Government was signed. In this France recognised the independence of Vietnam, and Vietnam agreed to be a member of the French Union as an Associated State; but actual independence was limited, and negotiations on cultural, diplomatic, financial, economic and military issues continued.[14] Gibbs noted that the new government was received with 'indifference' and doubted whether it 'will carry enough prestige to win over nationalist elements from the Vietminh'.[15] In Hanoi Trevor-Wilson continued to maintain contact with the DRVN on humanitarian issues.[16] The DRVN was weary of the French resurrection of Bao Dai and the challenge that this represented. Two former members of the Imperial Cabinet who were now ministers in the DRVN Government publicly denounced the authority and independence of Bao Dai, 'if you are fully informed of existing conditions in Vietnam, you will refuse to be a victim of the Machiavellian schemes of the French and you will make no action without prior agreement with President Ho Chi Minh'. The DRVN sought to legitimise its international standing with a visit to India by the Deputy Prime Minister. This included talks with Nehru, the President of the National Assembly, the Vice-Premier and the Secretary General of the Indian Socialist Party.[17]

In late July the US issued a policy statement which described continued US impotence in Indo-China.[18] The situation in Paris reflected poorly for Indo-China. Bollaert pressed the government to debate the Bao Dai solution and the Along Bay Accords, the French Socialist Party were calling for negotiations to be reopened with Ho, and the Army was becoming dissatisfied.[19] At the Foreign Office Mackworth Young noted that one French Government had just fallen over the issue of military credits and Indo-China was one of the largest items in the military budget: 'if the new government is forced to curtail military expenditure, the outlook will be even gloomier'.[20] J.O. Lloyd briefed Bevin that 'we cannot justly interfere in Indo-China, but we should do nothing to impede the French from reaching a settlement, whether by political or military means'.[21]

During the summer the British Military Liaison Officer in Saigon toured Cambodia and reported on the military situation in Indo-China. He observed that the Vietminh had linked up with Cambodian nationalist rebels, the Khmer Issarak, thereby broadening the conflict. He concluded that the Provisional Government's chances of success were slim due to the French delay in ratifying the June protocol and noted that as the Provisional Government had no offices or money it appeared to be merely the government of Southern Vietnam rather than the whole of the country. In the meantime, both General Xuan and Bao Dai were sentenced to death for treason by the Vietminh and Bollaert threatened to resign unless the Along Bay Agreement was ratified by the French Government.[22] The French Prime Minister accepted the principles of the 7 December 1947 and 5 June 1948 agreements and stressed that the mission of France and its constitution was 'leading the peoples of whom she has charge to the liberty of self-government and of democratically administering their own affairs'.[23] The Chamber of Deputies, however, voted for a postponement of the full debate. The ambiguity that this caused made it unclear whether Bollaert would continue when his mandate expired in September.[24] The French Government pressed Bollaert to persuade the Vietnamese that the Chamber had voted in their favour but to be ratified there needed to be an elected government in Vietnam. A counter argument emerged in Paris that the unity of the *Kys* could not take place until the French Assembly had considered the issue. The British Embassy noted that the situation had stalled in the legal interpretations of the French Constitution.[25]

Bollaert departed from Indo-China and was replaced as High Commissioner by Leon Pignon. France's Indo-China policy appeared in danger of disintegration and the situation on the ground remained perilous. In September the anti-French, anti-Sihanouk and pro-independence Cambodian National Assembly was dissolved.[26] In Vietnam Bao Dai's personal secretary announced that Bao Dai would soon return to power and include the majority of the DRVN, excluding the communists, in a new government.[27] The British Foreign Office regarded this new farce as the 'height of wishful thinking'.[28] The

Minister of Information in the Provisional Government proposed going to Paris to establish an official Vietnamese information service. Gibbs observed that the Minister of Information held the personal ear of Bao Dai but was critical of Xuan for being too pro-French.[29] Vietnamese nationalist unity under Bao Dai appeared weak and on the verge of division. Gibbs noted the fruitlessness of the French situation: 'the conjuror has waved his wand, but he has not even produced a rabbit'.[30] From the British Embassy in Paris Ashley Clarke informed Dening that, due to Indo-China creating 'fierce controversies' in the National Assembly, many in the French Government felt inclined 'to let things slide'.[31]

A State Department policy statement rejected either a reconquest or withdrawal. The US was in an 'essentially passive position of accepting a French policy with which it could not agree'.[32] On 12 November Graves, in Washington, was asked by Reed, now Chief of the Southeast Asia Section of the State Department, if there was some way of galvanising the French into action to protect the country against the potential communist menace.[33] As the prospect of a communist victory in China intensified, Harvey conveyed to the British Government the French fear of having a communist territory bordering Indo-China, 'they feel that this would mean a very powerful accession of strength to the Vietminh; so much so that it might be impossible to negotiate with Bao Dai'.[34] The US Consul-General in Saigon relayed to the British Consul, Donald Hopson, that the US Embassy in Paris had obtained a report of a French plan to evacuate Tonkin and Northern Annam to concentrate on Cambodia, Cochinchina, and Southern Annam. Hopson reflected that this measure could only be activated when the Chinese communists reached the Indo-Chinese frontier.[35]

On 6 December Clarke wrote to Dening that the French Cabinet was reluctant to give further concessions to Bao Dai.[36] In the US, Reed confided to Graves that he feared Pignon would resign 'after some months of frustration'.[37] Gibbs noted that the political situation in Vietnam had been complicated even further by the emergence of a new clandestine political organisation established to unify the various nationalist groups. Apparently the new organisation was supported by the Catholic Youth Parties in Hanoi and Saigon and was in contact with the nationalist politician Ngo Dinh Diem.[38] It involved also the Dai Viet, Dong Minh Hoi, Vietnam Quoc Dan Dong, the Socialists, and possibly, according to Gibbs, General Xuan and Bao Dai. The organisation was strongly nationalist, anti-French and anti-communist.[39]

Dening was dispatched to Paris at the invitation of the French Government to discuss Eastern questions but, as the Cabinet Far Eastern Committee noted, he would not be able to participate fully until the British Government had decided its whole policy.[40] Bevin agreed that Dening's approach should be not to 'press' the French nor to exasperate them but to 'convince' them of the need to clear up the situation in Indo-China before the Chinese communists reached the Indo-Chinese borders.[41] Upon his return Dening recorded that:

> The impression obtained ... during his visit was that the French officials principally concerned, and the Minister for Overseas Territories, are impressed with the need to find an urgent solution to their problem in Indo-China. Their chief difficulty lies in the stresses of internal politics in France, which make it very difficult for them to adopt bold and comprehensive measures.[42]

Considering the sensitivity of the French to colonial problems Bevin concluded to Attlee that 'It is satisfactory that the French should have welcomed these discussions, and it is to be hoped that continuing consultation may ensue which should encourage them to settle their affairs in Indo-China'.[43] In the meantime, the internal French political situation remained weak. The JIC considered the implications on French colonial policy of a change of government in Paris. It concluded that a third force government would not change the current policy or framework, a de Gaulle-led government would increase military effort to impose a settlement and a communist government would hand Indo-China over to Ho.[44]

Following a number of internal government scandals a Cambodian government of national unity was formed.[45] Bao Dai, in France, appeared as unwilling as the French to conclude a settlement for Vietnam. It seemed that 'enjoying the flesh pots of Paris and Cannes he was in no hurry to return to a more precarious and less comfortable existence in the Far East'. In frustration Bevin noted that France 'deserve[d] to lose the show'.[46] On 11 January 1949 the Foreign Office briefed Bevin that Britain could not give France the impression of support in Indo-China but it had no solution to offer. Bevin held talks with the French Foreign Minister, Robert Schuman, about the apparent stalemate in Indo-China and the need to find or form a credible indigenous government.[47] Schuman summarised the problem that France was facing: 'There was no great question of principle in dispute. The problem was to find leaders to carry out policies on the basis of agreed ideas, which he thought the French and British shared in common'.[48] Was Schuman now unsure of the Provisional Government and the Bao Dai solution? At the same time guerrilla activity in Cambodia increased. On 12 January the Sa Ang district headquarters in Kandal was attacked.[49] Coset Floret, now the Minister for Overseas France, accepted that the Along Bay Agreement was coming into force. In conversations with Clarke, Baeyens of the French Foreign Office confirmed that agreement had been reached with Bao Dai on many of the major issues; but the status of Cochinchina continued to remain a major obstacle to a settlement.[50] In the State Department Southeast Asia Division, Charlton Ogburn concluded that 'we are heading into a very bad mess in the policy we are now following toward Indo-China'.[51]

During February, as the political and military deadlock in Vietnam continued, in Cambodia a government report indicated the growth of rebel numbers and activity.[52] It was estimated that 50,000–60,000 troops had been killed or wounded in Indo-China. If North African and colonial troops were included then the total would need to be doubled.[53] At the Foreign Office Mackworth Young pessimistically noted 'there are speculations in the French press that Ho Chi Minh has signed a secret agreement with Mao Tse-Tung'. Robert Scott concurred – 'The omens are not good' – and even Dening admitted to being 'a little worried about the delays in the negotiations over French Indo-China'. He predicted that 'if the French do not hurry up they may find that the communist successes in China will strengthen the hands of Ho Chi Minh and make it more difficult than ever to reach a settlement'. At the same time Britain received intelligence that the Chinese communists were organising activities in Indo-China.[54] On 15 February the new US Secretary of State, Acheson, stated that it was a race against time to prepare the Vietnamese for self-government.[55] Ten days later he concluded that support for Bao Dai depended on vital concessions by France for its success.[56]

By March negotiations between Bao Dai and the French Government were completed and he agreed to return to Vietnam. It was hoped that the agreement would be submitted for ratification to the French Assembly on 11 March. The Foreign Office observed that France finally appeared to be making 'the best of a bad job'. It welcomed the French action but cautioned that 'it does not in itself mean that a positive step forward has yet been made, as its action will certainly have to await constitutional action ... by the French Assembly'. This would have to include a vote for a change in the status of Cochinchina.[57] On 8 March the Elysee Agreement was signed, but the delays had not aided France or Bao Dai's position.[58] The Foreign Office noted that 'French intransigence has gone a long way to alienating Annamite public opinion'.[59] The Assembly voted to rejoin Cochinchina to Vietnam with the electoral consent of the Cochinchinese but did not ratify the 8 March Agreement.[60] Gibbs wrote to Bevin concerning the local reaction to the agreement between President Vincent Auriol and Bao Dai, 'Everyone is agreed that this is France's last card, but many suspect that she is only playing it in the hope of getting American aid, and she has had it up her sleeve for so long that when it appears on the table it is likely to be rather limp'.[61] Dening concurred, 'depressing but probably correct'.[62] During a visit to Singapore, Pignon highlighted France's attitude towards Bao Dai as being supportive, 'not to control him but to make things easy for him'.[63] A paper by Reed reported that US diplomats believed that France was losing.[64] Press reports indicated that Chinese forces had crossed into Tonkin.[65] Baeyens confirmed to Clarke that about 18,000 Chinese irregulars were operating in Northern Tonkin under the command of Chinese communist General Chu Kia Pi.[66]

The US Consul in Hanoi confirmed to the State Department on 2 April that the Vietminh were co-operating with the Chinese communist army.[67] Gibbs reported to the Foreign Office a week later that the French were now pressing for diplomatic recognition of Bao Dai. Lloyd advised 'we must certainly wait a while and see how Bao Dai develops before considering the question of recognition. It would be futile if we were to recognise him prematurely and he should turn out to be a flop (as many people expect he will be)'.[68] Gibbs was advised of this policy and instructed to sound out the opinion of his US opposite in Saigon; at the same time the Foreign Office would consult the State Department.[69] Meanwhile Gibbs assessed the situation in the rest of Indo-China. In Cambodia, he believed that Sihanouk was looking towards achieving the same sort of political arrangement that Vietnam was negotiating with France. However, the position was complicated by the presence of a large Vietnamese population of over 400,000 in Cambodia. Gibbs noted that historically Cambodia had feared domination by both Thailand and Vietnam. He believed that the Cambodians had forgotten their need for French protection. He considered that the Cambodians were 'ambitious and indolent; more evolved than the Laotians, they lack their sense of reality and are a classic example of people who are trying to run before they can walk'. Gibbs noted that Khmer Issarak rebels continued to operate in Siem Reap and Battambang, they were in liaison with the Vietminh in Bangkok whilst the Vietminh operated independently along the Mekong amongst the Annamite population. Similarly the Laotians feared Thai and Vietnamese domination and in return for French protection appeared loyal to France.[70] On 30 April the League for the National Salvation of the Vietnamese Residents in Cambodia statutes proposed a Vietnamese-Khmer alliance against the French.[71]

In May Pignon visited MacDonald in Singapore. MacDonald concluded that 'good progress' was being made that would be 'crowned with success'.[72] MacDonald hoped that the recent agreement between the French and Bao Dai would 'help to restore the influence of liberal and constitutional Indo-Chinese leaders'.[73] By contrast the Foreign Office said that 'prospects don't look too bright'.[74] On 17 May Dening observed uneasily: 'I don't think the French Government as a whole show much concern, but M. Baudet told me the other day he was very worried'.[75] On the same day Reed informed Butterworth that 'the chances of saving Indo-China were slim'. The State Department Western European and Southeast Asian offices agreed that 'the US should not put itself in a forward position in the Indo-China problem' as there was nothing that could be done to alter the prospects.[76] US experts predicted that there was little chance of French concessions or that Bao Dai would appeal to the nationalists.[77] Ideological differences between the Europeanists and Asianists at the State Department continued to dog a cohesive Indo-China policy.[78] Both Bao Dai and General Xuan attempted to broaden their nationalist appeal by indicating that if Ho could demonstrate that he was a true nationalist, he need not be excluded from a new government. Hopson regarded such overtures as examples of 'the permanent state of bewilderment in which politics are carried on in this country' but against the international development of Titoism the Foreign Office asked its consulate in Saigon to reassess the extent of communist control on the Vietminh.[79]

Bao Dai proposed that his first diplomatic mission would be to send representatives to the Vatican, hoping that this would rally the Catholic minority to his side in Vietnam.[80] The State Department decided that now was the time to develop a common approach to Indo-China with other interested governments, particularly Britain, India and the Philippines.[81] Acheson reiterated to the US Consul in Hanoi the communist purposes of Ho and his men.[82] Acheson believed that the 'question whether Ho as much nationalist as Commie is irrelevant. All Stalinists in colonial areas are nationalists'.[83] Hopson cautioned against hasty recognition by Britain and the US of Bao Dai as this could result in Bao Dai being seen as a 'Western puppet'.[84] The Foreign Office regarded the argument that Britain should wait for the Southeast Asian nations to recognise Bao Dai was strong but questioned if any would really do so. Hopson was advised that ratification of the Auriol Agreement and publication of its terms was necessary before according recognition.[85]

By June the French National Assembly had rejoined Cochinchina with the rest of Vietnam. In the US a paper by Ogburn dismissed bringing Ho into the Bao Dai Government. It discussed the possibility of a communist Indo-China causing a chain reaction in the rest of the subcontinent. The US had dismissed the idea of Ho as an Asian Tito and instead appeared more willing to pamper the French. The State Department wrote to the Paris Embassy stressing that insufficient concessions had been made to attract nationalists away from Ho. The embassy and Acheson agreed that such pressure being placed upon France was harsh rather than encouraging.[86] A French cabinet minister informed the US Military Attaché in Paris that the battle in Indo-China was essentially against international communism rather than nationalism and that the US and France should draw a line north of the Sino-Indo-Chinese border to halt its advance.[87] The US urged Britain to advise the French Government to speed up the transfer of power to Bao Dai.[88] Similarly the US considered it important to issue a statement in support of the Elysee Agreement. This was edited and approved by the French.[89] Britain did not propose to make any similar statement, preferring to wait and see whether Bao Dai succeeded in forming a stable government.[90] However, in response to press enquiries Britain 'expressed agreement [with] State Department views' and Prince Buu Loc issued a statement on behalf of Bao Dai thanking the British Government for its declaration of 'good wishes'.[91] The State Department approached the Foreign Office about canvassing Southeast Asian nations in support of Bao Dai. The US Minister in London agreed with the Foreign Office the need to keep Anglo-US policy 'in step' regarding the recognition of Bao Dai.[92] Although Nehru disagreed with the US statement he decided not to criticise the US stance.[93] Nehru regarded Ho as a 'nationalist communist' rather than a 'Kremlin communist' and therefore found it difficult to support Bao Dai.[94] The Thai Government had been impatient to receive a Vietnamese diplomatic representative, perhaps due to the imminent communist victory in China. However, it now appeared reluctant because it regarded Bao Dai's chances of maintaining power as diminishing.[95] Likewise the Philippines expressed a willingness to extend recognition but only when the Vietnamese Government had established control.[96]

The French requested information from Britain about the administration of the Dominions which could be used in discussions with Bao Dai. Britain obliged but the Foreign Office pessimistically reflected that the Bao Dai regime was built upon the support of 'French bayonets'. Comparing Bao Dai to 'Canute' it summarised the situation as 'bleak' with the French offering insufficient military or political aid.[97] In contrast a speech by MacDonald stressed that, although division and weakness had been caused by disagreements between the French and Vietnamese nationalists, he considered this had now changed and praised Bao Dai for 'endeavouring to show his countrymen that a better destiny than communist enslavement awaits them'.[98] Meanwhile, on 19 July a Franco-Laotian Convention established Laos as an Associated State within the French Union.[99]

The French experienced some success in September with the split of the Khmer Issarak in Cambodia when large numbers surrendered.[100] The Foreign Office considered it impossible to offer economic or military support until Bao Dai's success was assured. It regarded it important not to give the US firm proposals until the Commonwealth had been consulted.[101] On 6 September the French Ambassador in London, Massigli, wrote to Attlee and requested that the Bao Dai-Auriol Agreement be presented to King George VI who expressed his personal hopes for success to President Auriol.[102] A week later in Washington, Bevin met Acheson at the State Department's request for discussions on Indo-China prior to the Tripartite Economic Conference between Acheson, Bevin and Schuman. Dening briefed Bevin that 'our legal advisers tell us that we cannot recognize *de jure* until the plan envisaged in the 8 March Agreement is carried out and completed'.[103] Bevin told Acheson that he felt that it was important to raise the Indo-China matter with Schuman and that the 'French Government must decide whether they were going to ratify the agreement with Viet Nam'. It was agreed that this 'was an essential condition to recognition' and that it was 'unreasonable' of the French to ask Britain or the US for recognition of Bao Dai 'before they themselves had really committed themselves'.[104] At the tripartite meetings France declared that it was fighting for all the democratic powers and needed help.[105] At the meeting on 17 September Schuman asked Britain and the US to use 'their influence to secure recognition of Viet Nam by Asiatic powers'. He agreed that recognition could not happen until France had ratified the 8 March Agreement but expected that this would happen before the end of the year. Nevertheless Bevin believed that Britain would have to remain cautious and that more could be done only upon ratification. Acheson pressed for France to strengthen Bao Dai by transferring Indo-Chinese affairs from the Overseas Ministry to the French Foreign Office and begin 'increasing the extent of his [Bao Dai's] representation abroad'.[106] The Foreign Office, confused as to the direction of French policy on Indo-China, presented the French, through Lord Hood at the British Embassy in Paris, with a list of questions for clarification. Scott wrote to Hood 'What in fact do the French want us to do? ... We are frankly very puzzled about the constitutional, legal and diplomatic niceties of the whole affair'.[107]

During October the situation in Indo-China continued to deteriorate. Vietminh influence and operations continued to extend into Cambodia and Laos. In Cambodia 3000 Vietminh troops occupied Kampot and Kompong Speu.[108] When interviewed by the Thai press Ho responded to accusations of him being a communist with close contacts to Mao and the Kremlin as 'French imperialist propaganda'.[109] On 19 October the CIA advised Truman that the French were at a stalemate in Indo-China. The CIA considered that the possible loss of Indo-China in two years time might be a 'critical breach' in the containment of communism.[110]

The French partly replied to the British Foreign Office list of questions for clarification, raising further legal debate in the Foreign Office concerning recognition.[111] The French 'begged us [the British] not to be too legalistic in the matter of recognition'.[112] Attlee pessimistically wrote to Bevin 'I rate the chances of French rule and influence in Indo-China very low. I think that France has missed the bus'. Attlee agreed with Bevin's direction of Britain's Indo-Chinese policy.[113] Dening curtly observed: 'Whatever the reason for them, there have been vacillations and delays in French policy towards Indo-China ever since the last war: what the situation now calls for is boldness and consistency, of neither of which ... is there much evidence'.[114] On 27 October the Lao Issara Government, in exile in Bangkok, dissolved itself.[115] The leader, Souphanouvong, went to the Vietminh where under its guidance the Lao Issara continued as the basis for Pathet Lao.[116] Bao Dai requested diplomatic recognition from King George VI. The Foreign Office informed Washington that no reply could be issued until Vietnam was recognised and the French Government ratified the 8 March Agreement.[117] Bao Dai also approached Southeast Asian nations for recognition including Australia, Ceylon and Thailand. Thailand decided to wait and see what the US approach to recognition would be. Britain advised the Commonwealth High Commissioners that they should stress to Commonwealth Governments 'our sympathy with Bao Dai and our hope that they will give as cordial a reply as possible to approaches made to them on Bao Dai's behalf. Obviously we cannot suggest to them that they should grant formal recognition to Vietnam as an independent sovereign state when we are not prepared to grant such recognition ourselves'.[118]

Between 2–4 November, MacDonald assembled a conference of regional British officials at Bukit Serene. The conference recommended that Bao Dai be accorded *de facto* recognition after the transfer of power to him by the French. It was felt that *de jure* recognition could only be given upon French ratification of the Auriol Agreement.[119] In contrast the conference agreed with the British Ambassador to China and the Governor of Hong Kong that China should be granted *de jure* recognition as soon as possible.[120] The delegates believed that the US, Commonwealth and Asian Governments should apply a similar policy regarding Vietnam and that Britain should encourage further concessions to Bao Dai.[121] Likewise they stressed 'the necessity of discussing our attitude with Pandit Nehru ... and securing at least his "neutrality"' concerning the recognition of Bao Dai.[122] Attlee appeared surprised by the existence of the conference, asking 'what is the Bukit Serene Conference'?[123] Bevin explained that '"Bukit Serene" is [sic] the name of Mr MacDonald's house. This was the name given to the conference of His Majesty's Representatives in the Far East'.[124] Was this a genuine oversight or did Attlee fear the robust intention of MacDonald's policy in Singapore? Two weeks later Attlee eventually conveyed his appreciation of the success of the conference to the Colonial Secretary Arthur Creech Jones.[125]

The Franco-Cambodian Treaty was signed on 8 November establishing Cambodia as an Associated State within the French Union.[126] Le Roy of the French Embassy in London called on Scott: 'he hoped that too much emphasis would not be placed by foreign governments on the question of ratifying the President Auriol-Bao Dai Agreement of 1949. The French Government were [sic] anxious to avoid a debate in Parliament on this subject as it might endanger their position'. He pressed that ratification was not essential as the agreement was in reality already in operation and suggested that the British should raise the rank of their consul-general in Saigon to that of minister.[127] At a meeting of the Western powers Foreign Ministers in Paris, 9–10 November, Schuman confided to Bevin that the French position regarding China was difficult due to the situation in Indo-China. They agreed that this would have to be discussed with Acheson.[128] The next day Schuman asked Bevin and Acheson whether it was possible not to 'recognise Bao Dai at this stage' but to 'inform Bao Dai that our Governments approved of him and French policy towards him' as 'an expression of goodwill'? Acheson told Schuman that the US wanted to be as helpful as possible but that previously it had been agreed that it was necessary for Bao Dai to obtain Asian support to avoid the implication of his government being a Western puppet. Acheson considered that the US was sympathetic to proposals put forward by France, but in the meantime France must sort out its constitutional position. Similarly Bevin too felt that the immediate issue was the French failure to ratify the Auriol Agreement. He pressed for France to transfer administration of Indo-China from the French Colonial Office to the French Foreign Office. Bevin 'undertook to consider the matter further' and do whatever was possible to help Schuman although he was not optimistic about Bao Dai's chances of success.[129]

Following Bukit Serene, MacDonald visited Indo-China from 10–22 November, where symbolically he had meetings not just with the French but also with Bao Dai, with whom he was 'impressed', and Sihanouk. MacDonald handed Bao Dai a goodwill message from Bevin.[130] This was to be an encouragement without committing Britain to recognition: 'The Secretary of State has instructed me to express to Your Majesty his personal good wishes and his hope that you will succeed in the establishment of a stable, representative government which will bring peace to your country and restore its prosperity'.[131] Bao Dai placed greater importance for his government on support and diplomatic recognition from Britain and the US than from India or other Asian nations.[132] Likewise, Sihanouk hoped for British and US recognition of Cambodia now a new treaty had been signed with France.[133] MacDonald assessed that the Bao Dai regime had a 50% chance of success and urged Pignon that the transfer of powers to Bao Dai 'should include every possible item of administrative and diplomatic power which could be handed over at this time'.[134] MacDonald added that the handover of power was essential before the end of the year but noted that although Bao Dai trusted Pignon the Vietnamese remained doubtful about the faith of the politicians in Paris.[135] Pignon cautioned MacDonald that officials in Paris feared the transfer of powers to Bao Dai 'lest Moroccan and Algerian politicians should demand for their colonies any and all the concessions made to Indo-China'. Pignon and Roger Du Gardier favoured granting Vietnam the same powers as a British Dominion, but Pignon had met with opposition to his views when in Paris and his future was uncertain.[136] MacDonald proposed that a personal note to Massigli was needed in support of the Bao Dai solution, Pignon's role and the early implementation of the 8 March Agreement.[137] MacDonald recommended to the British Government that if Britain recognised China before Bao Dai then Bao Dai should be kept informed of British intentions. Bevin agreed with MacDonald's recommendation and noted that any recognition of Bao Dai would have to be *de facto*. MacDonald concluded that Britain would need to persuade the US, India and other Asian nations to do likewise.[138]

During December Vietnam continued to be plagued by insurgency. Strikes by the Vietnamese brought about chaos in Saigon.[139] MacDonald considered that the struggle between Bao Dai and Ho was 'an evenly balanced affair, with victory still within the grasp of either of them'.[140] He wrote to Dening that 'a lot depends on the sincerity and zeal of the French Government in Paris supporting Pignon's liberal policy. I greatly hope that we can influence them to do the right thing'.[141] The British Acting Consul-General in Saigon believed that if Bao Dai was not attracting significant nationalist support by mid 1950 then the French could withdraw, and paradoxically the BDCC believed that even if Bao Dai was successful then high casualty numbers could force a French withdrawal. Therefore the BDCC suggested it was necessary to ascertain French intentions in the event of the failure of Bao Dai despite both JIC London and JIC Far East advice that any withdrawal was unlikely in the near future.[142]

Britain had been forced into not taking 'any unilateral action in recognising Bao Dai before the Ceylon [Colombo] Conference' as the matter had been placed on the agenda by Pakistan. It appeared that Britain would be unable to afford recognition until after 9 January 1950 but it was hard for Britain to finalise a policy as 'the position in Indo-China was still somewhat uncertain' and Bao Dai had added to this by suddenly deciding to go to Paris on 20 December.[143] Bao Dai later decided to postpone this untimely visit.[144] On 14 December Bevin circulated a memorandum to the Cabinet containing the brief for the United Kingdom delegation to the Colombo Conference. This stated that 'the solution to the Indo-China problem is essentially political. Our objective should be to do all we can to inspire confidence in Bao Dai among the Commonwealth and foreign countries in the area and in Indo-China itself; and to encourage the real transfer of power to him'.[145] Acheson had 'already stated at the tripartite meetings in Paris that the United States Government were anxious to help Bao Dai' and the British Government hoped that the US would be prepared to follow a similar line to themselves. Britain had decided against the idea of an Asian Tito. Ho could not be a 'democratic nationalist comparable … to Dr Hatta' (the Vice-President and Prime Minister of Indonesia) and Britain was satisfied that Ho was a communist and was 'not the right man to back'. Following the Colombo Conference the Foreign Office hoped to raise the status of the Consul-General at Saigon to minister and establish a legation only after *de jure* recognition.[146] A brief for the Commonwealth meeting on foreign affairs concluded that there was no risk of British troops being drawn into Vietnam if trouble erupted between the Vietminh and Bao Dai.[147] Anxious about the French reaction to the British recognition of China before Bao Dai, Bevin wrote to Schuman to justify the British policy, 'we cannot go on indefinitely ignoring the effective government of a territory like China'. Bevin highlighted that he understood if France was not as content as Britain to accord recognition towards China. He empathised that he shared the French anxiety over Indo-China and hoped that Britain would be able to recognise Vietnam in the near future but that this depended upon a transfer of power by the French.[148]

Sir Oliver Franks, the new British Ambassador in Washington, dined with Acheson who announced US aid of $75 million for Indonesia, Indo-China and possibly Siam. Franks reported that:

> Acheson interpolated a paean of praise about French achievements in Indo-China. They had done far more than they had ever let on. Bao Dai had a good chance and the thing to do was to press early recognition on the French. The American Government in distinction from its earlier views would be ready to recognise and help Indo-China as soon as the French had acted.[149]

MacDonald pressed the Foreign Office that 'the maximum degree of recognition which is technically possible' should be accorded to Bao Dai by Britain and the US upon the transfer of power and before British recognition of the PRC. In the meantime, he believed that military aid should be offered by Britain to the French.[150] On 22 December Schuman replied to Bevin that in the light of Mao's visit to Moscow could Britain now recognise Bao Dai before China? He hoped that the transfer of power would take place before the end of December.[151] Bevin met with Massigli and 'cross examined' him about developments in France and Indo-China. He pointed out that Britain had withheld recognising China for as long as possible, while Massigli urged British recognition of Bao Dai. Dening reiterated Britain's commitment to recognition after the Colombo Conference. Bevin concluded by stating that he would carefully review the British position and come to some conclusions on the following day.[152] The next day the British Embassy in Paris reported that ratification was only being delayed by the French parliamentary timetable and their budget debate.[153] Bevin informed Attlee that he intended to accord *de jure* recognition to China on 6 January 1950.[154] Massigli informed Sir William Strang, the Permanent Under-Secretary at the Foreign Office, that 30 December had been set to transfer powers from the France to Vietnam and that therefore France hoped for the British recognition of Bao Dai.[155] McNeil replied that Britain was to postpone the recognition of China until 6 January 1950 and that Britain would accord *de facto* recognition for Vietnam but that this would not be announced until after the Colombo Conference at which there would be an appeal to Commonwealth Foreign Ministers to follow suit.[156] MacDonald cautioned the government that it was too premature to accord *de jure* recognition at this stage.[157] McNeil informed Attlee about the deliberations concerning the recognition of Bao Dai and the PRC, and their relative chances of success.[158] Attlee agreed with the line being taken.[159]

Rice, relief, regionalism and military aid

Tension on the world stage escalated and British regionalism in Southeast Asia became interwoven with relief and military assistance. Rice remained an important British policy facet both regionally and towards Indo-China but was increasingly overshadowed.

In April 1948 the British War Office had not yet determined a line in the Far East beyond which it was necessary to stop Russian advances; however, it considered either plans or action without the US pointless.[160] Bevin instructed P.F. Grey to warn British representatives in Southeast Asia that a new tactic was being employed by the communists in the region 'of doing everything possible to undermine and hamper the reconstruction and economic development of the whole area'.[161] A Foreign Office paper prepared for Bevin to take to the Hague concluded that: 'There is no direct evidence of co-ordination by Russia of communist activities throughout Southeast Asia, though it is strongly suspected'.[162] In Singapore MacDonald was concerned about 'the status of Chinese in British Southeast Asia' and proposed the need to hold a conference on the 'Chinese question in the near future'.[163] In the meantime US Foreign Services Officers held a conference in

Bangkok in June to discuss communism in Southeast Asia.[164] This conference determined that 'The intention of the Soviet Mission in Bangkok is to pick up the threads of communist movements and to wind them onto the Soviet reel'. It was felt that 'Moscow appears to be nervous that, under Chinese direction, the doctrines may become heterodox'.[165] The conference discussed the possibility of establishing an 'anti-communist intelligence web' in Bangkok in opposition to the Soviet Legation.[166] It concluded that 'Anglo-American co-operation in the area is the only safeguard against serious political and economic deterioration'.[167] During talks at the State Department Dening noted with irony that the US 'who at one time seemed to think every nationalist must be good, now seemed to see a communist behind every nationalist bush'. The US appeared to be 'toying' with some kind of intervention in Indo-China but Dening advised that there was little that could be done for the moment especially due to the 'hypersensitive' attitude of the French.[168] An Australian goodwill mission to Southeast Asia was 'disgruntled' at the 'scant courtesy' that was accorded to their visit to Saigon by the French; perhaps the offer of education facilities by one dominion to another potential dominion was for the moment too embarrassing for the French.[169] Macmahon Ball of the mission believed that 'the French were afraid he was trying to pick up first-hand information about French Indo-China before bringing the situation to the attention of the [UN] Security Council, as the Australians had done in Indonesia'. The Australians did not confirm to the Foreign Office whether such fears were justified.[170] In Bangkok the mission had been approached by the Vietminh but had been 'scrupulously careful' to have nothing to do with them.[171] Dening, who had been in Canberra and who had had talks with Macmahon Ball shortly before the mission left, noted that the Australians had neglected to inform him of the mission and therefore doubted whether they had even approached the French Minister in Canberra. He concluded: 'I do not think we should say anything to the French'.[172]

On 26 July Lloyd briefed Bevin that if French Indo-China fell then this would have grave implications for regional security.[173] He advised that the US was 'fully alive' to such dangers and was similarly 'convinced that it would be disastrous if the French were to quit Indo-China'. Lloyd recommended that, although Britain could not interfere, it should do nothing to prevent a French political or military settlement and 'that we should not encourage any move to bring the matter up in the Security Council or in the General Assembly of the United

Nations'.[174] Mackworth Young noted that 'Indian opinion considers General Xuan a puppet of the French'. Sir Girja Bajpai, the Indian Foreign Secretary, threatened to deny French aircraft the right to fly over Indian territory.[175] On 13 August Reed cautioned the State Department that Moscow was turning more and more attention to the Far East.[176]

Similarly in May, the US decided to end the purge of war-related concerns. A report urged a programme for Japan's economic stability, including a revival of trade with the rest of Asia. Tonkin coal, Malaya tin and rubber, Indonesian oil and Burmese and Siamese rice were important components within this economic regionalism.[177] In Indo-China economic stability remained precarious. A reconstruction budget of 846 million Piastres had been apportioned for 1948, 80% paid for by France and 20% from Indo-China. As the crisis in Vietnam continued, rice mills were targeted and burnt in Cholon. The cost of living for both European and the indigenous population continued to rise during 1948.[178] Gibbs regarded this as part of a strategy of economic warfare that included the destruction of dykes for rice irrigation, the terrorisation of labour, the sinking of junks and the burning of shipyards.[179] The French requested British assistance in the supply of ammunition to their troops in Indo-China but the War Office declined. The Foreign Office urged the War Office to reconsider its position, 'in view of the present situation in Indo-China, anything that can be done to assist the French forces is of value' as a Vietminh success would threaten Britain's strategic position in Southeast Asia.[180] Again the War Office refused, considering its own stocks were below minimum requirements.[181] However, the Foreign Office appeared split over military supplies to the French. In July 1947 Britain had loaned an aircraft carrier to the French navy. This was now *en route* to Saigon with French aircraft supplies for Indo-China. A Foreign Office telegram to Saigon insisted that the chances of the ship being involved in fighting were remote but Mackworth Young believed the image of Anglo-French solidarity could prove embarrassing to the British in other parts of Southeast Asia.[182] The US had declined to allow the direct export of arms and ammunition to Indo-China but permitted 'the free export of arms to France ... for reshipment to Indo-China or for releasing stocks from reserves to be forwarded to Indo-China'.[183]

During the autumn, tension on the world stage escalated further. In Indonesia, communists at Madiun attempted to stage a revolution within a revolution whilst in China continued communist successes indicated the likelihood of an eventual collapse of the nationalist government. On 13 October the US warned its diplomatic missions in Asia that Moscow was turning more attention to the Far East.[184] The British and French exchanged information on communist leaders who had been expelled from Indo-China and could cause further agitation in the region.[185] The Chinese communist Liu Shao Chi announced that the solution to the colonial problem was to establish anti-imperialist collaboration with nationalist movements.[186] On 12 November Graves, in Washington, was asked by the US if there was some way of galvanising the French into action to protect the country against the potential communist menace.[187] Sargent, at the Foreign Office, increased Mac-Donald's remit to include Foreign Office defence matters (MacDonald already dealt with Colonial Office defence issues).[188] The Foreign Office then asked MacDonald to review the US query regarding galvanising the French during his forthcoming conference.[189] On 19 November the US issued NSC 20/4. This concluded that 'Soviet domination of the potential power of Eurasia ... would be strategically and politically unacceptable to the US'.[190] Three days later the DRVN applied to join the UN.[191] The Foreign Office proposed to evade the issue because the Security Council had not taken any action and the British delegation had not requested any instructions.[192]

By December the US appeared to be preparing for greater global intervention with the formation of the Foreign Assistance Correlation Committee.[193] The British Embassy in Paris believed that the US was 'not prepared to accept any responsibility for Southeast Asia'. It held that as it was for the regional powers to counter the 'communist menace' it was essential to resolve the situation in Malaya and sound out Anglo-French suggestions for future co-operation and to combat clandestine arms traffic.[194] In Britain there was no perception of an imminent crisis and no need for preparation, planning and infrastructure for a possible intervention. A Commanders-in-Chief Far East paper saw no threat of military invasion of Southeast Asia but stressed the psychological need of a will to resist communism in Hong Kong.[195] The Cabinet Far Eastern Committee considered that it could do nothing 'to combat the advance of communism in China'. It recommended that 'our main line of action must be therefore directed towards building up resistance in surrounding countries ... to resolve political disputes ... to improve the economic position' and to achieve co-operation of interested powers.[196] Indo-China was regarded as a 'poor buffer' to a communist China and it was predicted that economic disturbances especially centred on rice production would result from the success of a communist controlled China. This would lead to a decrease in regional rice consumption and 'provide fertile ground for communist agitation', which could disrupt other commodities such as rubber, tin and oils that 'are of such importance to world economic recovery'.[197] The CIA cautioned that the current situation in Asia was favourable to the Soviets and that the US was caught in the middle between Asian nationalists and the European states.[198] Dening considered that it was regionally important to convince France of the need to resolve Indo-China before the Chinese communists reached its borders.[199] Likewise, MacDonald was eager to seek diplomatic action 'to strengthen co-operation between friendly governments against the communist menace in Southeast Asia'.[200] In a meeting with the French Government in Paris, Dening volunteered that 'in future there should be frequent consultation on Far Eastern problems, not only by local authorities on the spot but also between the United Kingdom and French Foreign Offices'.[201] Meanwhile the total adverse visible balance of trade in Indo-China reached 1186 million Piastres, due to the high level of imports.[202] Considering potential food exports from Indo-China the British Procurement Office concluded that 'continual inflation has made cost of living abnormally high but official salaries have not risen in proportion with the result that corruption has closed in'.[203]

Bevin met Schuman in London on 13 and 14 January 1949 for a series of talks. The two discussed various means for the exchange of information between Britain and France through the Commissioner-General's office in Singapore.[204] Schuman also hoped that settlement of the Indonesian crisis would aid the situation in Indo-China.[205] He was quick to state that 'the French Union was quite different from the British conception of the Commonwealth. The latter was much wider in scope, with greater autonomy for its component parts'.[206] On 20 January Truman announced during his inaugural second term address that 'Point Four' assistance, US technical aid for under-developed countries, was a vital weapon against communism which grows 'on tissues made gangrenous by disease, poverty and exploitation'.[207] The COS considered that the strategic implication of the situation in China necessitated prompt settlement of the crises in Indo-China and Indonesia 'so that the solidarity and military strength of the Commonwealth and Western European countries is not impaired'. It concluded that for Indo-China and Indonesia the 'policy of withholding military aid must continue until the political situation changes'.[208]

Rice supply remained an issue in Southeast Asia. India had already found French rice prices too high and suggested that they together with Malaya should attempt to purchase Indo-Chinese rice as a bulk purchase to achieve a cheaper price based on economies of scale.[209]

Meanwhile, the progress of communist forces in China continued despite Stalin's scepticism. Mao's revolutionary strategy was vindicated following the People's Liberation Army crossing of the Yangzi in the spring of 1949 and the rapid conquest of the Southern provinces. The French suspected that Chinese communities in Southeast Asia could be used as a vehicle for subversive activities and welcomed an exchange of information with Britain on communist leaders, arms smuggling, communications and airfields. They also supported joint economic development and technical aid through the office of the Commissioner-General and the UN Economic Commission for the Far East. France urged Anglo-French-US co-operation in Southeast Asia to combat regional communism and the threat from communist China.[210] MacDonald complained to Killearn about the urgency of the situation 'in the face of the threat from China ... I am afraid that we are building with diplomacy rather than with military and economic resources'. He expressed a 'good deal of faith in the new Secretary of State, Dean Acheson' to change the momentum.[211]

During March a paper prepared for Bevin by Dening indicated that without help Southeast Asia would fall victim to a communist advance.[212] On 9 March a Foreign Office assessment of Indo-China noted that although the US was worried about the situation in Southeast Asia it did not believe that it had any responsibility for counteracting communist influence in the region. Anglo-French understanding was needed and 'British and French military commanders have already met and arranged for exchange of military and security intelligence'.[213] Attlee established a ministerial committee under himself comprising the Chancellor, the Lord President, the Minister of Defence and Secretaries of State for the Colonies, Commonwealth Relations and Foreign Affairs to consider the problems of China and Southeast Asia.[214] Continuing the spirit of co-operation begun by Killearn, MacDonald welcomed delegates including Indo-China to the Indo-Pacific Fisheries Council in Singapore on 24 March 1949.[215] Meanwhile, talks were orchestrated in London between Baeyens and Dening which 'were designed to convey to the French a sense of urgency in Far Eastern Affairs in view of the situation in China and the advance of communism in Asia'. The Foreign Office held that neither India nor Australia would recognise the Auriol Agreement as real independence.[216] Likewise MacDonald held private talks with Pignon, who seemed to understand the 'importance of the time factor'. He regarded that the French and Bao Dai needed between six months and a year 'before the Chinese communists become too powerful along the border'.[217]

On 29 March the US paper PPS51 concluded that Southeast Asia had become the target of an offensive by the Kremlin.[218] Meanwhile, about 18,000 irregular Chinese troops had begun operating in Northern Tonkin, and the British Foreign Office doubted whether France would be able to successfully reinforce troop numbers in Indo-China.[219] From September 1945 to December 1948 14,158 French troops had been killed in Indo-China not including North Africans or those seriously wounded.[220] Bevin travelled to Washington to sign the North Atlantic Treaty. Two days prior to the signing ceremony he wrote to Acheson that in 'parallel with our efforts in Europe and the Middle East' we should 'encourage a spirit of co-operation and self-reliance in Southeast Asia with the view to the creation of a common front against Russian expansion in that area'. He went on to urge Acheson that such containment could 'influence the situation in China and make it possible to redress the position there' but that the Asian Governments would also have to be included, and technical advice, assistance, capital goods and arms would need to be provided.[221] Graves sensed US wariness to the proposal: 'they have burnt their fingers so badly in China that they are at present in a very cautious mood'.[222] Ironically at the same time, in Singapore, MacDonald protested to Strang about the Foreign Office's attempts to postpone a Commonwealth Governments' conference until the autumn or the following year with the warning that both Burma and Indo-China could be further in communist hands if the situation was ignored.[223] On 4 April the North Atlantic Treaty was signed creating a regional defence organisation for Europe; Bevin, however, did not regard this as a precedent for other regional defence alliances. Three weeks later he stressed to Attlee that there were too many internal conflicts for a Southeast Asian NATO.[224]

Britain remained eager to ascertain the direction of US policy in the region and in May a working party was set up to study the Far East in the context of the January 1949 Truman address.[225] US policy appeared to be moving towards advocating the attainment of regional agreement with other attracted powers. On 20 May the State Department suggested that the US should try and 'meet common attitude with other interested governments, particularly UK, India and Philippines'.[226] MacDonald hoped that the US would 'tackle the problem of Southeast Asia with the same constructive energy as they have put into the problem of Western Europe and the North Atlantic'. He felt that 'we can hold a line against communism which keeps all the Southeast Asian countries on our side' but warned that 'time is running short'.[227] In Indo-China, France placed a blockade on rice production in Cochinchina in order to deny the Vietminh the revenue they were collecting from the internal movement of rice. This led to further regional problems with the cessation of rice exports from Saigon.[228]

Between June and August Britain was becoming increasingly concerned about the 'dollar gap' and the falling income from dollar exports by the sterling area nations. Britain was still bankrupt following the Second World War. It possessed an insulated imperial economy which allowed 'British Sterling debts to be discounted by imports and it secured markets and supplies for Britain which might otherwise have been lost'.[229] In Southeast Asia Malaya was strategically and economically important to Britain as the largest net earner of dollars of the British colonies, in 1948 $172 million.[230] Bevin believed that if the dollar and sterling areas achieved the right co-operation then it would be possible to use Truman's 'Point Four' assistance to raise living standards.[231] The dollar crisis resulted in talks with the US for the devaluation of sterling in September.[232]

At this time Russia increased pressure on the Far East with an Orientalist Conference in Moscow. *Pravda* published on 7–9 June the Chinese communist solution of the colonial question announced by Liu Shao Chi in November 1948.[233] In the US an Ogburn paper discussed the possibility of a communist controlled Indo-China causing a chain reaction in rest of the sub-continent.[234] The French pressed the US to draw a line to stop communism north of the Sino-Indo-Chinese border.[235] On 5 July the Philippines and nationalist China called for a regional anti-communist alliance. Six days later Acheson decided to send PPS51 to Europe and Asia as a source of information.[236] Reed remarked that for US policy 'the restoration of political stability was the prime necessity' in Burma, Indo-China and Indonesia.[237] A Foreign Office paper concluded that Russia was an expansionist power working towards domination in Europe and 'challenging British strategic and economic position [in] the Middle East and the Far East'.[238]

During August Russia exploded its first atomic bomb and the US White Paper foresaw an eventual Sino-Soviet Alliance.[239] The COS was warned by the BDCC that a French withdrawal from Indo-China would have 'extremely serious effects' on 'British interests in Southeast Asia'.[240] Similarly, the Colonial Office feared that a French withdrawal from Northern Indo-China would facilitate communist supplies into Burma and Thailand, and withdrawal from Cambodia and Cochinchina would result in 'a direct strategic threat to Malaya'.[241] In September Truman publicly acknowledged that Russia had exploded an atomic bomb.[242] The Commanders-in-Chief Far East considered that Britain should support the French in Tonkin to enable a friendly government to be established which would ultimately enable French forces to be re-deployed for the defence of Europe.[243] The US remained anxious about the heightened communist activity in Southeast Asia. On 8 September US Vice-Admiral Badger warned that if the Chinese communists were not stopped in Southern China then Indo-China, Burma and Malaya would fall.[244] The next day during talks at the State Department Dening revealed that in a Vietnamese radio broadcast Ho had thanked Stalin for the supply of arms against the French.[245]

At a meeting between Bevin and Acheson prior to tripartite meetings with France in Washington Bevin raised the situations in Malaya and Indo-China. Acheson acknowledged 'that the situation in Malaya was quite different from that prevailing in Indo-China since the Malays looked to the British for protection against the Chinese and were not at the present seeking a further degree of independence'.[246] In London a COS committee report by the JPS considered views from the JPS, the JIC and the BDCC on the further implications of a French withdrawal from Indo-China on British interests in Southeast Asia and other theatres. It concluded that 'A partial French withdrawal from French Indo-China would adversely affect British interests in Far East and Southeast Asia. A complete withdrawal would have the most serious implications for which the release of several French divisions for service elsewhere would be an inadequate compensation'.[247]

On 1 October the PRC was formally inaugurated in Beijing. British plans for the aerial photography of Indo-China were halted by the Foreign Office as such an operation could be interpreted by the communists 'as a prelude to active intervention', especially when considered against an active programme of visits to Indo-China by Britain which included two frigates and the CIGS in October, the Commissioner-General and the Commander-in-Chief of Far East Land Forces in November and Admiral Madden in December.[248] On 18 October, due to the lack of reliance on Indo-Chinese rice supplies, neither France nor Indo-China was included in a regional co-ordinating body at the Singapore Rice Conference.[249] On the same day British long-term policy 'to contain Soviet Russia and Communist China' and prevent 'the spread of communism in South and Southeast Asia' was set out in Cabinet Paper CP(49)207. This was 'the creation of some form of regional association between all the Governments in the area for political, economic and (if necessary) defence co-operation, this association working in partnership with the association of the North Atlantic Powers on the one hand and with Australia and New Zealand on the other'.[250] Bevin briefed Attlee that communist success in China had resulted in the Chinese communities of Southeast Asia favouring a Chinese communist government. He felt that there would now be 'greatly increased pressure from the communists in all the territories of Southeast Asia'.[251] Attlee 'agree[d] with the analysis' of CP(49)207.[252] Bevin warned the Cabinet that 'communist influence has recently been extended over a large part of China. There is a grave risk of its further extension into Southeast Asia'.[253] The Cabinet endorsed the policy of working towards regional, political and if necessary military co-operation through economic co-ordination, eight days later.[254] MacDonald believed that the Indian attitude towards Indo-China was improving and he urged close liaison with France about Indo-China and PRC aggression.[255] On 28 October the Mutual Defence Assistance Act Section 303 was passed in the US. Truman could now send any non-combatant military advisers to any nations or agencies.[256]

Considering MacDonald's optimism towards the Indian approach to Indo-China November did not begin well. During a visit to the US, Nehru did not demonstrate confidence in the Bao Dai solution and declared to Acheson that 'in his opinion Bao Dai was certain to fail'.[257] From the 2–4 November the Bukit Serene Conference of British regional representatives endorsed the recognition of the PRC, the long-term British policy objective of regional organisation through economic co-operation and the recognition of the Bao Dai regime.[258] The conference concluded that Southeast Asia was in a state of emergency where action against communism 'cannot be deferred until the policy of economic co-operation bears fruit'. It considered that it was 'unlikely that the Chinese communists will attempt military aggression against China's neighbours for some time to come'.[259] It was felt that the PRC would sponsor guerrilla operations in Southeast Asia and that Indo-China was currently the weakest part of the region. It was feared that if the communists could dominate the rice areas of Indo-China, Siam and Burma then this would strangle the region.[260] The conference agreed that the exchange of military intelligence with the French was limited due to current restrictions, and recommended that this problem be considered by the COS or the BDCC.[261] At the fifth session of the Economic Commission for Asia and the Far East in Singapore (a regional commission for the UN), Bao Dai's application for membership as an associate member was passed by eight votes to one (Russia).[262] A similar DRVN application was defeated with only India and Russia supporting the application, India had also voted in favour of Bao Dai.[263] Britain considered that no economic or social development assistance could be accorded to Indo-China 'until the fighting stops'. It regarded Indo-China's immediate problems as military and political rather than economic although it would take the necessary steps 'when the fighting stops, to restore Indo-China's rice exports' which would help to restore the region's food supply.[264]

Bevin asked Attlee to discuss the communist threat to Indo-China with Nehru during his current London visit, but Attlee was too busy and asked Bevin to broach this with Nehru.[265] The French regarded Indian Foreign Office policy with hostility, 'a feeling of solidarity against the white[s]'.[266] During a visit to Indo-China MacDonald held talks with the Indian Consul-General who predicted that 'the Bao Dai experiment would fail, and that the Vietminh would remain the most powerful representatives of nationalist feeling in Indo-China'. However, the Indian Consul-General felt that 'if the French prove as good as their word and begin to transfer substantial power to Bao Dai in the way suggested ... the Vietminh will lose a great deal of support'.[267] MacDonald urged Pignon to have talks with the Indian Consul-General 'to remove his deep suspicion of the French authorities' and result 'in wiser advice to his government in New Delhi'.[268] MacDonald desired the British and US Governments to issue a declaration similar to Acheson's concerning Hong Kong, that if the Tonkin border were attacked then the crisis would be referred to the UN Security Council and acted upon.[269] Dening and Strang were against this idea and therefore did not pursue it further.[270] Following a visit to Indo-China General Revers, Commander-in-Chief of the French Army, informed the British Military Attaché in Paris that it was essential for Britain and France to develop a united policy towards the communist threat and proposed a regional conference in Singapore.[271] Politically, the COS considered that British policy in the region had been placed in an awkward situation. If Britain failed to recognise the PRC then this could cause the Chinese population in Malaya and Singapore to regard Britain as anti-Chinese but recognition could be disastrous for Bao Dai and thereby lead to a French withdrawal from Indo-China which could threaten Singapore and Malaya.[272]

Late in 1949 the Chinese Peoples Liberation Army reached the Indo-Chinese border. Vietminh radio relayed Ho and Mao's exchanges of good wishes on the formation of the PRC.[273] The British Foreign Office was delighted with this evidence linking Mao and Ho as 'ideological brothers'.[274] In December the US paper NSC 48/1, 'The Position of the US with respect to Asia', concluded that there was a need to counter the Chinese threat to Asia but did not specifically mention the crisis in Indo-China.[275] Similarly NSC 58/2 concluded that it was important to use Titoism to roll back Soviet influence in the world.[276] Strangely the DRVN could not be applied to the Titoist model.

On 1 December the British Cabinet endorsed a policy of 'promoting regional co-operation in Southeast Asia, and improving economic and social conditions in the area with the aim of checking communism and Russian expansion'. It identified India as the critical area for US financial assistance due to its 'size, population, low standards of living and strategic position'. Because of the financial pressure caused by the problems with sterling balances Britain could not provide any investment or maintain current assistance in dependent territories. The International Bank, the Export-Import Bank, public loans floated abroad, private assets and the use of assets already held were identified as possible sources of funding, although it would still 'be desirable to induce the US to recognise the need for provision of additional finance'. US technical assistance was available under Truman's 'point 4' but this 'would only be fully effective if it is accompanied by the necessary finance'. The policy stated that assistance would have to be assessed upon the lines of vulnerability to communism, economic merit, regional and international benefits and how far a nation could apply self help. Indo-China, Indonesia and Burma were identified as countries 'where when conditions return to normal, rehabilitation must precede new development' as this 'could yield a higher return' and build up 'political resistance to communism'.[277] It reiterated Britain's stance that upon cessation of violence it was important to restore Indo-China's rice exports.[278] The next day the Foreign Office decided to withdraw its objections to the British aerial survey of Indo-China.[279] On 9 December the US decided upon a Military Aid Programme Bill of $75 million for Southeast Asia thereby giving finance to Truman's Point Four.[280]

The French Commander-in-Chief in Indo-China, General Carpentier, indicated that during a forthcoming visit to Paris, to review Indo-China, he would call on the British Military Attaché, probably to discuss the possible exchange of secret military Information with Britain, joint Anglo-French staff talks in the Far East and British supply of military equipment to Indo-China. In discussion the COS were in favour of achieving an Anglo-French-US policy towards Indo-China and believed that the Foreign Office should 'approach the State Department'. The COS supported the idea of Anglo-French talks provided that the boundaries 'were agreed in London beforehand'.[281] At a second meeting, three days later, the COS decided that any submission by the French for the supply of equipment 'should be given sympathetic consideration' and also instructed the JPS and JIC to consider how to execute Anglo-French staff talks 'with authorities in French Indo-China'. Likewise, it supported the idea that an aerial survey of Indo-China should be conducted as soon as possible.[282] The French asked the BDCC whether Britain would support France if Indo-China was attacked by the PRC and if Britain was not committed elsewhere.[283] On 16 December ministers on the China and Southeast Asia Committee chaired by Attlee ruled that Britain was not to become militarily involved in Indo-China. A week later the Foreign Office instructed the COS not to undertake staff talks or any talks that implied military action by Britain. The Foreign Office agreed that Indo-China was vital in the battle against communism but stressed that the Foreign Office was giving political support for the development of Cambodia, Laos and Vietnam. It welcomed the idea of talks with France on Southeast Asian defence but insisted that Britain would also need to inform the US and said that Britain would not become militarily involved in Indo-China even if the Chinese communists invaded Vietnam.[284] Meanwhile on 17 December the US JCS divided the Military Aid Programme budget between French Indo-China, Burma and Thailand.[285] Acheson informed Franks that he believed in 'a geopolitical division of responsibilities. The Americans would look after Indonesia, Philippines, and Indo-China with a little to spare for Siam. The Commonwealth would see to the help of the countries in the Indian Ocean. He had in mind especially Burma: then there was our own position in Malaya and our interest overlapping theirs in Siam'. Franks concluded that 'Acheson clearly was hoping that in some way India and the United Kingdom would be able to tidy up the mess in Burma so as to prevent the Chinese appearing over the hump'.[286]

Whilst a bankrupt Britain waited on the outcome of the Colombo Conference, the US appeared galvanised into beginning a policy of assistance towards Southeast Asia. The US dispatched the Ambassador-at-Large Philip Jessup on a fact-finding mission to the Far East on 15 December for three months. On 6 January 1950 Britain recognised the PRC. The US did not.[287] The Ministry of Supply contacted the Colonial Office and indicated that 'if the scale of the attack is increased by the occupation by the enemy of bases in Burma, Siam or Indo-China the defences [in Singapore] should be increased'.[288]

The escalation of a crisis

On 30 December France transferred administrative powers for Vietnam to the Bao Dai Government, although the Auriol Agreement still had not been ratified. The French delay had strengthened Ho, who had aligned with Stalin and Mao. Although diplomats had debated Ho's nationalist, communist and even Titoist credentials they had discounted that he could be both a nationalist and a communist. 'For him, nationalism and communism, the ends and the means, complement[ed] one another; or rather they merge[d] inextricably'.[289] Likewise, the creation of the PRC had symbolically linked Vietnam to the socialist bloc.[290] A DRVN military delegation had been dispatched to Peking to negotiate with the Chinese as the DRVN approached the second stage of Maoist insurgency warfare, 'equilibrium'.[291]

Britain had emerged from its wait-and-see strategy and consultations with its US ally with a clearer perspective of US policy. The US was committed to the containment of communism. France was a vital component of this containment in Europe as a member of NATO. The failure of US policy in supporting the nationalists in China made Indo-China a vital bulwark in US strategy and necessitated US aid.[292] The US belief in a monolithic world communist menace orchestrated by Moscow left no room for Indo-Chinese nationalism to be developed according to Titoism.[293] The US expected Britain and the Commonwealth to assist in Southeast Asia but here British policy remained unclear. The US interpreted this as a British attempt to disassociate itself from French policy in Indo-China.[294]

In contrast to the US and France, Britain had chosen to recognise the PRC but had delayed doing so in an attempt to allow France time to transfer power to Bao Dai. However the French were unable to take advantage of the British delay and for Britain to delay PRC recognition a second time would have been an unnerving experience as Britain sought not just to exploit any possible rifts between Moscow and Peking but also to protect its regional strategic and economic interests in Hong Kong, Malaya and the rest of Southeast Asia.[295] To balance the recognition of the PRC Britain had agreed to the *de facto* recognition of Bao Dai following the Colombo Conference but, conscious of the need for Bao Dai not to appear a Western puppet, Britain would need to appeal to the Commonwealth Foreign Ministers – especially India,

Ceylon, Burma and Pakistan – to do likewise. Britain and the US had hoped to persuade Nehru that Ho was a communist rather than a nationalist but Nehru's Pan-Asian sympathy for Ho as a nationalist communist rather than a Kremlin communist appealed to him more than France's nationalist masquerades with Bao Dai.[296] Unfortunately, Britain failed to get Commonwealth nations to recognise the Bao Dai regime at the Commonwealth Conference in Colombo.[297]

5
Consequences, January–June 1950

The French transfer of administrative powers to the Bao Dai Government on 30 December 1949 did little to reduce the growing international concern or the internal crisis in Indo-China. French failure to ratify the 8 March Agreement made the transfer of administrative powers an empty gesture. It provided Ho with the opportunity to counter ratification and any subsequent international recognition. Continued DRVN control of large areas of Vietnam justified Nehru's assertion that in reality there were 'two governments in Indo-China'.[1] On 18 January the DRVN was formally recognised by the PRC.[2] As French complacency continued, so did Ho's diplomatic offensive. In late January he held further talks with the PRC before proceeding to Moscow for negotiations with Stalin who rejected DRVN requests for direct Soviet aid, regarding this as the PRC's task. Russia formally recognised the DRVN on 30 January.[3] Ho appeared to have achieved if not a diplomatic advantage over the French and Bao Dai then at least equilibrium. The Indo-Chinese Communist Party declared Indo-China one battlefield and the Vietminh were prepared to provide leadership for the Cambodian and Laotian revolutionary movements.[4] Cambodia was an important source of finance for the Vietminh, through the control and taxation of fishing, pepper and rice production.[5] Coincidentally, Jessup, the US Ambassador at large, visited Hanoi and Saigon at the end of January as part of his tour to assess the growing crisis in the Far East.[6] Following the fall of the Chinese Nationalist Government the US needed to revise its Far Eastern policy and address its own internal criticism that 'it has had no consistent plan of action that could be described as a long-term policy.'[7] The US had long abandoned the principle of neutrality, if it had ever existed, in Indo-China. The precedent for US assistance in Southeast Asia was established on 9 January when five million dollars was granted to newly independent Indonesia to establish a police force.[8] Three days later the validity of the challenge was projected by Acheson during his 'Crisis in Asia' speech to the National Press Club. Acheson stated that the 'Real interest of American people was in maintenance of national independence of other peoples and it was because communism was hostile to that interest that America opposed it. To say merely that United States interest was to stop the spread of communism was putting the cart before the horse'.[9] The internal Indo-Chinese crisis had indeed escalated and exploded upon the world stage, creating two camps locked over Indo-China.

In Vietnam the political situation remained weak and perilously unstable. Bao Dai relinquished his position as Prime Minister and dissolved the government so that he could assume his duties as Head of State.[10] The Cao Dai group in the government immediately withdrew their support for the new Prime Minister, Nguyen Pham Long, although they maintained their personal support of Bao Dai.[11] Although a new government was established the British Foreign Office appeared to agree with Gibb's prediction of 'serious danger if the present "state of flux" in Indo-China is allowed to persist'.[12] Likewise, British recognition of the PRC had not helped the confidence or the stability of the Vietnamese government and 'was not well received'.[13]

For Britain the same priorities remained: recognition of Bao Dai only upon ratification of the 8 March Agreement; the question of military supplies to the French; the regional need to contain communism to protect British interests in Malaya and Hong Kong; and the need to ensure the supply of rice within Southeast Asia. Bevin was committed to meeting the escalating crisis in Indo-China and Southeast Asia; the Labour Government, however, also had to contest a spring general election. Nevertheless, these other Cabinet preoccupations did not prove decisive, as Britain had to await French ratification and a diplomatic US lead. Britain's financial difficulties and own commitments in the region meant that any long-term burden adopted through recognition could only be borne by the US. Therefore Britain's ability to commit military assistance to Indo-China was to prove limited at this stage and it had to accept second place. However, Britain's position in the region was still reinforced by Commonwealth support although, in order to maintain its position, this was subject to the whims of its regional partners.

The blend of Britain's Indo-Chinese and regional policies

Bevin kept the US informed of proceedings at the January Colombo Conference through the US Ambassador to Ceylon, to whom he expressed frustration with the French inability to ratify their agreement with Bao Dai. MacDonald had presented the conference with an encouraging internal synopsis of the situation in Indo-China and Bevin believed that 'if the French had ratified, all the government representatives here, with the exception of India, would have come down in favour of *de facto* recognition'. Instead there was 'a good deal of mistrust of French intentions'. Bevin feared that British recognition before French ratification would 'upset some of the hesitant members of the Commonwealth'. He was eager to support Bao Dai, and French ratification would demonstrate their 'good faith' in which, with the exception of India, the Commonwealth Governments would follow a British lead and accord recognition. Despite his non-committal assessment of India's reaction to recognition following ratification, Bevin did not think that Nehru would pose any further problems but considered it important for Britain to 'carry the Asian members of the Commonwealth with us' who 'were hesitant as a result of French procrastination in the past'.[14]

Bevin's conclusions were relayed to Schuman.[15] In London, Baudet met with Dening to discuss the conclusions of the Colombo Conference. Dening only offered a 'general outline' in which he relayed Nehru's solution that 'Bao Dai should come to terms with Ho Chi Minh'. Baudet also enquired about the outcome of talks between Field Marshal Slim, General Sir John Harding and General Carpentier 'about the supply of arms and military equipment for the French in Indo-China'. As Dening was unaware of the current situation, and the French were eager to pursue the enquiry, Baudet suggested that the Military Attaché at the French Embassy should contact the British Ministry of Defence.[16]

From Washington, Franks ironically observed that the US people were convinced 'that the supreme danger confronting their civilisation is not old fashioned colonialism but modern communism'. Therefore the colonial powers were regarded as 'natural and indispensable allies' although there was an inherent failure 'to recognise that anything which weakens the colonial powers also weakens the United States'.[17] Senator Joseph McCarthy began a campaign a month later to have the State Department purged of communist employees. Meanwhile, the State Department held that in order to attain maximum assistance for Bao Dai 'some Asiatic countries should precede the United States in according recognition or at least at the same time'. Therefore the US hoped to persuade the Philippines, Thailand and Indonesia, and trusted Britain to do the same with India and Burma.[18] However, when asked about the Commonwealth discussions on Bao Dai, Nehru replied 'We are generally opposed to any foreign armies functioning in Asia. That is a general proposition, our policy in Indo-China is to watch events and not to make any commitments'.[19] Similarly, the US wanted France to issue a statement of '"liberal intentions" and a specific plan for the further evolution of Viet Nam', as well as removing Indo-China from the responsibility of the Ministry of Overseas Territories.[20] Jessup in Vietnam concluded his visit with a message of goodwill from the US and a personal message of success from Acheson to Bao Dai.[21]

Having returned to Singapore, MacDonald advocated according the *de facto* recognition even if the French parliamentary timetable delayed ratification further. He believed that early British action was required: British recognition of the PRC had prejudiced Bao Dai; the Vietminh and the PRC were increasing their action and propaganda against Bao Dai; Bao Dai and the French in Saigon could easily be discouraged; and other Commonwealth Governments would follow a British lead. However, if Britain chose to await ratification he would support the government in putting 'every pressure on the French to ratify'.[22] Du Gardier visited MacDonald and relayed the news of a further gradual improvement in the situation in Indo-China. MacDonald briefed him as to the conclusions on the question of recognition arrived at by the Colombo Conference, i.e.: the 8 March Agreement should be ratified; Indo-China transferred from the Ministry of Overseas Territories to the French Foreign Office or a French Commonwealth Relations Office; Bao Dai should be allowed to appoint diplomats overseas wherever he wanted; and France should declare this the start of a process towards full sovereign state status. Du Gardier agreed with these proposals and indicated that Pignon also advocated similar policies. Du Gardier informed MacDonald that the French intended to extend recognition beyond the 8 March Agreement. An inter-state conference planned for the third week in February between Cambodia, Laos and Vietnam would be followed by further power transfers to the three Indo-Chinese governments. Similarly, 80% of the powers reserved by the French were limited to the current crisis and would be removed upon its conclusion. The other 20% would expire when the Vietnamese state 'expands its trained personnel in various fields, for example the judiciary'.[23] Pignon's position remained vulnerable. MacDonald considered that any attempt by the French to replace Pignon with a military High Commissioner at this juncture 'would be an act of titanic folly' which would damage Commonwealth opinion and Bao Dai's prospects.[24]

The French were both surprised and out-manoeuvred by the PRC recognition of the DRVN whilst Acheson expressed surprise at Russian recognition.[25] The British Ambassador in Moscow observed that 'the Soviet and Chinese leaders have decided that French-Indo-China is the weakest link in the chain of Western defence in Southeast Asia, and that the maximum pressure should be exerted there'. Russia's recognition of Indonesia appeared to amplify this position.[26] The French protested to the Russian Ambassador in Paris concerning recognition of the DRVN.[27] On 1 February a State Department working party concluded that already the US was bound together with France in Indo-China. A failure to support Bao Dai would result in a communist Indo-China which would contribute to the defeat of US objectives in Europe.[28] MacDonald summarised his feelings about communist recognition to the Foreign Office 'in these last two weeks we have lost the diplomatic initiative in Indo-China which has passed to the communist powers. In my view, unless we seize it again quickly and firmly, irreparable harm may be done'. MacDonald again pressed for an immediate *de facto* recognition based on the 30 December 1949 transfer of power to Bao Dai with a *de jure* recognition to follow ratification.[29] Considering the British troubles with communism in Malaya, MacDonald viewed this as the 'extension of the communist movement in China'.[30] After a delay by the French Government, on the 27 January the COS ordered the aerial survey of Indo-China to commence.[31] Three British officers were attached to French units in Indo-China as part of a local exchange scheme between British and French Officers in Indo-China and Malaya.[32] Reflecting the turmoil in Vietnam, the political situation in Cambodia was destabilised by the murder of Ieu Keos, President of the National Assembly, whilst visiting Laos, and there was 'considerable Vietminh infiltration into the Sam Neua area' of Northern Laos.[33] In the British Foreign Office it was cynically suggested that 'a "facade of democracy" is about the most that can be expected in a country such as Viet Nam even under more peaceful conditions. A similar facade in Indonesia is serving quite a useful purpose'.[34]

The Colombo Conference supported a plan by Percy Spender, Australian Minister for External Affairs, for the economic and technical development of South and Southeast Asia; this was to be co-ordinated by a Consultative Committee of Commonwealth countries.[35] The Australian Government agreed to host the first meeting of the Consultative Committee.[36] The Colombo Conference demonstrated that

Australia and New Zealand agreed with Britain over Indo-Chinese recognition, with Nehru in opposition. Therefore Attlee agreed to press France to ratify and transfer power by the end of January. Britain would only accord *de facto* recognition upon ratification.[37] Two days later the Foreign Office advised Attlee that British recognition 'should be neither *de facto* nor *de jure* but "in accordance with the terms of the agreement made between Bao Dai and President Auriol"'.[38] Attlee agreed.[39] Britain would recognise the Associated States in accordance with the 8 March 1949 Auriol-Bao Dai Agreement, the 19 July 1949 Franco-Laotian Treaty and the 8 November 1949 Franco-Cambodian Treaty. The Commonwealth Governments were informed and King George VI approval sought to upgrade the Consul-General in Saigon to the rank of a minister accredited to Cambodia, Laos and Vietnam.[40] MacDonald pessimistically noted 'my hunch is that we are in for an extremely tense year'. He was unsure if Indo-China, Siam and Burma could be held against communism and if not feared that Malaya would be threatened by the loss of its Southeast Asian food supply. He concluded ironically, 'it will at least be exciting'.[41]

Bevin returned to London from Colombo via Paris, where he held talks with the Acting French Foreign Minister Schneiter. Bevin expressed his continued disappointment at the French failure to ratify the 8 March Agreement. This had prevented the Commonwealth Governments making a definitive decision concerning recognition.[42] Bevin was in favour of Anglo-French co-operation, believing that 'Indo-China was a key point in the communist expansion programme'. Schneiter held that without 'moral and possibly armed support' France would possibly have to evacuate Indo-China.[43] Bevin explained that it was the intention of the British Government to place the recognition of Cambodia, Laos and Vietnam before the Cabinet on 7 February and hopefully accord recognition later that day. Schneiter was anxious about the deepening international crisis; already Russia and Czechoslovakia had recognised the DRVN. Further recognition by other communist bloc nations would follow. Schneiter considered that immediate recognition was needed by Britain and the US to slow the escalating crisis. Bevin was unmoved by Schneiter's plea, preferring to wait for a Cabinet decision, especially as he now favoured *de jure* recognition which needed further consultation. He also wanted to consult the Commonwealth Governments to ascertain which would support recognition. Bevin believed that Russia was aware of British intentions, but Britain would not be rushed into making any decision. He agreed to discuss the issue urgently with Attlee and inform the French

Government if 'an immediate decision could be taken'.[44] In Russia, Zhukov writing in *Pravda* denounced 'the criminal designs of the Franco-American imperialists in Indo-China, which are directed to the establishment of bases for aggression against [the] People's Democratic China and to preparing a new war'. Zhukov blamed the current crisis in Vietnam on French and US banks and 'American monopolies, which are interested in seizing the tin, zinc, coal and other natural riches of Vietnam, and by the American General Staff who are desirous of having strategic bases at the approaches to the Chinese People's Republic'.[45]

On 7 February the British Cabinet met to discuss the recognition of Cambodia, Laos and Vietnam. Bevin remained unconvinced of French sincerity to liquidate the vestments of the colonial regime and transfer real power to the Associated States. He emphasised to his Cabinet colleagues that it had been essential for British recognition to await French ratification in case the French Socialist Party vetoed the proposals which would have thereby caused British diplomatic embarrassment. Now that ratification had been enacted and US recognition accorded, Bevin recommended that Britain and the US should encourage France to stand against communism in Indo-China. The Cabinet agreed to British recognition of Cambodia, Laos and Vietnam.[46] The Commonwealth Governments were informed of Britain's decision and of the promotion of the Consul-General in Saigon to the rank of minister.[47] The Secretary of State for Commonwealth Affairs expected Australia, Canada and New Zealand to accord recognition; India would not, Pakistan remained undecided and it was hoped that Ceylon would follow the British lead. It was proposed that if Egypt or Persia 'could be persuaded' to recognise Bao Dai then Pakistan might do likewise.[48] The Foreign Office advised the British Embassy in Washington that 'our recognition is not qualified by the words *"de facto"*'. Britain had recognised the Associated States 'under French constitutional law' and did not regard them as 'independent sovereign states' or 'as eligible for membership of the UN'. Additionally, due to communist bloc recognition of the DRVN, Britain was against *de facto* recognition as 'this might have been interpreted by them as a snub'.[49] By contrast the US had accorded unqualified recognition and raised the rank of its representative in Saigon to a minister in charge of a legation.[50] The Foreign Office was not pleased with US accusations that its actions were 'skittish and timorous'.[51] Britain received also a request from the DRVN inviting the 'establishment of diplomatic relations'; however, the government decided not to respond to the request.[52] On 8 February

Massigli conveyed France's thanks for recognition to Bevin and requested Britain to contemplate further steps such as the appointment of a military representative or mission to Indo-China. Bevin declined: 'our hands were already full with the problems of Malaya and Hong Kong, and there might, I added [*sic*] be intensification at the present time of the Malaya question in particular'.[53]

The French Consul-General in Singapore, Guibant, wrote to Mac-Donald thanking him for his efforts in securing the recognition of Cambodia, Laos and Vietnam by Britain. He stated that this was 'I venture to hope the beginning of an active policy by the democratic nations, against opponents who until now have been able to take the initiative with impunity'. Guibant believed that Asiatic support would be forthcoming 'if we demonstrate a common and really firm willingness to defend them against a menace which they are too tempted to consider unavoidable'.[54] MacDonald replied that he was 'impressed by Bao Dai's steadiness and ability' and the 'firmness and the wisdom of Monsieur Pignon'. He considered that Pignon's success during the last year was the highlight in Southeast Asian politics since the Second World War.[55] However, although MacDonald supported British recognition of Cambodia, Laos and Vietnam, he regretted that Gibbs would only acquire the personal rank of a minister. MacDonald believed that Britain should follow the US example and establish a full legation in Saigon and that Britain's limited recognition had been diminished further 'by the full *de jure* recognition given by Russia and her satellites to Ho Chi Minh'.[56] MacDonald continued to press the Foreign Office for the raising of the status of the British Consulate in Saigon to a legation.[57]

On 10 February, following the established Indonesian precedent, the US controlled Export-Import Bank, predecessor to the International Bank, granted Indonesia a hundred million dollar loan, and Jessup attended the Bangkok Conference which had been arranged to discuss communism in the Far East and US aid to Southeast Asia.[58] US willingness to supply large quantities of financial assistance was not overlooked by the French. Six days later the French Ambassador in Washington called on Acheson and proposed a joint Franco-British-US statement 'to ensure the inviolability of the Indo-China frontier', plus setting up talks between the US and France on economic and military aid.[59] Already both the State Department and the French Embassy in Washington had informally questioned the British Embassy 'about military supplies for the French in Indo-China'. The State Department had indicated that the US was close to making a decision to contribute military or financial aid and were eager for Britain to supply light bombers. The British Embassy noted the US trap that 'the State Department would like to avoid too close association with items whose provenance would be so patent'. The embassy replied that it could not deal with such a request and, implying the need to refer the issue to London, it warned that Britain was already stretched with 'responsibilities in Malaya and Hong Kong'.[60] MacDonald supported economic aid to Indo-China and had suggested a joint British, US and Commonwealth survey party to assess the situation.[61] Similarly a report by the Organisation for European Economic Co-operation concluded that a European recovery would be enhanced if the US gave assistance to developing nations.[62] However, US officials were concerned at the amount of assistance that France had requested and were startled by the French claim that 'unless this aid could be furnished the French Government might be compelled to evacuate Indo-China'. The US Ambassador in Paris interpreted the requests as requiring from the US 'nothing less than 100% participation, including troops'.[63] Two days later Schuman clarified the claim, 'there was no question of a voluntary French withdrawal from Indo-China'.[64] In contrast, the French remained distressed at the perceived 'inconsistency' of US policy on colonial issues and Bao Dai, which they believed 'weaken and embarrass France'.[65] Acheson continued to be fearful of congressional 'criticism of French "colonialism" in Indo-China'.[66] On 21 February Massigli delivered to Strang a list of the 'immediate' military requirements needed by the French in Indo-China from the British. He indicated that France was hoping for US aid in equipping local Indo-Chinese forces on a long-term basis.[67] However, British assistance could only be limited. The British Embassy in Washington was instructed to discuss short term economic aid with the US on an '*ad hoc* basis in order not to prejudice discussions with the Commonwealth on the Colombo resolution and aid to Southeast Asia as a whole'.[68] US army planners concluded that once the US had recognised Bao Dai it was imperative to prevent him failing.[69] The US had lost its leverage on France and its commitment to containment gave the French increased influence over the US.[70]

The procurement of rice for British territories remained an important aspect of British Southeast Asian policy. The Sino-Soviet agreements, the PRC and Russian recognition of the DRVN, and the French appeals to Britain and the US suggested an escalating crisis. MacDonald feared that the Sino-Soviet Pact threatened Southeast Asia as it would 'increase respect for Chinese Government among overseas Chinese communities' and encourage other governments to believe that they could 'compromise with Soviet Russia or Communist China without sacrificing their independence'.[71] This could effect severely rice exports from Burma and Siam. Therefore, in Southeast Asia, it was essential that deficit territories achieved 'self-sufficiency', stockpiles were established and a 'comprehensive study of alternative or new sources' was undertaken.[72] Paradoxically, US rice growers considered prices too uneconomical to increase production.[73] The British Cabinet therefore decided to establish a working party to monitor the rice situation in Southeast Asia. The deficit for the current rice year was estimated by MacDonald's staff at over 800,000 tons. However, as reconstruction in Japan continued so its demand for rice increased. It had been estimated that Japan would only be allocated 200,000 tons of Southeast Asian rice but already it had contracted 330,000 tons from Siam and 170,000 tons from Burma, and reports indicated that it was willing to purchase a further 1,000,000 tons from Burma and Siam. Indo-China was estimated to have a 200,000 ton rice surplus, which had not been accounted for at the December allocation meeting; this would probably be absorbed by France and its territories.[74]

Meanwhile, a British Army team successfully visited the International Horse Show in Phnom Penh. MacDonald believed that this would help to improve British prestige in Indo-China.[75] MacDonald and the JIC Far East held that the PRC had enhanced its troop numbers on the Tonkin frontier to increase pressure there but that further troop movements were preparations for an invasion of Tibet.[76] The JIC, in London, concluded in its regional assessment that the PRC posed no threat to Formosa, Hong Kong or Indo-China. Instead Tibet was regarded as a distinct possibility for PRC aggression and, worryingly for Britain, the Malaya situation continued to deteriorate.[77] On 22 February the Canadian Secretary of State for External Affairs, L.B. Pearson, addressed the Canadian House of Commons. He identified Southeast Asia and the Middle East as targets for communist expansion due to recent decolonisation and the growth of nationalism. Concerning Southeast Asia he persisted with the common theme that there needed to be a rise in living standards by self-help and mutual aid to fight communism. Despite the continued violence in Vietnam, he praised the French for their efforts already taken in Cambodia, Laos and Vietnam which 'will provide a means by which the national aspirations of the people of Indo-China will be met'.[78]

From February to April the Vietminh conducted Operation Le Hong Phong 1, a limited offensive operation in Northwestern Tonkin. On 14 February the Sino-Soviet Friendship Treaty was signed between Russia and the PRC.[79] Five days later Ho called for a total mobilisation against the French colonialists and their US allies.[80] Dening met with Baudet and pressed him that the French Government had not yet given any reaction to the PRC, Russian and associated satellite states' recognition of the DRVN. The Foreign Office held that 'there was a danger that world opinion would come to regard Bao Dai and Ho Chi Minh as two rivals in a civil war with virtually equal status' and questioned the French response if the PRC or Russia sent diplomatic representatives to Ho. Baudet believed that such officials held no diplomatic status and would therefore be arrested.[81] However, French procrastination on Indo-China continued. Bevin instructed Harvey, the British Ambassador in Paris, to lobby the French about 'taking steps to try to dispel the suspicions of the Pakistanis and others about French intentions in Indo-China', although India still 'had no intention of recognising either side in Indo-China'.[82]

In addition to discussions with the US and Commonwealth Governments, Britain had lobbied Belgium, Burma, Denmark, Egypt, Greece, Indonesia, Italy, Norway, Persia, the Philippines, Portugal, Siam, Sweden, and Switzerland, to recognise Cambodia, Laos and Vietnam. Although it was impossible to assess the depth of British influence upon the decision-making process of these governments, Australia, Belgium, Brazil, Greece, Italy, New Zealand, and Siam had all accorded recognition by 2 March. Siamese recognition was symbolically important 'as being the first instance of a small independent Asiatic power taking the plunge'.[83] The Cambodian Government, perhaps due to the logic of Cambodian-Siamese historical rivalry, asked Siam not to grant it recognition.[84] The Pakistan Government and others, however, remained reluctant to accord recognition 'owing to doubts about the real nature of Indo-Chinese independence' that still persisted.[85] Lord Hood at the British Embassy in Paris met with Baeyens who maintained that the main difficulties facing France were the removal of Ho and 'finding competent Vietnamese to staff the administration'. He revealed that the US was no longer pressing for a general declaration of French policy on Indo-China but 'for a timetable for the transfer of powers to Bao Dai'.[86] However, whereas the US had been prepared to press the Philippines into recognition of the Associated States and hoped that Britain would be prepared to do likewise with Ceylon, the British Government maintained a firm line that 'no (repeat no) pressure should be brought to bear on Ceylon in this matter'.[87]

Bevin met Massigli on 2 March. Massigli advised Bevin that the French Government had asked the US for material assistance in Indo-China, Siam had recognised the Bao Dai regime and that the Chinese communists were aiding Ho. Massigli wanted to produce a 'common approach' to the crisis with Britain and the US but cautioned Bevin that the US was wary of further nations recognising the PRC. Bevin retorted that British recognition of the PRC had strengthened Mao against Stalin.[88] At this juncture Bevin regarded any Anglo-French staff talks on external defence in the Far East as premature.[89] In parallel the COS assessed that Britain could spare no Army or RAF forces to send to Indo-China; there were possibly limited Royal Naval resources available for off-shore patrolling only.[90] Nonetheless the JIC continued to prepare intelligence on the military situation in Indo-China whilst the JPS examined the issue of Anglo-French staff talks. Five days later Bevin met Schuman for talks during President Auriol's visit to Britain. Bevin was eager for the French to strengthen Bao Dai's position as this would encourage the Commonwealth nations to support France's Indo-China policy. He felt that the handover of the palace at Saigon would symbolically strengthen Bao Dai's position and encourage recognition. Schuman stated that it was France's desire to increase Bao Dai's powers and that his representatives were being appointed to London and Washington. Although he acknowledged that Cambodia, Laos and Vietnam could no longer remain under the jurisdiction of the Ministry of Overseas Territories they were still administered by this ministry as no decision had yet been taken regarding their future. It could be that a new ministry would be created based upon the British Commonwealth Relations Office. Likewise, as the Ministry for Overseas Territories still administered Vietnam, Schuman indicated that he would pass on the question of the palace to his ministerial colleague, giving the recommendation his support. Bevin was encouraged and Schuman used the opportunity to press Bevin on the issue of British aid to Indo-China, stating, 'France was now the principal obstacle for communism in the Far East ... and the commitments in Indo-China prevented the re-organisation of the French Army in Europe. It was not only a question of defending French interests in Indo-China; the matter had to be looked at as a wider problem'. Bevin acknowledged that Massigli had already delivered 'a list of military requirements' which was being studied. However, due to Britain's 'many commitments' Bevin was 'not sure how much we would be able to do'.[91] Schuman attempted to snare

Bevin into an aid commitment by referring 'to the sum of $75 million which the United States had at their disposal'. He elaborated that although the French did not know what percentage of this they would be allocated, 'any military aid which the United Kingdom and the United States might furnish for Indo-China would have a good psychological effect on French troops'. Bevin avoided the snare. He agreed that 'France was a good candidate for United States aid in Indo-China' and failed to mention any British aid commitment.[92] Following on from Bevin's meeting with Massigli on 2 March, Schuman stated that if the PRC had not recognised the DRVN then France as well as Britain would have recognised the PRC.[93]

A week later Jessup held encouraging discussions with Schuman in Paris. Agreement was reached on the transfer of US arms within Vietnam and Jessup pressed the French about the status of the palace at Saigon.[94] Truman had already approved the allocation '"in principle"' of fifteen million dollars for military aid to Indo-China.[95] However, the US did not approve of the proposal to transfer Indo-Chinese affairs from the French Ministry of Overseas Territories to a new ministry. Instead the State Department wanted the transfer to be to the French Foreign Office and lobbied Britain for a joint Anglo-US approach to the French on this issue. Bevin held that Britain had pressed France far enough on the transfer of Indo-Chinese affairs to an appropriate ministry and that the issue should 'be allowed to rest' as further pressure 'could be interpreted by the French as undue interference in their internal affairs' and 'might also make M. Schuman's position more difficult'.[96] The State Department had ascertained that Nehru was considering calling a conference to discuss the Indo-China crisis. The US regarded this as unhelpful and asked if Britain was prepared to '"throw grit into the machinery"'.[97] However, because of India's stated policy of non-interference, Bevin was sceptical about the likelihood of a proposed conference and advised 'I should be inclined to let the idea die a natural death'.[98] Meanwhile the French Government suggested to Vietnam that it would be appropriate to send diplomatic missions to both London and Washington.[99]

The COS decided to consider international developments against a possible wartime strategy.[100] The Commanders-in-Chief Far East and MacDonald believed that the transfer of French powers to Bao Dai had slowly increased his nationalist credentials but that the British recognition of the PRC had resulted in a negative effect on Bao Dai's support. They recommended the development of a 'regional security plan including friendly Asian countries' and, because of the increased likelihood of a communist Indo-China, Burma and Siam, a 'reassessment of the military defences of Malaya in relation to the common frontier with communism'.[101] Malaya remained an important contributor of dollars to the British economy in the continuing world dollar shortage and a significant exporter of supplies to Western Europe.[102] MacDonald wrote to Jessup to encourage further US support for Indo-China and Southeast Asian nations against the threat of communism.[103] On the 17 March the parameters for the Anglo-French information talks between the Commanders-in-Chief Far East and the French authorities were finalised by the JPS. The talks were to fortify French morale, assess military needs, comprehend French plans and exchange information on internal communist threats.[104] A JPS paper considering a strategy for a major war in 1957 pessimistically warned 'Indo-China will have a communist government in control of most of the country'.[105] At a COS meeting on 24 March Dening held that Schuman was attempting to blackmail Britain into aiding the French in Indo-China with the threat that no assistance would result in a French withdrawal. Lt.-General Brown-John considered that it was impossible now to separate the internal and external threats to Indo-China. Dening explained that the Foreign Office believed it credible to discuss the internal Indo-Chinese situation in any Anglo-French information talks but that Britain could not be drawn into assisting France internally in Indo-China. He added that Bevin had expressed to Schuman that it was unwise for Britain, the US and France to be appearing to resolve the situation without consulting the Asian powers, especially India. The French press had already exaggerated the significance of the Bevin-Schuman negotiations. The Foreign Office was prepared as a last resort to inform Russia that any activity in Southeast Asia was not acceptable to Britain. The COS agreed to begin Anglo-French informal information talks about French Indo-China.[106]

In the meantime MacDonald met with R. Allen Griffin who had been dispatched by the US on a fact-finding mission to Southeast Asia. The Griffin mission was 'to make urgent recommendations on the kind and the extent of American assistance which would be most immediately effective in the campaign against communism'. Although the parameters for this were 'immediate needs in the economic field', Griffin was 'to interpret "economic" aid in a wide sense to include police and quasi-military assistance'. Griffin informed MacDonald that only the Presidential fund of $75,000,000 was currently available for Southeast Asia and 'much of this was intended for direct military aid but use for semi-military and political purposes was not excluded'. However, a further $100,000,000 from the remnant of the China aid programme could be available, if agreed by Congress, before this returned to US Treasury funds on 30 June 1950. Likewise, funds could also be available under the Point Four programme but the appropriate legislation was still being considered. MacDonald reported to the Foreign Office 'Viewing the area as a whole, Mr Griffin said that he gave first priority to Indo-China'.[107] Griffin confirmed the importance of Indo-China during a press conference as 'one of the most important places in the world and one where American aid could help mutually'. He predicted that economic aid such as medical supplies would be distributed within 90 days but warned that 'American aid would not duplicate any aid to Asian countries that might be given under any plan agreed to by the Commonwealth. The US were [sic] very interested in the Canberra meeting and would undoubtedly have observers there'.[108] Despite Griffin's intention of sending immediate aid to Indo-China 'he was exercised about the problem of giving help to Bao Dai without involving the French loss of prestige. There were difficulties both as regards offering American technical assistance and ... about the distribution of aid'. Griffin observed 'the French in Indo-China were very jealous of the treaty of rights which gave them priority (and in their interpretation, an almost exclusive right) in furnishing advice and expert assistance in any schemes of public character'. Therefore, despite the perilous situation, the local French denied the need for technical assistance.[109] The French feared 'American economic domination and bad moral effect on the expeditionary force'; paradoxically the Vietnamese also feared technical aid as this could lead to the 'continued control of Western powers through economic necessity'.[110] By contrast, Pignon was concerned with France's excessive military expenditure in Indo-China. In 1949 military expenditure in Indo-China had cost France 160,000 million francs. Pignon held that in the struggle against communism both in Indo-China and Southeast Asia 'France had already made heavy sacrifices. It was time to state frankly that her ability to continue to bear such responsibility depended on degree of understanding accorded to her'.[111] Likewise concerning the distribution of aid, the Governments of Cambodia, Laos and Vietnam favoured bi-lateral agreements with the US as the machinery of distribution, whereas the French 'favoured an organisation which had the United States on one hand and France, Vietnam, Cambodia and Laos on the other'. MacDonald and Griffin agreed that due to the unhelpful attitude of the local French in Indo-China it appeared necessary 'to take parallel action in Paris' to clarify the situation.[112]

The situation in Vietnam remained chaotic and unstable. A visit by the US Navy, 16–20 March, was greeted by Vietnamese student demonstrations against the US naval presence. On 25 March the Vietnamese Government was plunged into further turmoil with the resignation of three leading ministers. A political stalemate ensued until 28 April when Bao Dai was forced to dissolve the Nguyen Pham Long Government and invite Tran Van Huu to form a new administration.[113] The French approached MacDonald's office to request details of the security agreement between Malaya and Siam concerning police frontier co-operation in order to replicate such an agreement between Cambodia, Laos and Siam.[114] Similarly a request was made to the British High Commissioner in New Delhi for information concerning British relations with the Maldives Islands. A copy of the 1948 agreement with the Sultan of the Maldives Islands was given to the French. It was believed that France was considering a similar arrangement with the Indo-Chinese islands, especially Poulo Condore.[115] Despite the political crisis and security problems rice production increased in Southern Vietnam during the rice year 1949–50. Prices in the south were in decline but in the north prices were increasing due to the added misfortune of a drought.[116]

On 29 March the Ministry of Defence requested that Attlee consider the military implications of the deterioration in Vietnam. It had already assessed that as the French were heavily stretched a decisive victory was unlikely but that a PRC offensive was also unlikely in the near future. It feared that if the French received no assistance then a withdrawal was possible, and a subsequent Vietminh victory could threaten the Malaya anti-bandit campaign. It estimated that the Vietminh had 188 battalions of 86,000 regular and 90,000 irregular forces by comparison to France's 135,800 regulars, Vietnam's 50,000 regulars, Cambodia and Laos's 6000 regulars and 41,000 Indo-Chinese irregular forces. France was suffering heavy casualties but could not inflict a severe defeat on the Vietminh due to the Vietminh tactic of conducting a war of attrition. Time was on the Vietminh's side.[117] The COS concluded that 'everything possible, therefore, should be done to support the French in Indo-China' but acknowledged that Britain would be unable to contribute any forces and could only offer military discussions. These would be on an informal basis and were supported by Bevin.[118] Attlee agreed and the Commanders-in-Chief Far East were instructed 'to proceed as soon as possible'.[119] The Secretary of State for the Commonwealth Relations Office thought it important to inform the Commonwealth Governments. Australia was likely to be in favour of, but India against, such talks.[120] Nehru was opposed to any direct foreign intervention in Indo-China and regarded France as administering 'oppressive imperialism which ought to be got rid of'.[121] The Secretary of State for Commonwealth Relations feared that there was an implicit danger in engaging in talks to boost French morale if Britain could not actually offer any assistance. The Vice-COS agreed. Dening held that if the Commonwealth Governments were informed of the talks in advance then this could encourage deeper suspicion, especially from India. He favoured releasing a statement after the talks, that British officers had been to Saigon in order to study the developing situation.[122]

By 3 April the Associated States had been recognised by Australia, Belgium, Bolivia, Brazil, Britain, Costa Rica, Cuba, Greece, Honduras, Italy, Jordan, Luxembourg, New Zealand, South Africa, South Korea, Spain, Thailand, the US and the Vatican, whilst the DRVN had been recognised by North Korea, the PRC, Russia, the Soviet European satellites and Yugoslavia.[123] The Heads of State of Cambodia, Laos and Vietnam were supported by the extended visit during April of Kenneth Landon, Head of the State Department Southeast Asia Bureau. He presented them with personal messages of goodwill from Truman.[124] Acheson warned Schuman that the US was opposed to the French negotiating with Vietnamese communists or recognising the PRC.[125] US NSC 68 endorsed the strategic concept of the defence of a perimeter to contain communism and thought that any military threat could be interpreted as psychological as well as physical.[126] This paper emphasised the need to increase the military strength of the Western European nations, but France was restricted by its commitment in Indo-China.[127] Likewise, NSC 64 committed the US to prevent communist expansion in Southeast Asia. It included what would later be called the Domino Principle that if Indo-China fell to communism then Thailand and Burma would also fall.[128] Ho visited Peking for talks with the PRC leadership.[129]

The COS began planning for the evacuation of British subjects in the event of a war in the Far East; a Cabinet Defence Committee Sub-Committee already had approved of such an evacuation.[130] On 19 April the COS decided that the US should be informed of the Anglo-French information talks before they commenced.[131] In the meantime, by 6 April the JPS had assessed and prepared a brief on British strategy and defence policy in Southeast Asia and the Far East. This was brought before the COS on 2 May. It stated that, although the defence of Indo-China in a major war would have to depend on its internal security forces, Indo-China was strategically important. A Vietminh victory could act as a potential catalyst and stepping stone for communism to spread into the rest of Southeast Asia. This would threaten Malaya and the South China Sea. There was also an economic threat due to the potential loss of Indo-Chinese rice exports. The Bao Dai regime was assessed as the only hope for Indo-China but the French needed to restore law and order. The strategic key to Vietnam was the control of the rice-producing regions and the destruction of DRVN factories within these areas, thereby depriving the DRVN of resources. Likewise, the French would need to acquire aid from the US. In conclusion the JPS considered it important for Britain to encourage France to complete the transfer of power to Cambodia, Laos and Vietnam. India's reaction needed to be monitored. Britain would also have to aid France with intelligence information, arms and equipment, and other forms of material assistance.[132]

Meanwhile MacDonald liaised with British representatives in Southeast Asia to organise an informal conference in Singapore, after the proposed Sydney Commonwealth Conference, between the heads of British diplomatic missions in the region 'to review policy in the area in the light of developments since [the] Bukit Serene Conference last autumn'.[133] However the Foreign Office, to MacDonald's 'disappointment' and perhaps in relation to Attlee's reaction to the Bukit Serene Conference in November 1949, was to veto his plans.[134]

The French were irritated with the US attitude towards the Indo-Chinese crisis. During April a mission to Indo-China of Korean businessmen accompanied by a member of the US mission to Korea had explored the possibility in obtaining raw materials in exchange for manufactured goods.[135] Du Gardier informed MacDonald that although US interest in Indo-China was welcome and the French appreciated US 'readiness to give practical help', the 'Americans were now overdoing things in some directions'. The Vietnamese had become disillusioned by empty US promises of aid. The local French were irritated with the US arrogance at being the only nation able to assist, and the promise of US technicians and investors 'sounded dangerously like American "imperialism"'. The French military questioned whether they 'were fighting to make Indo-China safe for the Americans'. Du Gardier proposed that a consignment of British aid would moderate any DRVN negative publicity against US aid. He reported that, although the military situation had improved, the political situation remained delicate and Bao Dai's situation weak. Pignon remained optimistic of Bao Dai's chances of success, but this was no longer believed by Du Gardier.

However, Pignon was convinced that, due to the attitude of the US, the nervousness of the local French and pro-Bao Dai Vietnamese, and the hardened attitude of Paris towards policies that could have repercussions in North Africa, it was no longer possible to issue a statement of evolution towards full sovereign state status although he still supported an evolutionary policy. Du Gardier and Pignon believed that the forthcoming Foreign Ministers Conference should issue a 'declaration of policy regarding Southeast Asia'. Du Gardier envisioned that this would be a regional statement rather than specific to Indo-China. He hoped that Britain, France and the US would declare a resolution 'to do everything possible to assist the peoples of Southeast Asia in attainment of their democratic aims, and that they would do everything possible to prevent communism from gaining control of any Southeast Asian country, either by aggression from without or by subversive activities from within'.[136] MacDonald was in favour of the statement despite the difficulties of the current Indo-Chinese situation. He feared that if Indo-China fell to communism then the rest of Southeast Asia would rapidly do likewise.[137] Du Gardier had also revealed to MacDonald in confidence his own and Pignon's frustrations with the direction of Indo-Chinese policy from Paris. The single 'greatest stumbling block to progress' appeared to be the French President, who 'seemed to be averse to any more liberal policy towards Indo-China'.[138]

By 2 May the PRC had occupied Hainan. MacDonald lobbied the Foreign Office concerning the conference. He advocated supporting the French declaration and supported the need for a discussion about material aid. MacDonald held that this needed to be supplied to both the French and Indo-Chinese but that even if this was agreed immediately it could take nearly six months to deliver due to current stock levels, logistics and finance. MacDonald, the British Consul-General's staff and the French High Commissioner's staff were all united and supported the need for a token shipment of British equipment. MacDonald proposed that a consignment of wirelesses could be shipped from British Far Eastern Land Forces in Singapore to Indo-China. MacDonald reiterated and contrasted the PRC's commitment to the DRVN with continued reports of arms being delivered across the Tonkin border. The French feared that the PRC victory against the Chinese nationalist forces on the island of Hainan would release extra PRC regular troops to pressurise the PRC-Tonkin frontier and allow for the release of 50,000 irregulars to infiltrate Vietnam. Similarly, junks would be able to smuggle arms from Hainan to the Red River delta. MacDonald considered that recent Vietminh operations in Cochinchina had been intended to cause as much chaos and destruction as possible before any US aid arrived; although these operations had failed, any delay in assistance to the French and the Indo-Chinese would enable the Vietminh to reinforce and attempt a second offensive. He concluded 'it seems to me emphatically a case where "he gives twice who gives swiftly"'.[139]

In Paris Pignon dined at the British Embassy, where he admitted that politically 'Indo-China had suffered from the intervention of French internal politics, which had delayed constitutional development until the concessions made were too late to have their full effect'. Regarding Bao Dai, he believed that 'the Emperor had lost his prestige ... owing to his temporizing policy. His Majesty though very intelligent, was lazy'.[140] However, France still had not transferred the Associated States from the Ministry of Overseas Territories. Despite the establishment of US and Italian Legations in Saigon, Britain remained cautious not to change the status of the consulate or its terms of recognition too rapidly. The Foreign Office held 'The basic difficulty is the difference between the French and British theories about colonies. Whilst we regard it as a matter of course that colonies should be guided towards independence the French policy is to integrate and centralise, so that the overseas territories and France form a unit and colonials share in governing the whole'. The Foreign Office believed that France wished to use the forthcoming Foreign Ministers Conference to compel Britain and the US 'to underwrite the French position' without having to make any political concessions or grant independence.[141] Schuman had already expressed to the international press his incredulity that the US kept on discussing the future of Vietnamese independence when what was at risk was Vietnamese independence from communism.[142] Britain appeared to approach the conference from a position of strength. Until the Commonwealth Conference in Sydney there was little the Foreign Office required of the US. France was negotiating from a position of weakness.[143] The Indian Ambassador-designate to China observed 'Britain realises that the way of peace, greatness and effective authority in the world for her lies in a compromise with New Asia'.[144] An Indo-Chinese delegation in Paris requested information from Britain on how the Commonwealth operated and the role and status of the Commissioner-General in Southeast Asia.[145] Britain agreed to the request, including information on the 'machinery for the exchange of information and consultation on foreign affairs between the United Kingdom and Commonwealth Governments'.[146] Meanwhile in Cambodia the first National Congress of the Khmer Resistance

(communist) was held in the Southwest, and a governmental ministerial crisis erupted in Phnom Penh due to friction in Siem Reap between
the Cambodian army and former elements of the Khmer Issarak rebel
movement. Ministers were alleged to have supported the rebels to the
detriment of the army, and therefore the army was threatening a *coup
d'état*. This resulted in the dismissal of the government by Sihanouk.[147]

On 8 May the US announced that it was prepared to donate military
equipment, as well as diplomatic and possibly economic aid to Indo-
China.[148] Meanwhile Britain prepared to host the London Conference of
bipartite and tripartite meetings between the representatives of Britain,
France and the US. Against the escalating threat from Russia in Europe,
the Cabinet held that it was important to build up the military strength
of France for the defence of Western Europe.[149] On 13 May Schuman
reviewed the current situation in Indo-China and insisted 'that France
was serving the interests of the common cause and that the French
Government needed urgently extensive military help'. The Ministers
agreed that although the general security of Southeast Asia was strategically important to the US, both Britain and France held 'direct responsibilities in the area which make its security of even greater concern to
them'. The Ministers linked the conflicts in Indo-China and Malaya with
the conviction that in either area 'forcible expulsion ... would be a military and political disaster'. Britain reaffirmed its commitment to its interests in the region and France declared likewise, 'within the framework of
close and active co-operation with the United Kingdom and United
States Governments'. Bevin stressed that local British representatives in
Southeast Asia had discouraged either individual or joint declarations by
the British, French or US Governments regarding Southeast Asia due to
the possible hostile attitude of Ceylon, India and Pakistan. He preferred
therefore not to make a conference declaration. Schuman recognised
Bevin's difficulties with the Commonwealth nations but considered that
'a joint declaration should be made'. It was agreed that this suggestion
should be returned to by Britain, France and the US after the forthcoming Commonwealth Conference when it might be implemented more
successfully.[150] To Foreign Office alarm the Vietnamese Government
announced through the international press the appointment of Tran
Van Don as Ambassador to Britain as well as representatives to Cambodia, Laos, the US and the Vatican. The Foreign Office replied that
Britain was 'not yet ready to receive an Ambassador' and asked for a
formal request to be made through normal diplomatic channels.[151] In
the meantime the State Department established the Interdepartmental
Southeast Asia Aid Committee.[152]

Bevin communicated the results of the London Conference to the Commonwealth Prime Ministers. Nehru replied that India had 'never questioned the necessity of military and other necessary action in Malaya ... to maintain law and order' but that in Indo-China 'military or economic efforts will not by themselves solve what is pre-eminently a political problem, *viz.*, satisfaction of nationalist aspirations'. Nehru believed that non-communist nationalist groups in Indo-China were dissatisfied with the French because 'real independence' had not been granted. He stressed that Indo-China, rather than the individual countries of Cambodia, Laos and Vietnam, needed an elected assembly comprising all parties including the Vietminh. This assembly would not only determine 'the form of the Government of Indo-China but its relations with the French Union'. As the French Minister for Overseas Territories had already declared that 'independence for such territories must be founded within the French Union', the Indian Government predicted that in Indo-China there would be a 'prolonged but unpredictable deterioration of the present troubles'.[153] Bevin met the Indian High Commissioner in London and proposed that a close study would be made of Nehru's proposals. He also indicated that Britain had been trying to secure PRC admission to the UN but that this had been stalled by the Russians 'walking out of the Security Council and trying to dictate to the rest of us'.[154] Meanwhile General Carpentier informed Britain that the French Government had not yet given permission for Anglo-French information talks on Indo-China to commence. The COS requested that the Foreign Office pursue the matter with the French Government.[155] However, four British officers had already embarked on a two week attachment to French units in Indo-China as part of the local exchange programme.[156] Likewise Admiral Sir Patrick Brind, Commander-in-Chief Far East Station, had been in Indo-China for talks with 'the leading naval and military authorities' and Brigadier-General Marsden, Head of Medical Services Far East Land Force, visited Saigon as a guest of the French Medical Inspector-General.[157] The French believed that Brind had offered British naval assistance to patrol the Indo-Chinese coast to prevent contraband reaching the Vietminh.[158]

The Commonwealth Consultative Committee agreed at the Sydney Conference in May to form a Commonwealth Technical Assistance Scheme based in Colombo.[159] Kenneth Younger, Foreign Office Minister of State, informed Massigli of the results of the Sydney Conference and indicated that Britain wanted Cambodia, Laos and Vietnam to be invited to partake in a plan of economic co-operation.[160] Mac-Donald had predicted that the 'most important result of the Sydney deliberations would be an effective start of work on proper long-term development programmes for Southeast Asia'.[161] The issue of rice supply in Southeast Asia still prevailed as 'only a third of pre-war exports were available'.[162] At the beginning of June Australia envisaged that an approach should be made to the Associated States through the British Minister in Saigon and not through the French Government. However, India and Pakistan did not want to be associated with this proposal and Canada and New Zealand offered no response.[163] The British Cabinet agreed that the non-Commonwealth countries of Burma, Cambodia, Indonesia, Laos, Siam, and Vietnam should submit development plans so that economic development in South and Southeast Asia would cover the whole region. It also decided to offer two British officials to assist in developing such a plan if required.[164]

Meanwhile US General MacArthur, Commander Occupational Forces Japan, was convinced of the need for urgent military supplies to both the French and the Vietnamese.[165] MacDonald stressed to the BDCC that 'the security of Indo-China was the key to the whole situation. If Indo-China was lost to communism then Siam and Burma would undoubtedly follow and the communists would be on the borders of India and Malaya and dominate the rice bowl'. General Harding assessed that the French urgently needed further military equipment in Indo-China.[166] MacDonald recommended that Bao Dai should immediately receive British or US aid.[167] Britain had already offered to sell military equipment to the French but this had not been accepted as the French were waiting 'to see what they are likely to get free from the US'.[168] Australia, Canada, New Zealand and South Africa had been informed of Britain's intention to sell equipment to the French and to exchange Far Eastern information with them in informal talks in Saigon and Singapore. The first of these talks was to take place in July in Singapore.[169] Due to the sterling crisis Britain could not afford to donate military equipment to the French. But because of security concerns for Malaya, it was suggested, during a BDCC meeting in Singapore, that Britain should 'adopt a policy of making a free gift to the French of such British equipment as is essential to the successful conduct of their campaign'. Government policy had been constructed around the fear that if financially an exception was made with the supply of free arms to the French then this would cause a watershed of free arms requests from Burma and Siam. However, following Admiral Brind's tour of Indo-China, the BDCC disagreed as they thought it better to offer a little aid immediately rather than in six months.[170] The French were likewise hampered by their own economic needs, especially the drain of Indo-China on French resources. France also lacked sterling reserves to purchase British equipment.[171] The COS reached an agreement that further consideration should be given to donating, or selling at a reduced rate, equipment to the French.[172] The French already had been informed what requests for military equipment Britain could meet. The COS noted that the lack of a reply indicated that the French were still waiting to see what the US would supply.[173] The Defence Committee of the Cabinet, chaired by Attlee, continued to advocate charging the French for surplus British equipment but doubted whether sufficient reserves would be found to meet French demands.[174] As the French were not forthcoming with any further specific requests the COS recommended that the British Minister of Defence should contact his opposite number in Paris to ascertain French needs.[175]

At the beginning of June a US economic mission was established in Saigon under Robert Blum. In order to facilitate an economic aid programme immediately, members of the mission liaised with the governments of the three Associated States. Indo-China had already been allocated 'a credit of twenty-three million United States dollars' of which 'six million will be earmarked for medical and pharmaceutical supplies, drugs and hospital equipment'.[176] In the US the Act for International Development, technical aid, was created.[177] The Indo-Chinese states remained perilously weak. US army intelligence predicted that within a year the Vietminh would be so sufficiently strengthened by PRC aid that the French might have to withdraw from Northern Indo-China.[178] In Cambodia the governmental crisis was ended by the formation of a new government under Prince Monipong; but in Vietnam the Bao Dai regime was further undermined by 'rumours' in Saigon that 'prominent Vietnamese politicians backed by General Xuan' intended to form 'a compromise solution involving a "third force" government to replace Bao Dai and to include Vietminh nationalists'.[179] The French hoped for further political development in Indo-China through an inter-state conference arranged to take place at Pau on 29 June. Prior to this 'preliminary meetings of the various delegations were held in Saigon'.[180] This had been delayed from May due to the previous crisis in the Vietnamese government.[181] The Cambodians, Laotians and Vietnamese all regarded the Pau Conference as a significant event in their political evolution and the three respective Prime Ministers attended the opening session. The High Commissioner and his officials were also present having first attended a meeting in Paris about 'the creation of the *Haute Conseil* of the

French Union'. Unfortunately the downfall of the French Government combined with the news of the crisis in Korea 'caused uneasiness' amongst the French and Vietnamese which was countered by only 'the firm attitude adopted by the United States Government'.[182] The US Senate had already passed the Economic Co-operation Authorisation for 1951, which permitted the $100 million dollar China aid fund to be distributed in the '"general area of China"' (Southeast Asia) and Truman proposed that a further $75 million fund be allocated for military assistance.[183] On 29 June 'eight C.47 (Dakota) transport planes arrived at Saigon ... as the first consignment under the military aid programme' and a US company arranged for the import of 170 British Land Rover vehicles.[184]

Meanwhile on 21 June, despite France having not moved the administration of Indo-Chinese affairs from the Ministry of Overseas Territories to a new ministry, Britain informed France of its intention to raise the office of its Consulate-General in Saigon to a legation. This was intended to demonstrate British confidence in French policy, and Cambodian, Laotian and Vietnamese chances of successfully establishing prosperous democracies within the French Union.[185] However, the rapid fall of a second French Government resulted in the move to a legation being suspended.[186] French parliamentary politics reflected the instability within Vietnam. The French Socialist Party continued to cause problems in Paris, demanding that the government should raise the Indo-Chinese crisis at the UN, give real independence to Vietnam within the French Union and withdraw French troops if the Vietnamese Government required once peace had been established.[187] Following a Vietnamese request, Britain was able to supply the French and the Vietnamese with information concerning the Malaya Emergency Legislation, and support Cambodian, Laotian and Vietnamese full membership of the World Health Organisation.[188] Vietnam was also admitted to the International Labour Organisation in Geneva but the Associated States were unlikely to apply for membership of the UN due to the Russian veto.[189]

Both Russia and the PRC had observers operating with the Vietminh.[190] The Russians were adept with the implicit threat of their UN veto. Just as for Britain, France and the US, Southeast Asian diplomatic recognition was important for the DRVN and its allies, Russia and the PRC. In comparison with US pressure upon the Philippines, Russia pressed Indonesia to recognise the DRVN in return for a Russian diplomatic mission and Russian support for Indonesian membership of the UN. The implied threat of the Russian veto in the UN for non-compliance was evident in the demands. This prompted debate in the Indonesian Parliament on the recognition of the DRVN but, despite both Russian incentives and threats, a government resolution was narrowly passed postponing DRVN recognition until more information was known about the Vietminh.[191]

British policy denouement

On 25 June Kim Ilsung ordered his forces to cross the 38th parallel into South Korea commencing the Korean War. Two days later Truman, against the disintegration of containment policy, announced the US intention not only to support the Korean Government against communism but to strengthen Formosa and the Philippines and 'acceleration in the furnishing of military assistance to the forces of France and the Associated States in Indo-China and the dispatch of a military mission'.[192] A day later the PRC Foreign Minister, Chou En Lai, condemned Truman's statement and expressed 'sympathy' with 'the people of Korea, Vietnam, the Philippines and Japan' who were victims of 'American imperialism' and 'aggression'. The challenge was set: 'The Chinese people firmly believe that all the oppressed nations and peoples of the East are undoubtedly capable of burying the vicious and hated American imperialist war-makers'.[193] The Indo-Chinese conflict had escalated for the US from a French colonial crisis to a vital battle-ground in the containment of communism which had to be defended. However, 'America's initial commitment to Indo-China in 1950 established the pattern for its future involvement: large enough to get America entangled, not significant to prove decisive'.[194]

Britain did not have the stamina or the resources to compete with the US in meeting the crisis in Indo-China or the new global challenge to containment policy. Following the outbreak of the Korean War the Cabinet approved of US actions in Indo-China and the Philippines.[195] The COS had held that British foreign policy should achieve 'a unity of policy between the British Commonwealth, the United States and France' that would enable the reduction in British and French resources in Indo-China and Malaya to allow for the defence of Western Europe. This would have to involve the expansion of local security forces.[196] Despite the escalated crisis in the Far East the COS was primarily concerned with the defence of Western Europe. With the arming of the East German Police for what Bevin believed could be possible use in a civil war, he predicted 'how troublesome it could be if there were a big civil war in Indo-China and one in Europe at the same time'.[197]

MacDonald visited Indo-China in late June and early July for a holiday and discussions with the French and the Vietnamese. Dr Benham, his economic and financial adviser, accompanied him on this trip.[198] MacDonald returned from Indo-China encouraged that the situation in Indo-China was 'still improving, both militarily and politically' and that 'Ho Chi Minh's stock has sunk quite a lot'.[199] However, despite MacDonald's optimism for Bao Dai and the Associated States, British action in Indo-China, whether diplomatic, military, economic or political, was severely limited. The symbolism of Britain's decline internationally, regionally in South and Southeast Asia and locally in Indo-China in contrast to the US, Russia, the PRC and even the Commonwealth was ironically illustrated by MacDonald's departure from the twelfth century temple of Angkor Wat in Cambodia.

I kissed some of the Asparas 'Goodbye' on the top terrace of Angkor Wat at noon. It had been a hot morning, and their smiling lips were warm, sunny, shapely and stony. They seemed both pleased and indifferent, as if both gratified at feeling mortal man's lips on their mouths again, and yet sad that the kisses of the Twentieth Century lacked something of the fervour of the Thirteenth.[200]

Conclusion

British foreign policy towards Vietnam 1943–50 is an important case study illustrating the decline of the Western European imperial powers and the dynamics of the emerging new world order – US Western hegemony, Cold War bi-polarity and the rise of Asian nationalism. It involved not only British bi-lateral relationships with France and the US but also the regional relationships with Australia, Burma, Canada, Ceylon, China, the Dutch East Indies, India, New Zealand, Pakistan, the Philippines, Siam (later Thailand) and others. Often these relationships were complex, and Britain's policy towards Vietnam had to take into account these complexities as prerequisites to any attempt to establish a consistent policy. It would be a mistake to consider that such policy was purely political in nature: the policy towards Vietnam was both political and economic; it reflected Vietnam's vital strategic position within Southeast Asia and Britain's post-war world position. Finally the policy was not just limited to Vietnam; many of the same policy concerns and aspirations involved to a lesser extent Cambodia and on occasion consideration was given too to Laos.

Britain

British policy towards Vietnam was conceived and subsequently evolved in response to Roosevelt's World War Two concept of trusteeship for French Indo-China. Britain feared that any change in the post-war sovereignty of Indo-China would act as a dangerous precedent which could threaten its own colonial territories, especially Hong Kong and India, and establish a method for European imperial decolonisation. Similarly, Britain was concerned with the aspirations of the US sponsored Chinese nationalist government whose apparent imperialist

desires to annex Southeast Asia, with its large indigenous Chinese populations, were to remain an active feature of British Southeast Asian
policy. Elements in the Foreign Office, motivated by such fears and traditionally sympathetic to France, suspected a wider hidden US economic agenda rather than just a tradition of anti-imperialism. The logic
of recent European history dictated that the Francophile Foreign Office
believed that a strong France was needed to protect British security in
Europe and potentially to reinforce Britain in the hierarchy of any new
post-war global geopolitics. However, as the Foreign Office attempted to
formulate a coherent response towards Roosevelt's plans for Indo-China
it was restricted repeatedly by Churchill who regarded the intimacy of
his special relationship with Roosevelt as paramount to Britain's war
effort and the maintenance of its global status. Churchill and Roosevelt
both understood some of the domestic complexities and limitations
that affected their respective positions, a degree of subtlety and appreciation that was lost at times by others on both sides of the Atlantic.
Churchill's frequent silences, stalling techniques and sporadic ramblings on the Indo-Chinese issue, which were independent from and at
times in direct opposition to both the Foreign Office and the War
Cabinet, revealed just how isolated within the British Government his
position was on this issue. If Churchill had been forced to clarify
Britain's Indo-Chinese policy earlier then the political drift that ensued
would have been avoided, but at what cost? Ironically, the relationship
that Churchill had sought to preserve had changed fundamentally by
1944 to one of British dependence on the US; a point not lost on
Roosevelt. Churchill was not aided in his Indo-Chinese conspiracy to
preserve his Anglo-US relationship by the SACSEA Mountbatten, whose
manipulation of Roosevelt, Churchill and the CIGS Brooke concerning
the Gentleman's Agreement with Chiang Kai-Shek further complicated
the Indo-Chinese debate, and threatened Anglo-US relations within the
SEAC and China theatres. Eventually, changing external factors such as
the decline in the nature of the Anglo-US relationship, the ascendancy
of de Gaulle, the rehabilitation of France, the Japanese coup in Indo-
China and the death of Roosevelt eroded Churchill's non-committal
position and unified British policy in support of a French return to
Indo-China.

Nevertheless, Britain did not unilaterally restore Indo-China to
France, neither did Britain crush the aspirations of emergent Indo-
Chinese nationalism, nor was Major-General Gracey the true miscreant
of Britain's liberation duties but rather the more Machiavellian Mountbatten. The Labour Government's commitment to the restoration of

France in Europe and the demobilisation of British and Common-wealth forces compromised the resources and operations of the ALF. Political interference prevented Mountbatten and Gracey from treating the situation in Cambodia in a similar way to the methods used in Burma where Britain worked alongside indigenous nationalists: by not doing this the limited resources were stretched further. In Southern Vietnam the ALF inherited a dangerous power vacuum with no one political grouping in the ascendancy and with unworkable directions from London. Britain discovered too that it now had to contend with humanitarian relief and rehabilitation as well as the complexities of the Cambodian-Siamese border dispute with France technically still at war with Siam. Britain's ALF duties were not without failings of judge-ment or missed opportunities but the end of World War Two marked a watershed for Britain. Britain was almost financially bankrupt and attempting to redefine its global status. There were bigger and more important immediate post-war priorities than Indo-China and any coherent change in policy would have to be developed by the Foreign Office who remained both pro-French and focused upon European priorities.

The appointment of Killearn allowed British policy to be developed bi-laterally towards Indo-China, in co-ordination with Britain's other regional commitments and in relation to British decolonisation. The continuing Cambodian-Siamese border dispute and the importance of Indo-Chinese rice production to alleviate regional food shortages meant that Killearn paid close attention to the escalating Franco-DRVN dispute. The US, France and Britain maintained correspondence con-cerning the developing crisis; all were concerned with the growth of Asian nationalism and communism. But the British, reflecting their own desire to come to terms with emergent nationalism and through raising living standards to defeat communism, were suspicious of labelling all nationalists as communists and were prepared to maintain a dialogue with the DRVN. However, the financial constraints that had plagued Britain since the end of war accelerated. The growing dollar gap restrained government expenditure and prevented Britain from operating independently from its Commonwealth allies. Regionally this dependence made Britain susceptible to appeasing the pan-Asian nationalist policies of Nehru, and Britain's other former Asian territo-ries, in case they decided to support and thereby legitimise the struggle of the DRVN.

The amalgamation of the functions of the Special Commissioner and Governor-General reflected Britain's continuing financial decline.

MacDonald had to cope with many of the same Indo-Chinese problems as Killearn – rice supply, raising living standards to combat communism, fears concerning the growth of Chinese communism and its relationship to the indigenous Southeast Asian Chinese populations – and in addition repeated requests by the French for the recognition of Bao Dai. MacDonald sought to maintain the same dynamic and independent direction that had characterised Killearn's administration, but the growth of Cold War tensions, coupled with Britain's financial decline, meant that greater direction was given by London. The Labour Government sought to balance its foreign policy with its relationships with the Commonwealth nations and crucially, reflecting the change in the Anglo-US relationship, waited for the US to develop its own policies for Southeast Asia. Britain's decline meant that it could no longer maintain its position in Europe, the Middle East or Southeast Asia without external support. The Commonwealth alone was not strong enough to arrest this and US aid was required.

In 1950 Britain emerged from its deliberations with a clearer idea of US policy. Zealous US commitment to containment and provision for NATO made the support of France vital to its global position against a perceived advancing communist menace, a menace that allowed for no compromise and therefore no opportunity for the DRVN to be accredited according to the Titoist model. Britain was more circumspect of monolithic power struggles, preferring to exploit rifts between Moscow and Peking to protect its interests in Southeast Asia. Britain was cautious of any attempt to establish Bao Dai without proper nationalist credentials or the Asian support needed in order to avoid accusations of the creation of a Western puppet. The French delay in ratifying the Auriol Agreement allowed the DRVN to establish diplomatic relations with the communist bloc and thus critically attain diplomatic legitimacy before Bao Dai. British recognition of the PRC was not well received by the French or the Vietnamese, but the French had failed to address British concerns that would have enabled earlier recognition of Bao Dai. The subsequent recognition of Bao Dai created two Vietnamese governments upon the world stage, both diplomatically recognised by nations on opposite sides of the Cold War. As the escalation of the crisis intensified the question of military aid to support the French and, by default, defend Malaya and Hong Kong was raised. Britain's financial problems meant that aid would have to be sold to the French, something that France did not possess either the sterling or dollar reserves to do and in any case was not needed when the possibility of French leverage could result in arms and technical assistance coming from the US, paid for by the Truman Doctrine's Point Four assistance and the remnant of the Chinese nationalist aid programme. Neither Britain nor the Commonwealth had the resources to compete with the US but the British response through the development of the Commonwealth Technical Assistance Scheme was at least regional and not bi-lateral. The Colombo Conference and the Commonwealth desire to work together merged Britain's Vietnamese and regional policies. Technical aid and regional co-operation was an achievement that in theory allowed Britain to operate politically independent of the US, but it was also a denouement due to Britain's financial decline. Poor sterling reserves and a large dollar gap meant that economically Britain was subservient to the US. In Europe it was strategically linked to the US through NATO, and although in Southeast Asia US assistance would aid stability in Malaya, paradoxically, Britain's foreign policy towards Vietnam would be subject to the constraints of its Commonwealth partners.

France

Indo-China was integral to both French national rebirth and prestige. During World War Two France had been eager to secure participation in the war in the Far East and the concept of the French Union mirrored other European imperial powers' commitment to post-war colonial development. Therefore when the war was over France strove to re-establish itself as an imperial power. However, the resignation of de Gaulle as President plunged the metropole into a domestic political crisis which continued until his return in 1958. The political stability needed to rejuvenate both the metropole and imperial territories was lacking and subservient to the interests of party politics. Despite the failure of direction from Paris, Indo-China was returned to the French with British and US aid. No matter how soiled by collaboration with Germany and Japan, France, as a victorious Allied power under de Gaulle, would have expected nothing less. Cambodia and Laos rapidly developed under the auspices of the French Union but Vietnam remained an anathema to the French. The separation of Cochinchina from Tonkin and Annam with the creation of its own nationalist government and independent colonial status plagued efforts to create a coherent policy. French policy was disorganised and disjointed, reacting only to immediate crises. The roles of the High Commissioners reflected such instability; D'Argenlieu created a private conservative fiefdom independent from Paris, whilst Bollaert and Pignon were continuously undermined in their search for resolution by metropolitan political stagnation and infighting. The only consistency attained by French policy was its inability to come to terms with the DRVN. Whether labelled as nationalist, communist or both, France strove to avoid compromise and in doing so undermined the legitimacy of its alternative, the Bao Dai solution. Despite the inherent advantages associated with being a returning imperial power, France's arrogance towards the DRVN bordered on a complete ignorance of Vietnamese affairs. The French suffered the same tragedy as the US two decades later, 'a cultural vacuum ... that a great deal in the political culture of the country and of its people is not readily intelligible to the Western mind'.[1]

The French and the British possessed different attitudes to the dual challenges of nationalism and communism. The alternative direction pursued by Britain with its Commonwealth and that pursued by the French Union highlighted fundamental differences and misunderstandings concerning decolonisation and the challenges of the postwar world. Any attack, political or otherwise, upon the stability of the French Union was viewed from Paris as an attack upon the national interest but Paris failed to clarify the boundaries between union and metropole or to define the national interest of France or the union. Therefore, French requests to Britain for information concerning the administration of the Dominions, the Malay-Thai border treaty and the Malaya Emergency Legislation were highly embarrassing as they demonstrated that the French plans for their colonies were not as advanced as they believed. Indeed, French failure to transfer the administration of Cambodia, Laos and Vietnam from the Ministry of France Overseas to the French Foreign Office or a new Dominions Office following diplomatic recognition in 1950 revealed just how dormant French attitudes and plans really were, a mistake that was repeated with Algeria 1947–62. However, as the Cold War intensified with the communist victory in China, the French were able to develop adequate leverage upon the US to maintain their position in Indo-China as a vital bastion against communism in the line of containment. With US aid, French political dormancy was allowed to continue towards the tragedy of Dien Bien Phu.

The US

Roosevelt dominated US policy towards Indo-China during World War Two. He had stated that one of his major war aims was to prevent the return of Indo-China to France, this attitude reflected US deep-seated anti-colonialism. France had collaborated with Germany and with

Japan. It was the weakest of the allies and was therefore an ideal candidate for Roosevelt's trusteeship experiment. However, Roosevelt was an adept politician who constantly revised his Indo-China policy to suit his manipulation of wartime great power politics. As the State Department developed its Indo-China policy in response to the need for post-war planning Roosevelt's zeal for trusteeship did not wane but evolved. Roosevelt knew that the US would finish the war as the main Allied creditor nation and that short-term wartime diplomatic courtesy to the British, and to a lesser degree the French, could be dispensed with at the post-war conference table and by utilisation of the UN. US hegemony would be able to prevent a return to the pre-war imperial *status quo*, US finance being the ammunition behind Roosevelt's political weaponry. However, Roosevelt's death created a power vacuum in US foreign policy at a similar time to the power vacuum and revolution in Vietnam. Truman, a domestic politician, had to come to terms with a US foreign policy whose only consistency was in its being exclusive to Roosevelt himself. Thus US policy towards Indo-China stalled at a critical moment. The US-led compromise to the inter-theatre boundary crisis at the Potsdam Conference divided Vietnam between the Chinese and the British ALF in order to appease its Allied wartime partners but was devoid of any logic at either macro or micro level. The priority of European reconstruction and world food problems made the US reliant on Britain and France, especially as the perceived Russian threat intensified. As the US reversed and even denied Roosevelt's trusteeship policy it was left susceptible to French leverage for aid to return to Indo-China. Later, despite disengagement from the Indo-China debate, the US continued to support France militarily even though it knew that such supplies would be used in Indo-China.

While the State Department Far East and Southeast Asian sections grew in response to new US global responsibilities and the onset of the Cold War, the imminent defeat of US policy in China accelerated the importance of Indo-China and especially Vietnam in US planning. Strategically, Vietnam had enabled the Japanese to overrun Southeast Asia and threaten India and South Asia during the Second World War. The victory of the PRC repeated this threat especially with large indigenous Chinese communities already present in Southeast Asia and with the Malay Emergency underway. Such fears and US commitment to containment enabled France to encourage the development of a US Indo-Chinese policy as a bulwark of world freedom against the communist menace and with it copious amounts of US aid (even more so after the start of the Korean War). Unlike Britain, the US did not attempt to separate Vietnamese nationalists and communists. Ho could be no Tito, something that at least Britain explored before agreeing with France and the US. The US relationship with Vietnam was bilateral and often mono-focused on containment whilst Britain's constraints produced a multi-layered approach that allowed for a policy of realism through necessity. The US decision not to recognise the PRC and subsequent unqualified recognition of Cambodia, Laos and Vietnam, sharply contrasted with Britain's pragmatic recognition of the PRC and limited recognition of the Indo-Chinese states. It demonstrated that, although Britain required US participation in post-war geopolitics and despite US ascendancy in the Anglo-US relationship, the independence of British foreign policy could still be guaranteed. This was maintained at the 1954 Geneva Conference and ultimately prevented Britain from joining the US in the later Vietnam War.

Summary

British foreign policy towards Vietnam 1943–50 reflected the revision and decline of Britain's geopolitical status. During this period the Anglo-American relationship evolved from equality to dependence. Decolonisation altered the relationship between Britain and its colonies and Dominions, and between Britain and the other European imperial spheres of influence in Southeast Asia. The Commonwealth partially preserved Britain's global status and its ability to act independently of the US, however, this resulted in Britain being subject to the sentiments of its Commonwealth partners – notably India. Likewise the restoration of a strong France was thought to be vital, by a Francophile Foreign Office, to Britain's post-war security in Europe; this allowed France to place leverage upon Britain concerning Vietnam. British foreign policy certainly did not manage to produce a unified coherent approach towards Vietnam. Churchill and Mountbatten both followed their own autonomous policies detached from the War Cabinet and the Foreign Office; whilst Killearn and MacDonald's regional co-ordination was more dynamic and interactive than at times London desired. Gracey has been subjected unfairly to long-standing criticism for his actions. But it remained French paralysis and myopia that determined the plight and subsequent legacy of their colonial rule in Vietnam. This led to greater US involvement and resulted in 30 years of conflict for the Vietnamese people.

Select Personalia

BRITAIN

Attlee. Clement Attlee. Lord President of the Council and Deputy Prime Minister 1943–45; Prime Minister 1945–51.

Bennett. John Sterndale Bennett. Head of Far Eastern Department Foreign Office 1944–46; Minister in Sofia 1947–49; Deputy Commissioner-General Southeast Asia 1950–53.

Bevin. Ernest Bevin. Foreign Secretary 1945–51.

Brooke. General Sir Alan Brooke (Field Marshall 1944). CIGS 1941–46.

Cadogan. Sir Alexander Cadogan. Permanent Under-Secretary of State Foreign Office 1938–45; Permanent Representative UN Security Council 1945–50.

Churchill. Winston Churchill. Prime Minister and Minister of Defence 1940–45.

Cooper. Duff Cooper. Ambassador to France 1944–47.

Dening. Maberly Esler Dening. Chief Political Adviser to SACSEA 1943–46; Assistant Under-Secretary of State Foreign Office 1946–50.

Dixon. Pierson Dixon. Principal Private Secretary to Eden 1943–45 and Bevin 1945–48; Ambassador to Czechoslovakia 1948–50; Deputy Under-Secretary Foreign Office 1950–52.

Eden. Anthony Eden. Foreign Secretary 1940–45.

Franks. Sir Oliver Franks. Ambassador to US 1948–52.

Gibbs. Frank Gibbs. Consul-General Saigon 1948–50; Minister in Saigon 1950–51.

Gracey. Major-General Douglas Gracey. ALF Commander Indo-China 1945–46.

Halifax. Lord Halifax (Edward Wood). Ambassador to US 1941–46.

Harvey. Sir Oliver Harvey. Assistant Under-Secretary Foreign Office 1943–46; Deputy Under-Secretary 1946–48; Ambassador to France 1948–54.

Hollis. Major-General Leslie Hollis. War Cabinet Secretariat 1939–46; Deputy Military Secretary to Cabinet 1946–49.

Inverchapel. Lord Inverchapel (Archibald Kerr). Ambassador to US 1946–48.

Ismay. General Hastings Ismay. Chief of Staff to Churchill in his role as Minister of Defence 1940–45.

Killearn. Lord Killearn (Sir Miles Lampson). Special Commissioner Southeast Asia 1946–48.

Lawson. John Lawson. Secretary of State for War 1945–46.

MacDonald. Malcolm MacDonald. Governor-General Malaya and Borneo 1946–48; Commissioner-General Southeast Asia 1948–55.

McNeil. Hector McNeil. Foreign Office Minister of State 1946–50.

Meiklereid. E.W. Meiklereid. Consul-General Saigon 1946–48.

Mountbatten. Admiral Lord Louis Mountbatten. SACSEA 1943–46; Viceroy of India 1947; Governor-General of India 1947–48.

Murray. Lt.-Colonel E.D. Murray (Brigadier October 1945). ALF Commander Phnom Penh 1945–46.

Sargent. Sir Orme Sargent. Deputy Under-Secretary Foreign Office 1939–46; Permanent Under-Secretary 1946–49.

Slim. General William Slim. Commander-in-Chief ALF SEAC 1945.

Strang. Sir William Strang. Representative to the Europe Advisory Committee 1943–45; Political Adviser British Zone in Germany 1945–47; Joint Permanent Under-Secretary Foreign Office 1947–49; Permanent Under-Secretary 1949–53.

Thompson. Geoffrey Thompson. Minister and then Ambassador to Siam (Thailand).

Wilson. Field Marshal Henry Wilson. Head of British JSM Washington 1944–47.

Younger. Kenneth Younger. Foreign Office Minister of State 1950–51.

FRANCE
Auriol. Vincent Auriol. President 1947–53.

Baudet. Philippe Baudet. Chief of the Asia-Oceania Section of the Foreign Ministry.

Bidault. Georges Bidault. Foreign Minister 1944–46; Prime Minister 1946; Foreign Minister 1947–48; Prime Minister 1949.

Bollaert. Emile Bollaert. High Commissioner Indo-China 1947–48.

Bonnet. Henri Bonnet. Ambassador to US 1944–54.

Carpentier. General Carpentier. Commander-in-Chief Indo-China 1949–50.

Cédile. Jean Cédile. Colonial Administrator Indo-China.

D'Argenlieu. Admiral Thierry D'Argenlieu. High Commissioner Indo-China 1945–47.

de Gaulle. General Charles de Gaulle. Free French Leader London 1940–43; Head of the French Committee of National Liberation 1943; President of the French Provisional Government 1944–46.

Leclerc. General Philippe Leclerc. Liberated Paris 1944; Commander French Expeditionary Corps to the Far East; Commander-in-Chief forces in Indo-China 1945–46.

Massigli. René Massigli. Ambassador to Britain.

Pignon. Leon Pignon. Colonial Administrator Indo-China; Political Adviser to de Gaulle's General Delegate; High Commissioner 1948–50.

Schuman. Robert Schuman. Prime Minister 1947–48; Foreign Minister 1948–52.

INDO-CHINA
Bao Dai. Vietnamese Emperor 1926–45; abdicated; adviser to DRVN 1946; exile; returned as nationalist leader and Head of State.

Ho Chi Minh. Leader Vietminh; Leader of the Indo-Chinese Communist Party 1945–69; President DRVN 1945–69; Prime Minister 1945–55.

Khim Tit. Cambodian Defence Minister.

Norodom Sihanouk. King of Cambodia 1941–55.

Pham Van Dong. DRVN Minister of Finance 1945; Deputy Premier 1949–55.

Son Ngoc Thanh. pro-Japanese Cambodian nationalist; Foreign Minister 1945; Prime Minister 1945.

Vo Nguyen Giap. Indo–Chinese Communist Party Member; Commander Vietnamese Liberation Army 1945–47; Interior Minister 1945–46; Defence Minister 1946–80; Commander-in-Chief People's Army of Vietnam 1947–80.

US
Acheson. Dean Acheson. Under-Secretary of State 1945–47; Secretary of State 1949–52.

Byrnes. James Byrnes. Secretary of State 1945–47.

Hull. Cordell Hull. Secretary of State 1933–44.

Hurley. General Patrick Hurley. Ambassador to China 1944–45.

MacArthur. General Douglas MacArthur. Supreme Allied Commander Southwest Pacific; Commander Occupational Forces Japan 1945–51; Commander-in-Chief UN forces in Korea 1950–51.

Marshall. General George Marshall. Army Commander-in-Chief 1939–45; diplomatic mission to China December 1945; Secretary of State 1947–49; Secretary of Defence 1950–51.

Moffat. Abbot Low Moffat. Chief of Southeast Asia Section of the State Department.

Patti. Major Archimedes Patti. Head of OSS mission of Indo-China 1945.

Reed. Charles S. Reed. US Consul Saigon 1946–48; Chief of Southeast Asia Section of the State Department.

Roosevelt. Franklin Delano Roosevelt. President 1932–45.

Stettinius. Edward Stettinius. Secretary of State 1944–45.

Stilwell. Lt.-General Joe Stilwell. Commander-in-Chief US forces China and Chief of Staff to Chiang Kai-Shek 1942–44.

Truman. Harry Truman. Vice-President 1944–45; President 1945–52.

Wedemeyer. Lt.-General Albert Wedemeyer. Deputy Chief of Staff SEAC 1944; Commander-in-Chief US forces China 1945–46.

OTHER

Aung San. Chief of Staff Burma Independence Army 1941; Created Anti-Fascist Party 1944; Deputy Chairman Executive Council 1946; assassinated 1947.

Chiang Kai-Shek. President of China 1928–49; President of Taiwan 1949–75.

Nehru. Jawaharlal Nehru. President of the Congress Party 1929–64; Indian Prime Minister and Foreign Minister 1947–64.

Notes

Note: archival and file abbreviations used are listed in full in the archival sources section of the bibliography.

Introduction

1 D. Duncanson, *Government and Revolution in Vietnam*, London, 1968, p. 158.
2 A. Bourdain, *A Cook's Tour: in search of the perfect meal*, London, 2001, pp. 1–5, 52–64.
3 CAB 129/1, CP(45)112 Annex, Memorandum by Lord Keynes, 13 August 1945, R. Hyam (ed.) *British Documents on the End of Empire* [hereafter *BDEE*], *Series A. Volume 2: The Labour Government and the End of Empire 1945–51: Part 2 Economics and International Relations*, London, 1991, pp. 1–5.

Chapter 1   Churchill and Roosevelt, January 1943–July 1945

1 H. Kissinger, *Diplomacy*, London, 1994, p. 395.
2 J. Charmley, *Churchill's Grand Alliance: The Anglo-American Special Relationship 1940–57*, London, 1995, p. 37.
3 Kissinger, *op. cit.*, p. 396.
4 S.M. Habibuddin, 'Franklin D. Roosevelt's Anti-colonial Policy Towards Asia. Its Implications for India, Indo-china and Indonesia 1941–5', *Journal of Indian History*, vol.53, 1975, p. 498.
5 Charmley, *op. cit.*, p. 5.
6 S. Tonnesson, *The Vietnamese Revolution of 1945: Roosevelt, Ho Chi Minh and De Gaulle in a World at War*, London, 1991, p. 63; W.R. Louis, *Imperialism at Bay: The United States and the Decolonisation of the British Empire 1941–5*, New York, 1978, p. 26, citing E.R. Stettinius Jr, *Roosevelt and the Russians: the Yalta Conference*, New York, 1949, p. 237.
7 Kissinger, *op. cit.*
8 L.D. Epstein, *Britain: An Uneasy Ally*, Chicago, 1954, p. 209.
9 Tonnesson, *op. cit.*, p. 170; Charmley, *op. cit.*, pp. 11–12.
10 Lord Halifax, *Fulness of Days*, London, 1957, p. 253.
11 A. Eden, *The Memoirs of Anthony Eden, Earl of Avon: The Reckoning*, Boston, 1965, (second printing), p. 433; Charmley, *op. cit.*, p. 136.
12 Joint Chiefs of Staff Meeting, 7 January 1943, *Foreign Relations of the United States* [hereafter *FRUS*]: *The Conferences at Washington 1941–2 and Casablanca 1943*, Washington D.C., 1968, pp. 505–14.
13 C. Thorne, *Allies Of A Kind: The United States, Britain And The War Against Japan, 1941–1945*, London, 1979, p. 283; M. Viorst, *Hostile Allies: FDR And Charles De Gaulle*, New York, 1965, p. 191.
14 AP 20/53/107, British Embassy Washington to Eden, 5 January 1942.

15 M. Gilbert, *Winston Spencer Churchill, Volume 7: The Road to Victory 1941–1945*, London, 1986, p. 292.
16 AP 20/12/47, Churchill to Eden, M887/4, 20 July 1944.
17 Louis, *op. cit.*, p. 14.
18 D.C. Watt, *Succeeding John Bull, America in Britain's Place, 1900–1975*, Cambridge, 1984, p. 195.
19 G.R. Hess, *The United States' Emergence as a Southeast Asian Power, 1940–1950*, New York, 1987, p. 56.
20 AP 20/10/230A, 896 Circular to Washington, 14 June 1943.
21 G. Smith, *American Diplomacy During The Second World War 1941–1945*, New York, 1965, p. 92.
22 AP 20/11/13B, Roosevelt to Churchill, 31 December 1943.
23 Roosevelt to Churchill, no.559, 12 June 1944, W. Kimball (ed.), *Churchill and Roosevelt: The Complete Correspondence: Alliance Declining, 1944–1945*, Princeton, 1984, pp. 180–1.
24 J. Lacouture, *De Gaulle: The Rebel: 1890–1944*, London, 1993, p. 333.
25 J.M. Siracusa, 'The United States, Viet-Nam and the Cold War: A Re-appraisal', *Journal of Southeast Asian Studies*, 1974, p. 85.
26 *Ibid.*, p. 87; AP 20/10/184, Eden to Churchill, PM/43/184, 25 June 1943.
27 AP 20/10/314B, Paraphrase of State Department to Ambassador Winant, 8 October 1943.
28 AP 20/11/484, Eden to Churchill, PM/44/486, 2 July 1944.
29 PREM 3/187, Roosevelt to Churchill, T139/2, 29 January 1942.
30 AP 20/11/484, Eden to Churchill, PM/44/486, 2 July 1944.
31 Hess, *op. cit.*, pp. 71–2.
32 CAB 65/33, WM(43)30, 15 February 1943.
33 FO 371/35917/F1851/877/61G, Conversation between Welles and Halifax, 25 March 1943.
34 PREM 4/42/9, Halifax to Churchill, no.1470, T397/3, 28 March 1943.
35 CAB 65/38, WM(43)53, Conclusions, 13 April 1943.
36 FO 371/35927/F2116/1953/61, Paper by G. Wint, revised version, 19 May 1943.
37 FO 371/35930/F4023/4023/61G, Minute by G.F Hudson, 26 July 1943.
38 FO 371/35921/F4646/1422/61, Minute by N. Butler, 21 August 1943.
39 G. Bordinier (ed.), *La Guerre D'Indochine 1945–54: Textes et Documents, Volume 1, Le Retour de la France en Indochine 1945–1946*, Vincennes, 1987, p. 19.
40 PREM 3/180/7, R. Campbell to FO, no.4658, 14 October 1943.
41 PREM 3/180/7, Minute by Churchill, 16 October 1943.
42 PREM 3/180/7, Cadogan to Churchill, PM43/343, 21 October 1943.
43 PREM 3/180/7, Minute by Churchill, 22 October 1943.
44 PREM 3/180/7, Cadogan to Churchill, 3 November 1943.
45 PREM 3/180/7, Minute by Churchill, 19 November 1943.
46 PREM 3/180/7, Minute by Churchill, 22 November 1943; Minute by Churchill, 17 December 1943.
47 FO 371/35935/F6582/6582/61G, Brief for Cadogan, 22 November 1943.
48 PREM 3/178/2, Attlee to Churchill, no.1050, 30 November 1943.
49 PREM 3/178/2, Churchill to Attlee, no.554, 1 December 1943.
50 CAB 65/40, WM(43)169, Conclusions, 13 December 1943.

51 Watt, *op. cit.*, p. 199.
52 CAB 65/40, WM(43)169, Conclusions, 13 December 1943.
53 J. Lacouture, *De Gaulle: The Ruler: 1945–1970*, London, 1993, p. 85.
54 PREM 3/178/2, Eden to Churchill, no.699, 20 December 1943.
55 PREM 3/178/2, Churchill to Eden, no.769, 21 December 1943.
56 PREM 3/178/2, Eden to Churchill, no.786, 24 December 1943.
57 PREM 3/178/2, Minute by Churchill, 25 December 1943; FO 371/35921/F6656/1422/61, FO to Washington, no.8995, 29 December 1943.
58 CAB 122/812, Halifax to FO, 3 January 1944.
59 FO 371/35921/F6656/1422/61, Minute by Cavendish Bentinck, 22 December 1943.
60 FO 371/35930/F4461/4023/61G, Minute by Hudson, 27 December 1943.
61 FO 660/44, Duncannon to Reilly, 9 December 1943.
62 PREM 3/178/2, Eden to Churchill, no.1312, 11 January 1944.
63 PREM 3/178/2, Churchill to Eden, no.1255, 12 January 1944.
64 Hess, *op. cit.*, pp. 79, 86, 99–101, 105, 126–7.
65 PREM 3/178/2, Halifax to FO, no.258, 18 January 1944.
66 FO 371/40369/W376/15/E74, P.S Faller for Lord Hood to Lt.-Colonel Taylor, 20 January 1944.
67 PREM 3/160/7, COS(44)48th Meeting (0), 14 February 1944.
68 PREM 3/160/7, Dening to FO, 17 February 1944.
69 CAB 81/45, PHP(44)2(0) Final, Post-Hostilities Planning Sub-Committee, 22 January 1944.
70 FO 371/41723/F980/66/61G, Minute by Cadogan, 2 February 1944.
71 FO 371/41723/F980/66/61G, Minute by Eden, undated.
72 PREM 3/178/2, WM(44)25th, Conclusions, 24 February 1944.
73 AP 20/12/116, Churchill to Eden and Cranborne, M266/4, 11 March 1944.
74 PREM 3/178/2, Cranborne to Churchill, 31 March 1944.
75 PREM 3/178/2, Minute by Churchill, 1 April 1944; Louis, *op. cit.*, p. 36.
76 FO 371/41720/F4348/9/61G, Memorandum by Eden, 10 September 1944; Thorne, *op. cit.*, p. 469.
77 AP 20/12/416, Churchill to Eden, M886/4, 19 July 1944.
78 PREM 3/180/7, Mountbatten to COS, SEACOS 136, 13 April 1944.
79 PREM 3/180/7, Minute by Churchill, 4 May 1944.
80 CAB 120/708, Ismay to Sir M. Peterson, 6 May 1944.
81 FO 371/41723/F2223/66/61G, Minute by Cadogan, 12 May 1944.
82 PREM 3/180/7, Selborne to Churchill and Eden, 12 May 1944.
83 PREM 3/180/7, Eden to Churchill, PM44/349, 18 May 1944; Churchill to Eden, M580/4, 21 May 1944.
84 CAB 120/708, Mountbatten to COS, 1 June 1944.
85 CAB 120/708, Hollis to Churchill, 2 June 1944.
86 PREM 3/180/7, Churchill to Hollis, D.190/4, 11 June 1944.
87 CAB 120/708, Hollis to Churchill, 12 June 1944; PREM 3/180/7, COS to Mountbatten, COSSEA 113, 12 June 1944.
88 AP 20/12/744, Bracken to Eden, 9 June 1944.
89 AP 20/12/416, Churchill to Eden, M886/4, 19 July 1944.
90 AP 20/12/744, Bracken to Eden, 9 June 1944.

91   AP 20/41/26, P.J Dixon to Eden, 14 August 1944.
92   Eden, *op. cit.*, p. 528; AP 20/12/744, Bracken to Eden, 9 June 1944.
93   PREM 3/180/7, War Cabinet COS Committee, COS(44)668(0), 28 July 1944.
94   PREM 3/180/7, Minute by Churchill, 3 August 1944.
95   FO 371/41720/F4930/9/61G, Hollis to Churchill, 13 October 1944.
96   WO 193/195, JSM to COS, JSM 227, 30 August 1944.
97   PREM 3/180/7, Halifax to FO, no.4685, 30 August 1944; JSM to AMSSO, JSM 228, 31 August 1944.
98   FO 371/41724/F3677/66/61G, Minute by L. Foulds, 9 August 1944.
99   CAB 65/43, WM(44)106th, Conclusions, 14 August 1944; PREM 3/178/2, WM(44)106th, Conclusions, 14 August 1944.
100   FO 371/41719/F4028/9/61, Meeting between Eden and Massigli, 24 August 1944; FO 371/41720/F4348/9/61G, Memorandum by Eden, 10 September 1944.
101   PREM 3/180/7, Colville, Defence Office Aide Memoire, 12 September 1944.
102   PREM 3/180/7, Colville to V.G Lawford, 26 September 1944; FO 371/41720/F4681/9/61G, Sterndale Bennett to Churchill, 7 October 1944.
103   CAB 120/708, Mountbatten to COS, SEACOS no.231, 14 September 1944.
104   CAB 120/708, Minute to the Defence Office, 16 September 1944; COS to Vice-COS, no.206, 16 September 1944.
105   FO 371/41720/F4495/9/61G, Dening to FO, no.165, 30 September 1944.
106   FO 371/41720/F4495/9/61G, Minute by Eden, undated.
107   WO 203/5068, Mountbatten to Eden, SC4/1579/F, 2 October 1944.
108   M. Thomas, 'Free France, the British Government and the Future of French Indo-China 1940–45', *Journal of Southeast Asian Studies*, vol. 28, no.1, 1997, p. 153.
109   FO 371/41720/F4681/9/61G, Sterndale Bennett to Churchill, 7 October 1944.
110   FO 371/41720/F4681/9/61G, Minute by Eden, 8 October 1944.
111   FO 371/41720/F4495/9/61G, FO to Paris, no.211, 8 October 1944.
112   AP 20/12/486, Churchill to Eden, M(Tof1)4/4, 11 October 1944.
113   FO 371/41720/F4930/9/61G, Hollis to Churchill, 13 October 1944.
114   FO 371/41720/F4930/9/61, Eden to Churchill, 20 October 1944; PREM 3/180/7, Churchill to Eden, M(Tol)16/4, 21 October 1944.
115   PREM 3/180/7, CCS 708, 6 October 1944, Memorandum by US COS, Enclosure A, Vice-Admiral R. Fenard to Washington to CinC US Fleet, no.389, 19 September 1944, Appendix, 19 September 1944.
116   PREM 3/180/7, Colville to F.W Mottershead, 20 December 1944.
117   PREM 3/180/7, First Sea Lord to Churchill, 22 December 1944.
118   PREM 3/180/7, Minute by Churchill, no.1251/4, 31 December 1944.
119   HW 1/3314, no.138127, Spanish Embassy in Washington to Ministry of Foreign Affairs Madrid, 8 November 1944.
120   P. Ziegler, *Mountbatten*, Glasgow, 1985, pp. 242, 284–5.
121   CAB 120/708, COS(44)968(0), War Cabinet COS Committee, 13 November 1944.
122   FO 371/41721/F5303/9/61, Minute by Sterndale Bennett, 4 November 1944.

123 FO 371/41721/F5303/9/61, Minute by Eden, 8 November 1944.

124 *The Pentagon Papers, The Defense Department History of United States Decision Making on Vietnam, Volume 1,* [hereafter *The Pentagon Papers*] Gravel Edition, Boston, 1971, p. 11.

125 AP 20/12/718, Churchill to Eden, M1257/4, 31 December 1944.

126 PREM 4/31/4, Eden to Churchill, PM/45/11, 8 January 1945, S.R. Ashton and S.E. Stockwell (eds), *BDEE, Series A, Volume 1: Imperial Policy and Colonial Practice 1925–1945: Part 1: Metropolitan Reorganisation, Defence and International Relations, Political Change and Constitutional Reform,* London, 1996, pp. 215–18.

127 FO 371/41721/F6155/9/61, Halifax to FO, no.6888, 28 December 1944.

128 CAB 80/91, COS(45)64(0), Memorandum by COS Committee, 21 January 1945, Annex 2, Halifax to FO, no.32, 2 January 1945.

129 CAB 80/91, COS(45)64(0), Memorandum by COS Committee, 21 January 1945, Annex 3, Halifax to FO, no.168, 9 January 1945.

130 CAB 80/91, COS(45)64(0), Memorandum by COS Committee, 21 January 1945, Annex 4, Dening to FO, no.14, 6 January 1945.

131 CAB 121/741, COS(45)64(0), Memorandum by COS Committee, 21 January 1945; COS(45)27th Meeting, 25 January 1945; Eden to Hollis, undated.

132 Hess, *op. cit.,* p. 133.

133 PREM 3/185/4, Eden to Churchill, PM/45/32, 16 January 1945.

134 PREM 3/185/4, Churchill to Eden, 19 January 1945.

135 PREM 3/185/4, Eden to Churchill, PM/45/50, 23 January 1945; Churchill to Eden, M113/5, 25 January 1945.

136 Louis, *op. cit.,* pp. 457–60; PREM 3/178/3, Churchill to Eden, M(Arg)9/5, 13 February 1945.

137 Press Conference by Roosevelt, 23 February 1945, A.B. Cole, (ed.), *Conflict In Indochina and International Repercussions: A Documentary History, 1945–1955,* New York, 1956, p. 48.

138 FO 371/46304/F1269/11/61G, Dening to Sterndale Bennett, 16 February 1945.

139 PREM 4/31/4, Churchill to Attlee, M190/5, 10 March 1944.

140 FO 371/46325/F2144/127/61G, Minute by Sterndale Bennett, 5 April 1945.

141 FO 371/46325/F2144/127/61G, Minute by A.N Scott, 7 April 1945.

142 Declaration of the Provisional French Government Concerning Indochina, 24 March 1945, Cole (ed.). *Conflict In Indochina and International Repercussions: A Documentary History, 1945–1955, op. cit.,* pp. 5–7.

143 FO 371/46304/F1269/11/61G, Sterndale Bennett to Dening, 14 April 1945.

144 CAB 81/46, PHP(45)29(0) Final, 29 June 1945, Ashton and Stockwell (ed.), *BDEE, Series A, Volume 1: Imperial Policy and Colonial Practice 1925–1945: Part 1, op. cit.,* pp. 231–44.

145 AP 20/13/229, Churchill to Roosevelt, 17 March 1943.

146 Memorandum by the British COS, CCS 308, 15 August 1943, *FRUS: The Conferences at Washington and Quebec 1943,* Washington D.C., pp. 968–71.

147   Meeting of the CCS with Roosevelt and Churchill, 23 August 1943, Item 7, *FRUS: The Conferences at Washington and Quebec 1943, ibid.,* pp. 941–9.
148   MB 1/C50/13, Mountbatten to Brooke, 3 February 1944.
149   Ziegler, *op. cit.,* p. 242.
150   CAB 122/1067, Mountbatten to COS, 837/SEACOS, 9 November 1943.
151   PREM 3/90/3, Mountbatten to Roosevelt, 23 October 1943; MB 1/C205, Roosevelt to Mountbatten, 8 November 1943; WO 203/5131, Mountbatten to Lt.-General Sommervell, SC5/602/S, 17 March 1945.
152   PREM 3/90/3, Mountbatten to Roosevelt, 23 October 1943.
153   PREM 3/90/3, Mountbatten to Churchill, 23 October 1943; MB 1/C50/2, Mountbatten to Brooke, 23 October 1943.
154   MB 1/C205, Roosevelt to Mountbatten, 8 November 1943.
155   FO 371/41720/F4930/9/61G, Hollis to Churchill, 13 October 1944.
156   FO 371/41798/F4292/100/23, Mountbatten to COS, SEACOS 231, 14 September 1944.
157   MB 1/C280, Wedemeyer to Mountbatten, 29 January 1945.
158   CAB 80/91, COS(45)96(0), Memorandum by COS Committee, 4 February 1945.
159   MB 1/C42/62, Carton de Wiart to Mountbatten, 7 February 1945.
160   Thomas, *op. cit.,* p. 140; A. Short, *The Origins of the Vietnam War,* London, 1989, p. 58, footnote 28, citing P.M. Dunn, *The First Vietnam War,* London, 1985.
161   MB 1/C42/62, Carton de Wiart to Mountbatten, 7 February 1945; MB 1/C42/66/4, Minute by Air Vice Marshall Whitworth-Jones, 22 February 1945.
162   MB 1/C42/66/6, Air Vice Marshal Whitworth-Jones to Mountbatten, 27 February 1945; MB 1/C42/66/4, Minute by Air Vice Marshall Whitworth-Jones, 22 February 1945.
163   MB 1/C280, Wedemeyer to Mountbatten, 10 February 1945.
164   FO 371/46325/F1154/127/61G, Seymour to Sterndale Bennett, no.160, 9 February 1945.
165   J. Boucher De Crevecoeur, *La Liberation Du Laos 1945–46,* Vincennes, 1985, p. 15.
166   PREM 3/178/3, Carton de Wiart to Churchill, T211/5, 22 February 1945.
167   HW 1/3527, Secret 157, 8 February 1945.
168   CAB 80/92, COS(45)120(0), Memorandum by COS Committee, 21 February 1945.
169   CAB 120/708, Ismay to Churchill, 27 February 1945.
170   CAB 120/708, Wilson to Ismay, FMW14, 9 March 1945.
171   CAB 121/741, Churchill to Eden and Ismay for COS, 1 March 1945.
172   CAB 80/92, COS(45)143(0), Memorandum by COS Committee, 3 March 1943, FO to COS, 2 March 1945, Annex 1; CAB 80/91, COS(45)64(0), Memorandum by COS Committee, 21 January 1945, Annex 2, Halifax to FO, no.32, 2 January 1945.
173   AP 20/13/60, Eden to Churchill, PM/45/81, 4 March 1945; Minute by Churchill, 6 March 1945.
174   CAB 80/92, COS(45)143(0), Memorandum by COS Committee, 3 March 1943, FO to COS, 2 March 1945, Annex 1.

175 D. Lancaster, *The Emancipation of French Indochina*, London, 1961, pp. 104–7; B. Kiernan, *How Pol Pot came to Power: a History of Communism in Kampuchea, 1930–75*, London, 2004, p. 49.
176 AP 20/13/73, Eden to Churchill, PM/45/99, 11 March 1945.
177 PREM 3/178/2, Churchill to Ismay, D72/5, 12 March 1945.
178 PREM 3/178/3, Eden to Cooper, draft, 12 March 1945.
179 AP 20/13/229, Churchill to Roosevelt, 17 March 1945.
180 CAB 121/741, JIC(45)91(0), 18 March 1945.
181 CAB 120/708, Wilson to COS, FMW23, 18 March 1945.
182 Meeting of the CCS with Roosevelt and Churchill, 23 August 1943, Item 7, *FRUS: The Conferences at Washington and Quebec 1943, op. cit.*
183 CAB 120/708, COS to Wilson, 1746, 19 March 1945; Churchill to COS, 20 March 1945.
184 PREM 3/178/3, Churchill to Eden and Ismay for COS, M237/5, 19 March 1945.
185 CAB 120/708, Ismay to Churchill, 19 March 1945.
186 PREM 3/178/3, Churchill to Ismay for COS, 20 March 1945.
187 PREM 3/178/3, Wilson to Churchill and COS, FMW24, T307/5, 20 March 1945.
188 R.H. Spector, *The U.S. Army in Vietnam: Advice and Support: The Early Years*, Washington D.C., 1983, p. 31; WO 208/670, Sitrep 3, 15 March 1945; Sitrep 4, 15 March 1945; JBS/172, 14 March 1945; General Noiret to Lt.-Colonel Montgomery, 19 March 1945; Sitrep 5, 16 March 1945.
189 CAB 121/741, Mountbatten to COS, SEACOS 339, 22 March 1945.
190 CAB 121/741, CCS 644/21, 'Support for French Resistance Forces in Indo–China', 29 March 1945, Enclosure B, Fenand to CCS, no.17MN/SE 12TS, 27 March 1945; Enclosure C, Fenand to CCOS, no.18MN/SE 124TS, 27 March 1945.
191 CAB 121/741, JSM to Cabinet, JSM 646, 30 March 1945.
192 CAB 121/741, Sterndale Bennett to Air Commodore Beaumont, 30 March 1945.
193 FO 371/46306/F2065/11/61G, Wilson to COS, FMW40, 30 March 1945.
194 FO 371/46306/F2065/11/61G, Wilson to COS, FMW39, 30 March 1945.
195 PREM 3/178/3, Roosevelt to Churchill, no.724, T324/5, 22 March 1945.
196 CAB 120/708, Wilson to COS, FMW25, 20 March 1945.
197 PREM 3/178/3, Wilson to Ismay, FMW33, 27 March 1945.
198 CAB 120/708, Ismay to Churchill, 19 March 1945.
199 PREM 3/159/12, FO brief, 28 March 1945, Annex 1, Hurley, 28 March 1945.
200 PREM 3/159/12, FO brief, 28 March 1945, Annex 6, Indo-China, 28 March 1945.
201 PREM 3/159/12, Minute by Churchill, 11 April 1945; A. Danchev and D. Todman (eds), *War Diaries 1939–1945: Field Marshal Lord Alan Brooke*, London, 2001, p. 682.
202 PREM 3/178/3, Churchill to Hollis, D92/5, 31 March 1945.
203 PREM 3/178/3, Churchill to Hollis, D93/5, 3 April 1945.
204 CAB 120/708, Mountbatten to COS, SEACOS 359, 8 April 1945.

205 Memorandum by the Assistant to the President's Naval Aide (G.M. Elsey), undated, *FRUS: The Conference at Berlin 1945 (The Potsdam Conference) Volume 1*, Washington D.C., 1960, pp. 915–21.

206 PREM 3/178/3, Churchill to Roosevelt, no.943, T438/5, 11 April 1945.

207 PREM 3/178/3, Truman to Churchill, no.4, T478/5, 14 April 1945.

208 CAB 121/741, Churchill to Ismay, 15 April 1945; C.P. Price to Brooke, CAS, First Sea Lord, ref.COS 563/5, 15 April 1945.

209 CAB 120/708, Ismay to Churchill, 19 April 1945.

210 CAB 120/708, Churchill to Truman, no.9, T537/5, 20 April 1945.

211 PREM 3/180/7, Churchill to Cadogan, M339/5, 15 April 1945.

212 CAB 120/708, COS to Mountbatten, COSSEA no.249, 25 April 1945.

213 Memorandum by the Assistant to the President's Naval Aide (G.M. Elsey), undated, *FRUS: The Conference at Berlin 1945 (The Potsdam Conference) Volume 1, op. cit.*

214 CAB 120/708, Wilson to COS, FMW84, 10 May 1945.

215 MB 1/C280, Wedemeyer to Mountbatten, 12 May 1945.

216 MB 1/C280, Mountbatten to Wedemeyer, 21 May 1945.

217 PREM 3/178/3, Wilson to COS and Mountbatten, FMW95, 29 May 1945.

218 PREM 3/178/3, Wilson to COS, FMW100, 1 June 1945; Spector, *op. cit.*, p. 49.

219 CAB 122/1177, Marshall to Wilson, 5 June 1945.

220 CAB 122/1177, Wilson to COS, FMW106, 8 June 1945.

221 PREM 3/178/3, COS to Wilson, Cypher 3681, 11 June 1945.

222 WO 203/5291, WO to Mountbatten, 97099 Cypher CA4, 29 May 1945; A. Patti, *Why Vietnam?* Berkley, 1980, pp. 58, 67, 102, 125–9.

223 CAB 119/205, COS(45)161st Meeting, 26 June 1945.

224 CAB 119/205, FO to Terminal, no.38, 16 July 1945.

225 MB 1/C206, Draft record of a conversation with Truman, 24 July 1945.

226 PREM 8/33, FO to Terminal, no.259, 28 July 1945; Terminal to FO, no. 324, T12/45, 1 August 1945.

227 L.C. Gardner, *Approaching Vietnam: From World War Two Through Dienbienphu*, London, 1988, p. 47.

228 Hess, *op. cit.*, pp. 79, 86; Tonnesson, *op. cit.*, p. 64.

229 Hess, *op. cit.*, pp. 126–7; Short, *op. cit.*, p. 36.

230 Dunn, *op. cit.*, p. 86.

231 Hess, *op. cit.*, p. 94; W. La Feber, 'Roosevelt, Churchill and Indochina 1942–5', *American Historical Review*, vol.80, 1975, p. 1289.

232 Short, *op. cit.*

233 Hess, *op. cit.*, p. 128.

234 G.C. Herring, 'The Truman Administration and the Restoration of French Sovereignty in Indochina', *Diplomatic History*, vol.1, no.2, Spring 1977, p. 99.

235 Hess, *op. cit.*, p. 134.

236 Thorne, *op. cit.*, pp. 501, 631.

237 S. Tonnesson, 'The Longest Wars: Indochina 1945–75', *Journal of Peace Research*, vol.22, no.1, 1985, p. 11.

238 Thorne, *op. cit.*, p. 622.

239 Spector, *op. cit.*, p. 43.

240 Hess, *op. cit.*, pp. 135–6, 145.

241 Thorne, *op. cit.*, p. 631.
242 Louis, *op. cit.*, p. 489; Thorne, *op. cit.*, p. 600.
243 Thorne, *op. cit.*, p. 629.
244 Herring, *op. cit.*, p. 104; Acting Secretary of State Joseph Grew to Ambassador Jefferson Caffrey in Paris, 9 May 1945, A.W. Cameron (ed.), *Viet-Nam Crisis: A Documentary History. Volume 1, 1940–1956*, New York, 1971, p. 36.
245 FO 461/4, Halifax to Eden, no.642, 30 May 1945, Enclosure to no.2, R.D. Crockatt (ed.), *British Documents on Foreign Affairs: Reports and Papers from the Foreign Office Confidential Print: Series C, North America, Part 3: Volume 5: January 1945–December 1945*, University Publications of America, 1999, pp. 97–103.
246 AP 20/13/217, Eden to Churchill, T934/5, 14 May 1945.
247 FO 371/46307/F4240/11/61G, Minute by Butler, 10 July 1945.
248 C. Thorne, 'Indochina and Anglo-American Relations 1942–5', *Pacific Historical Review*, 1976, p. 96.
249 Tonnesson, *The Vietnamese Revolution of 1945: Roosevelt, Ho Chi Minh and De Gaulle in a World at War, op. cit.*, pp. 13–19; La Feber, *op. cit.*, p. 1277.
250 *The Pentagon Papers, op. cit.*, p. 2; Short, *op. cit.*, p. 38.
251 Charmley, *op. cit.*, p. 159.
252 Thorne, *Allies Of A Kind: The United States, Britain And The War Against Japan, 1941–1945, op. cit.*, pp. 600, 629, 631.
253 Viorst, *op. cit.*, p. 155, citing de Gaulle, *Memoirs de Guerre, Vol.2, L'Unite 1942–1944*, Paris, 1956, p. 80.
254 FO 371/46325/F234/127/61, Minute by J. Thyme Henderson, 14 January 1945.
255 F.R. Dulles and G. Ridinger, 'The Anti-colonial policies of Roosevelt', *Political Science Quarterly*, 1955, pp. 1, 10.
256 Thorne, *op. cit.*, p. 630; J. Sbrega, 'The Anti-Colonial Policies of Franklin D. Roosevelt: A Re-appraisal', *Political Science Quarterly*, vol.101, no.1, 1986, p. 77.
257 Thorne, *op. cit.*, p. 466.
258 S. Bills, *Empire and the Cold War: The Roots of United States – Third World Antagonism*, London, 1990, p. 73.
259 *The Pentagon Papers, op. cit.*, p. 16; R. Blum, *Drawing the line*, New York, 1979, p. 105.
260 G.R. Hess, 'Franklin D. Roosevelt and French Indochina', *Journal of American History*, vol.59, no.2, September 1972, p. 366.
261 D.G. Marr, *Vietnam 1945: The Quest For Power*, Berkley, 1995, p. 269; Tonnesson, *op. cit.*, pp. 168–70, 213–14.

Chapter 2 Liberation, July 1945–March 1946

1 N. Tarling, 'Some Rather Nebulous Capacity: Lord Killearn's Appointment in Southeast Asia', *Modern Asian Studies*, vol.20, no.3, 1986, pp. 559–60.
2 CAB 129/1, CP(45)112, Annex, Memorandum by Keynes, 13 August 1945, Hyam (ed.), *BDEE, Series A. Volume 2: The Labour Government and the End of Empire 1945–51: Part 2, op. cit.*, pp. 1–5.

3   R.F. Holland, 'The Imperial Factor in British Strategies From Attlee to Macmillan 1945–63', *Journal of Imperial and Commonwealth History*, vol.12, January 1984, pp. 166, 183.

4   Tonnesson, *op. cit.*, p. 365.

5   WO 203/5655, Dening to Mountbatten, 7 August 1945.

6   Charmley, *op. cit.*, p. 184.

7   A. Adamthwaite, 'Britain and the World 1945–9: The View From The Foreign Office', *International Affairs*, vol.61, no.2, Spring 1985, p. 226.

8   FO 934/3/12(7), Hollis to Cadogan, 20 July 1945, R. Butler, and M. Pelly (eds), *Documents on British Policy Overseas, Series 1, Volume 1, The Conference at Potsdam July–August 1945*, London, 1984, pp. 475–7.

9   Meeting of the CCS, 24 July 1945, *FRUS: The Conference at Berlin 1945 (The Potsdam Conference) Volume 2*, Washington D.C., 1960, p. 377; FO 371/F4715/47/23, Memorandum by Foulds, 1 August 1945, Butler, and Pelly (eds), *Documents on British Policy Overseas, Series 1, Volume 1, op. cit.*, p. 1145.

10 Meeting of the CCS, 24 July 1945, *FRUS: The Conference at Berlin 1945 (The Potsdam Conference), Volume 2, op. cit.*

11 Lin Hua, 'The Chinese Occupation of Northern Vietnam 1945–1946: A reappraisal', pp. 144–69, H. Antlov and S. Tonnesson (eds), *Imperial Policy and Southeast Asian Nationalism 1930–1957*, Surrey, 1995.

12 S. Tonnesson, 'Filling The Vacuum: 1945 in French Indochina, the Netherlands East Indies and British Malaya', pp. 123–5, Antlov and Tonnesson, *op. cit.*

13 CAB 121/741, Minute by Mountbatten, 9 August 1945.

14 Tonnesson, 'Filling The Vacuum: 1945 in French Indochina, the Netherlands East Indies and British Malaya', Antlov and Tonnesson, *op. cit.*

15 WO 203/5642, B.A.C. Sweet-Escott, no.7/16/45, 13 August 1945, A.J. Stockwell (ed.), *BDEE, Series B Volume 3: Malaya Part 1*, London, 1995, p. 110.

16 Bills, *op. cit.*, pp. 83–4.

17 R.E.M. Irving, *The First Indochina War, French and American Policy 1945–1954*, London, 1975, p. 16, citing B. Fall, *Street Without Joy*, p. 26.

18 Dunn, *op. cit.*, p. 16; R.B. Smith, *Vietnam and the West*, London, 1968, p. 111.

19 Dunn, *op. cit.*, p. 18; J. Saville, *The Politics of Continuity: British Foreign Policy and the Labour Government 1945–1946*, London, 1993, p. 178.

20 Dunn, *op. cit.*

21 Patti, *op. cit.*, p. 453; Dunn, *op. cit.*, p. 22; Bills, *op. cit.*, p. 89.

22 Spector, *op. cit.*, p. 56; J. Sainteny, *Ho Chi Minh and His Vietnam: A Personal Memoir*, Translated By H. Briffault, Chicago, 1972, p. 47.

23 Dunn, *op. cit.*, p. 123.

24 K. Nitz, 'Independence without Nationalists? The Japanese and Vietnamese Nationalism during the Japanese period 1940–5', *Journal of Southeast Asian Studies*, vol.15, no.1, March 1984, p. 131.

25 Dunn, *op. cit.*, pp. 23, 136; Gardner, *op. cit.*, p. 73.

26 Tonnesson, 'Filling The Vacuum: 1945 in French Indochina, the Netherlands East Indies and British Malaya', pp. 122, 143, Antlov and

Tonnesson, *op. cit*; Hess, *The United States' Emergence as a Southeast Asian Power, 1940–1950, op. cit.*, p. 164.

27 Hess, *op. cit.*, p. 181.

28 Balfour to Bevin, AN2597/4/45, 25 August 1945, Crockatt (ed.), *British Documents on Foreign Affairs: Reports and Papers from the Foreign Office Confidential Print: Series C, North America, Part 3: Volume 5, op. cit.*, pp. 276–9.

29 FO 371/46308/F6353/11/61, Government of India External Affairs Department to Secretary of State for India, no.7670, 1 September 1945.

30 FO 371/46308/F6353/11/61, Secretary of State for India to Government of India External Affairs Department, no.19530, 3 September 1945.

31 MB 1/C10/3, Mountbatten to D'Argenlieu, SC5/1766/A, 1 September 1945.

32 CAB 122/512, Dening to FO, 10 September 1945.

33 J. Buttinger, *Vietnam: A Dragon Embattled Volume 1*, London, 1967, pp. 311–12.

34 D.G. Marr, 'Vietnam 1945: Some Questions', *Vietnam Forum*, vol.6, Summer 1985, p. 171.

35 N. Tarling, *Britain, Southeast Asia and the onset of the Cold War 1945–1950*, Cambridge, 1998, pp. 56, 79.

36 F.S.V. Donnison, *British Military Administration in the Far East 1943–1946*, London, 1956, pp. 408–9.

37 CAB 120/708, Mountbatten to CO, SEAC(RL)91, 24 September 1945.

38 WO 203/5644, Saigon Control Commission to Mountbatten, 21 September 1945.

39 WO 203/2173, Mountbatten to Gracey, NGS106, 24 September 1945.

40 WO 203/2173, HQSEA 31st Miscellaneous Meeting, 28 September 1945.

41 FO 371/46308/F7269/11/61, Telegram to the Foreign Ministers Conference London, received 18 September 1945.

42 Patti, *op. cit.*

43 Bills, *op. cit.*, p. 88.

44 Gallagher's meeting with Ho, 29 September 1945, G. Porter (ed.), *Vietnam, the Definitive Documentation of Human Decisions. Volume 1*, Philadelphia, 1979, pp. 80–1.

45 G. Rosie, *The British in Vietnam*, London, 1970, p. 63.

46 WO 203/5644, Supreme Allied Commander 286th Meeting, 28 September 1945.

47 WO 203/5608, Control Commission to Mountbatten, 25 September 1945.

48 WO 203/5608, Lt.-General Sir B. Kimmins to Lt.-General Sir F. Browning, ADV28, 28 September 1945.

49 MB 1/C91, Mountbatten to Driberg, SC5/1988/D, 4 October 1945.

50 MB 1/C91, Mountbatten to Driberg, Autumn 1945 (undated).

51 Dunn, *op. cit.*, p. 233.

52 P. Dennis, *Troubled Days of Peace: Mountbatten and South-East Asia Command, 1945–46*, Manchester, 1987, p. 63.

53 WO 203/2173, Brain to Mountbatten, SGN.COS 40, 1 October 1945.

54 Dunn, *op. cit.*, p. 241; Ziegler, *op. cit.*, p. 332.

55 Saville, *op. cit.*, p. 195.

56 PREM 8/63, SACSEA to Cabinet Office and JSM Washington, SEACOS 489, 24 September 1945.
57 PREM 8/63, Hollis to Attlee, 28 September 1945.
58 PREM 8/63, 'R.B.' to Hollis, 29 September 1945.
59 FO 371/46309/F8070/11/G61, Hollis to Attlee, 4 October 1945.
60 PREM 8/63, DO(45)7th Meeting 18(Revise)(Secret), Defence Committee, 5 October 1945.
61 PREM 8/63, DO(45)7th Meeting 18(Revise)(Secret), Defence Committee, 5 October 1945, Annex 1, JP(45)258(Final).
62 CAB 80/97, COS(45)589(0), Memorandum by COS Committee, 25 September 1945.
63 CAB 80/97, COS(45)598 1(0), Memorandum by COS Committee, 3 October 1945, FO to Secretary COS.
64 WO 203/2173, Monitoring flash 445, 5 October 1945.
65 Bills, *op. cit.*, p. 126.
66 PREM 8/189, Memorandum by Sterndale Bennett, 9 October 1945, Stockwell (ed.), *BDEE, Series B, Volume 3 Malaya: Part1, op. cit.*, p. 169.
67 P. Ziegler (ed.), *The Personal Diaries of Admiral, the Lord Louis Mountbatten, Supreme Commander Southeast Asia 1943–1946*, London, 1988, p. 258.
68 Saville, *op. cit.*, p. 191.
69 MB 1/C113/2, Mountbatten to Gracey, SC5/2089/G, 13 October 1945.
70 CAB 120/708, Mountbatten to Cabinet, SEACOS 513, 12 October 1945.
71 WO 203/4454, Report 114/CA, 'French Indo-Chinese Situation', (undated).
72 Bills, *op. cit.*, p. 88.
73 Saville, *op. cit.*, p. 202.
74 *Hansard House of Commons Parliamentary Debates* [hereafter *Hansard*], Volume 414, 24 October 1945, pp. 2149–50.
75 Rosie, *op. cit.*, pp. 11, 55–6, 134–5, 140.
76 Saville, *op. cit.*, p. 191.
77 WO 203/5476, Sayers to Rayner, Rear 5527, 13 October 1945.
78 D. Duncanson, 'General Gracey and the Vietminh', *Journal of the Royal Central Asian Society*, vol.55, part 3, October, 1968, p. 294.
79 Gracey 4/8, Saigon Control Commission Political Report 13 September–9 October 1945.
80 Gracey 4/12, Gracey to Slim, 5 November 1945.
81 MB 1/C10/11, Mountbatten to D'Argenlieu, Mokan 128, 8 November 1945; Gracey 4/13, Mountbatten to Gracey, SC5/2205/G, 31 October 1945.
82 Dennis, *op. cit.*, p. 20; Patti, *op. cit*; WO 203/5440, Meiklereid to Dening, SGN.FO16, 25 October 1945.
83 W.C. Gibbons, *The U.S. Government and the Vietnam War, Part 1: 1945–1960*, Princeton, 1986, p. 25.
84 WO 203/5476, Ho to Stalin, M.156, 20 October 1945.
85 K.C. Chen, *Vietnam and China 1938–54*, Princeton, 1969, p. 128.
86 Hess, *op. cit.*, p. 183.
87 Spector, *op. cit.*, p. 77.
88 Herring, *op. cit.*, p. 114.
89 WO 203/4432, Saigon to FO, no.30, 19 December 1945.

90   CAB 122/512, Précis of Colonel Walker-Chapman's report on Indo-China, Autumn 1945.
91   MB 1/C113/12, Mountbatten to Gracey, SC5/2539/G, 4 December 1945.
92   CO 968/107/2, G. Hall to Sir H. Moore, 19 November 1945.
93   CO 968/107/2, Moore to Hall, no.357, 7 December 1945.
94   MB 1/C113/12, Mountbatten to Gracey, SC5/2539/G, 4 December 1945.
95   MB 1/C207, Mountbatten to Attlee, 14 December 1945.
96   MB 1/C207, Attlee to Mountbatten, 1 January 1946.
97   MB 1/C91, Mountbatten to Driberg, 17 December 1945.
98   Dunn, *op. cit.*, p. 329; Saville, *op. cit.*, p. 197.
99   MB 1/C130/6, Dening to FO, no.98, 14 January 1946.
100 MB 1/C130/10, Gibson to Captain Brockman, Singmo.62, 18 January 1946.
101 Nehru to the All India States People's Conference, 1 January 1946, Cole, *Conflict In Indochina and International Repercussions: A Documentary History, 1945–1955, op. cit.*, p. 50.
102 MB 1/C130/15, Governor-General New Delhi to Secretary of State for India, no.650, 22 January 1946.
103 MB 1/C10/15, Mountbatten to D'Argenlieu, SC6H/57/A, 24 January 1946.
104 FO 800/461/FE/46/9, Dening to Bevin, no.46, 29 January 1946.
105 FO 800/461/FE/46/10, Bevin to Dening, no.81, 29 January 1946.
106 Lin Hua, 'The Chinese Occupation of Northern Vietnam 1945–1946: A reappraisal', p. 165, Antlov and Tonnesson, *op. cit.*
107 Lancaster, *op. cit.*, p. 127.
108 CAB 121/742, Meiklereid to FO, no.8, 10 January 1946.
109 FO 371/46308/F65/45/11/61, Chiang Kai-Shek's statement to National Defence Council and Central Executive Committee, 24 August 1945.
110 Hess, *op. cit.*, p. 195.
111 WO 203/4432, HQSACSEA Commission no.1 Saigon to Mountbatten, 17 January 1946.
112 Dunn, *op. cit.*, pp. 342–3.
113 Irving, *op. cit.*, p. 15.
114 Hess, *op. cit.*
115 J.L. Gaddis, *Strategies of Containment*, New York, 1982, p. 19.
116 Spector, *op. cit.*, p. 84.
117 M. Gilbert, *Winston Spencer Churchill, Volume 8: Never Despair 1945–1965*, London, 1988, pp. 197–203.
118 WO 203/6057, HQSACSEA Interservice Mission to French Indo-China to HQSEA, no.1/364, 25 February 1946.
119 WO 203/6057, HQSACSEA Interservice Mission to French Indo-China to HQSEA, no.Int201, 3 March 1946.
120 Smith, *op. cit.*, p. 112.
121 B. Fall, *The Two Vietnams*, London, 1963, p. 3; Spector, *op. cit.*, p. 79.
122 CAB 121/742, Meiklereid to FO, no.61, 8 March 1945.
123 Fall, *op. cit.*
124 WO 203/6216, Mountbatten to Browning, msing.63, 4 March 1946; Browning to Maunsell, NGS.719, 20 February 1946.
125 Tarling, *op. cit.*, p. 85.
126 CAB 121/742, Meiklereid to FO, no.76, 21 March 1946.
127 Tarling, *op. cit.*

128 CAB 121/742, FO to Paris and Saigon, no.660, 27 March 1945.

129 CAB 121/742, Mountbatten to COS, SEACOS 662, 17 March 1946.

130 WO 203/6419, Saigon to FO, no.81, 27 March 1946.

131 D.P. Chandler, *A History of Cambodia*, Washington D.C., 1999, p. 170.

132 M. Vickery, *Kampuchea: Politics, Economics and Society*, London, 1986, p. 8.

133 Chandler, *op. cit.*, p. 171.

134 V.M. Reddi, *A History of the Cambodian Independence Movement 1863–1955*, Triupati, 1973, p. 108.

135 Kiernan, *op. cit.*, p. 51.

136 CAOM, GGI/65498, 'Etudes sur les movements rebelles au Cambodge 1942–1952', Annex, 'Le Nationalisme Khmer', pp. 19–21.

137 Chandler, *op. cit.*

138 CAOM, GGI/65498, 'Etudes sur les movements rebelles au Cambodge 1942–1952', Annex, 'Le Nationalisme Khmer', p. 3.

139 WO 172/7009, Secret War Diary Headquarters ALF Phnom Penh, ALF/PP/23/G, HQ 20th Division 9–31 October 1945, 4 November, Lt.-Col. Commanding Allied Force; WO 208/636, no.14569, 12 November 1945; CAOM, GGI/65498, 'Etudes sur les movements rebelles au Cambodge 1942–1952', Annex, 'Le Nationalisme Khmer', pp. 12–13.

140 WO 203/2151, Gracey to SACSEA, Signal 99, COS 29, 25 September 1945.

141 WO 203/5644, Supreme Allied Commander 31st Misc. Meeting Minutes, 28 September 1945.

142 WO 203/5644, Supreme Allied Commander 286th Meeting, 28 September 1945.

143 Reddi, *op. cit.*, pp. 108–11; Lancaster, *op. cit.*, pp. 94, 111.

144 N. Sihanouk, *Souvenirs Doux et Amers*, Paris, 1981, pp. 113–14.

145 WO 172/7009, Secret War Diary Headquarters ALF Phnom Penh, ALF/PP/23/G, HQ 20th Division 9–31 October 1945, 4 November, Lt.-Col. Commanding Allied Force.

146 WO 172/7009, ALF Phnom Penh, Instruction no.1, 10 October 1945.

147 WO 203/2178, Gracey to CGS, no.02210, 16 October 1945.

148 WO 172/7009, Secret War Diary Headquarters ALF Phnom Penh, ALF/PP/23/G HQ 20th Division 9–31 October 1945, 4 November, Lt.-Col. Commanding Allied Force.

149 WO 172/7009, Secret War Diary Headquarters ALF Phnom Penh, ALF/PP/23/G, HQ 20th Division, Appendix, no.J2, 12 October 1945.

150 WO 172/7009, Secret War Diary Headquarters ALF Phnom Penh, ALF/PP/23/G HQ 20th Division 9–31 October 1945, 4 November, Lt.-Col. Commanding Allied Force.

151 WO 172/7009, Secret War Diary Headquarters ALF Phnom Penh, ALF/PP/23/G, HQ 20th Division, Appendix, no.J3, 12 October 1945.

152 WO 172/7009, Secret War Diary Headquarters ALF Phnom Penh, ALF/PP/23/G, HQ 20th Division, Appendix, no.J4, 13 October 1945.

153 Gracey 4/8, Gracey to the Recorder SEAC, no.1/DDG, 3 October 1946.

154 WO 203/2178, Gracey to CGS, no.02210, 16 October 1945.

155 WO 172/7009, Secret War Diary Headquarters ALF Phnom Penh, ALF/PP/23/G, HQ 20th Division 9–31 October 1945, 4 November, Lt.-Col. Commanding Allied Force.

156 AIR 40/1451, Sum.172, 22 October 1945.

157 Report by Mountbatten to CCS, 30 June 1947, *Documents Relating to British Involvement in the Indochina Conflict 1945–65*, London, 1965, pp. 47–52.

158 WO 172/7009, Secret War Diary Headquarters ALF Phnom Penh ALF/PP/23/G, HQ 20th Division 9–31 October 1945, 4 November, Lt.-Col. Commanding Allied Force; D.P. Chandler, *The Tragedy of Cambodian History: Politics, War and Revolution since 1945*, Yale, 1991, p. 27.

159 CAOM, GGI/65498, 'Etudes sur les movements rebelles au Cambodge 1942–1952', Annex, 'Le Nationalisme Khmer', pp. 1–35.

160 WO 172/7009, Secret War Diary Headquarters ALF Phnom Penh, ALF/PP/23/G, HQ 20th Division, ALF/PP/1/G, 26 October 1945.

161 WO 172/7009, Secret War Diary Headquarters ALF Phnom Penh, ALF/PP/23/G, HQ 20th Division ALF Phnom Penh to 20th Indian Division, 31 October 1945.

162 WO 172/7009, Headquarters ALF Phnom Penh, ALF/PP/23/G, 1–30 November Report, 3 December 1945.

163 WO 172/7009, Headquarters ALF Phnom Penh, ALF/PP/23/G, 1–31 December Report, 4 January 1946.

164 Lancaster, *op. cit.*

165 CAB 121/741, Dening to FO, no.543, 27 September 1945.

166 WO 106/4820, Memorandum on the instructions to be given to SEAC regarding Cambodia, (undated).

167 FO 371/46323/F6043/52/61, Balfour to FO, no.5903, 28 August 1945.

168 FO 371/46323/F6043/52/61, Minute by A.C.S. Adams, 31 August 1945.

169 FO 371/46323/F6043/52/61, Minute by I.A.D. Wilson-Young, 1 September 1945.

170 WO 106/4820, FE(0)(45)19, 1 September 1945, Treatment of the boundary between Siam and Indo-China in the proposed Siamese settlement.

171 CAB 21/1950, Minute by E.A. Armstrong, 6 September 1945.

172 WO 203/894, Headquarters SACSEAC Joint Logistical Planning Committee, 1 September 1945.

173 CAB 121/741, Dening to FO, no.543, 27 September 1945.

174 CAB 121/741, Halifax to FO, no.6760, 10 October 1945.

175 CAB 21/1950, Cabinet Far Eastern Committee, FE(0)(45)31, Minute by Armstrong, 21 September 1945.

176 CAB 121/742, SEACOS to COS, no.560, 2 December 1945.

177 WO 203/4432, Gracey to HQSACSEA, COS 47, 15 December 1945.

178 WO 203/2463, Evans to Pyman, no.0/220, 20 December 1945.

179 WO 203/2463, HQSACSEA Commission 1 Saigon to HQSEA, no. COS/168, 28 December 1945.

180 WO 203/2463, Gracey to Evans, no.COS 184, 7 January 1946.

181 WO 203/2463, Evans to Gracey, no.03189, 9 January 1946.

182 CAB 121/742, FO to SACSEAC, no.1330, 21 December 1945.

183 CAB 121/742, Wilson-Young to Price, 22 December 1945.

184 CAB 121/742, COS to SACSEA, COSSEA 448, 24 December 1945.

185 CAB 121/742, SACSEA to CO for COS, SEACOS 611, 11 January 1946.

186 WO 203/4455, COS to Mountbatten, COSSEA 448, 30 December 1945.

187 CAB 121/742, Mountbatten to COS, SEACOS 626, 26 January 1946.

188   CAB 121/742, JIC(46)4(0), 6 January 1946, Annex, 14(45).
189   CAB 21/1950, Dening to FO, no.353, 3 March 1946.
190   CAB 21/1950, Dening to FO, no.354, 3 March 1946.
191   CAB 21/1950, FO to Bangkok, no.208, 9 March 1946.
192   CAB 21/1950, Bird to Saigon, no.25, 13 March 1946.
193   CAB 21/1950, Meiklereid to FO, no.66, 16 March 1946.
194   CAB 21/1950, Meiklereid to FO, no.67, 16 March 1946.
195   CAB 21/1950, Meiklereid to FO, no.68, 17 March 1946.
196   CAB 21/1950, Meiklereid to FO, no.66, 16 March 1946.
197   CAB 21/1950, Thompson to Killearn, no.296, 26 March 1946.
198   CAB 21/1950, FO to Killearn, no.56, 28 March 1946.
199   WO 203/4924, Chiang Kai-Shek to Mountbatten, 28 August 1945.
200   MB 1/C53/51, Mountbatten to Chiang Kai-Shek, SC(?)/1763/C, 1 September 1945.
201   CAB 21/1950, Cabinet 68/6th meeting, Conclusions of the working party of the Far Eastern Committee, 4 September 1945.
202   BT 64/2864. Kenrick to Fisher, 3 August 1945.
203   BT 64/2864, Kenrick to Fisher, 8 September 1945; D.B. Harden to C.W. Sanders, 28 September 1945.
204   WO 203/5291, Mountbatten to WO, SAX 23358/QOPS, 25 September 1945.
205   BT 64/2864, WO to Mountbatten, 74087 cypher CA17, 15 September 1945.
206   WO 203/4117, Leclerc to Brigadier Montague-Jones, no.180/ECO/LI, (Undated).
207   CAB 120/708, WO to Mountbatten, 78609, 9 October 1945.
208   WO 203/5476, Mountbatten to Saigon Control Commission, NGS 213, 9 October 1945.
209   AIR 23/2376, HQSACSEA to Air Attaché Chungking, 15 October 1945.
210   CAB 121/742, Brain to FO, no.688, 1 November 1945.
211   WO 172/1789, Gracey to Mountbatten, SGN.241, COS 67, 26 October 1945.
212   WO 172/7009, Secret War Diary Headquarters ALF Phnom Penh, ALF/PP/23/G, HQ 20th Division, ALF/PP/1/G, 26 October 1945; Gracey 4/8, Gracey to the Recorder, SEAC, London, no.1/DDG, 3 October 1946.
213   FO 371/46309/F9668/11/61, SLAO(Far East)(45)109, 1 November 1945, Cabinet Committee On Supply Questions In Liberated And Conquered Areas Sub-Committee on the Far East, Minute by Kenrick.
214   CAB 122/512, Saigon to FO, no.28, 22 December 1945.
215   WO 203/4454/114/CA, Minute by Mountbatten on Secretary's minute 5/S4, 2 December 1945.
216   WO 203/4432, Mountbatten to SACSEA Commission no.1, ngs.510, 15 December 1945.
217   CAB 122/512, Précis of Colonel Walker-Chapman's report on Indo-China, Autumn 1945.
218   CAB 121/742. JIC(46)4(0), 6 January 1946, Annex, JIC14(45).
219   WO 203/4432, 'Points discussed with General Gracey', Saigon, 5 January 1946.
220   WO 203/5440, Dening to Mountbatten, no.7a, 7 January 1946.

221 FO 371/53957/F1393/8/61, Meiklereid to FO, no.4, 7 January 1946.
222 CAB 121/742, Brain to FO, no.688, 1 November 1945.
223 CAB 121/742, Meiklereid to FO, no.25, 24 January 1946.
224 PREM 8/211, part 1, CP(46)26, 28 January 1946, Memorandum by the Minister of Food, Appendix 2.
225 CAB 121/742, Mountbatten to COS, SEACOS 627, 28 January 1946.
226 WO 203/6263, Brief for Mountbatten, Flag L, 28 February 1946.
227 WO 203/6263, Brief for Mountbatten, 28 February 1946.
228 CAB 121/742, Mountbatten to COS, SEACOS 662, 17 March 1946.
229 CAB 121/742, COS(46)45th Meeting, 22 March 1946; COS(46)88, 23 March 1946, FO to Secretary COS Committee, 22 March 1946.
230 PREM 8/211, part 1, CP(46)28, 29 January 1946, Memorandum by the Minister for Food, Appendix.
231 PREM 8/211, part 2, WFS(46)19, 10 February 1946, Memorandum by the Minister for Food.
232 PREM 8/211, part 2, WFS(46), 2nd Cabinet Meeting, 12 February 1946; *Hansard*, Volume 419, 21 February 1946, pp. 1360–1.
233 PREM 8/63, Mountbatten to Cabinet and JSM, SEACOS 489, 24 September 1945.
234 PREM 8/63, DO(45)7th Meeting 18(Revise)(Secret), 5 October 1945.
235 PREM 8/63, DO(45)7th Meeting 18(Revise)(Secret), 5 October 1945, Enclosure to Annex 1.
236 PREM 8/63, Mountbatten to Cabinet and JSM, SEACOS 489, 24 September 1945.
237 WO 203/2178, (G)SD4 to Gplans, Lt.-Colonel Dawson, no.79006/SD4, 28 August 1945.
238 WO 203/2235, Mountbatten to CinC India, SAC 21266, 8 September 1945.
239 PREM 8/63, Mountbatten to Cabinet and JSM, SEACOS 490, 24 September 1945.
240 PREM 8/63, Hollis to Attlee, 28 September 1945.
241 CAB 80/97, COS(45)570(0), Memorandum by COS Committee, 8 September 1945.
242 Field Marshal Viscount Wavell to Lord Pethick-Lawrence, L/PO/10/22, New Delhi, 1 October 1945, N. Mansergh (ed.), *Constitutional Relations Between Britain and India: The Transfer of Power 1942–7. Volume 6: The Post War Phase: New Moves by the Labour Government 1 August 1945–22 March 1946*, London, 1971, pp. 304–9; Wavell to Lord Pethick-Lawrence, L/PO/10/22, Kashmir, 9 October 1945, pp. 319–24.
243 WO 203/2235, CinC India to Mountbatten, no 99620/SD5, 16 September 1945.
244 CAB 119/200, Director of Plans London to Director Plans SEAC, Magneta 186, 9 October 1945.
245 CAB 80/97, COS(45)598 1(0), Memorandum by COS Committee, 3 October 1945 FO to Secretary COS.
246 CAB 80/97 COS(45)607(0), Memorandum by COS Committee, 9 October 1945, Annex, DO OCC/2B, Slim to Brooke, 6 October 1945.
247 CAB 80/97, COS(45)619(0), Memorandum by WO, 13 October 1945, Annex 1, Cabinet to Mountbatten.

248   WO 172/1790, Mountbatten to WO, signal SAC27379, 3 November 1945.
249   CAB 121/742, Mountbatten to COS, SEACOS 555, 27 November 1945.
250   CAB 121/742, COS(45)333, Memorandum by the First Sea Lord, 24 December 1945.
251   *The Pentagon Papers, op. cit.*, pp. 17–18; Herring, *op. cit.*; WO 203/2236, Major Weaver to ARM India, no.2131SD2, December 1945.
252   WO 203/2236, Troopers to East Africa, no.78730LM3, 10 October 1945.
253   WO 203/4292, WO to CinC India and Mountbatten, no.81090Q(AE), 2 October 1945.
254   WO 203/2236, Weaver to Troopers, no.146 (undated); Troopers to HQALFSEA, no.89364/WSC, 14 December 1945.
255   WO 203/2236, Weaver to Mountbatten, no.2120SD2, 24 December 1945.
256   WO 203/2599, Weaver to CG USF IBT, no.161, no.31512/SD2 (undated).
257   WO 203/6066, ALFSEA to Mountbatten, Report of GSO OPS1, I/SM to French Indo-China Saigon 6–9 March 1946, Summary Report, no. 10410/G(0)1, 11 March 1946.
258   WO 203/6419, Browning to Maunsell, SAC 7486, 22 February 1946.
259   WO 203/6419, WO to ALFSEA, 99235Q(OPS)1, 27 February 1946.
260   WO 203/6419, Mission French Indo-China to Mountbatten, ALFSEA COMD40, 8 March 1946.
261   WO 203/4292, DofST to PSTO Middle East, DST France, SSTO Southern France, 21 December 1945, ALFSEA to WO, 6 December 1945.
262   CAB 21/1950, Halifax to Cabinet, no.464, 20 January 1946.
263   CAB 119/200, JSM to Cabinet, JSM 175, 26 January 1946.
264   CAB 119/205, COS(46)14th Meeting, 28 January 1946.
265   CAB 121/742, Annex to JP(46)30(Final), 19 February 1946, COS Committee JPS, draft telegram Cabinet to JSM, sent 20 February 1946.
266   CAB 121/742, COS(46)31st Meeting, 25 February 1946.
267   CAB 121/742, COS to Mountbatten, COSSEA 480, 1 March 1946.

Chapter 3   Lord Killearn, March 1946–May 1948

1   CAB 134/280, FE(0)(46)52, 16 April 1946, 'British Policy in the Far East', 31 December 1945.
2   CAB 124/1007, no.62, 17 August 1946, Proposed Statement revised by Morrison for Committee on Overseas Information Services, (01(46)10), R. Hyam (ed.), *BDEE, Series A. Volume 2, The Labour Government and the End of Empire 1945–1951: Part 1: High Policy*, London, 1991, pp. 306–9.
3   Lampson 6/2, p. 69, 18 February 1946.
4   Tarling, *op. cit.*; FO 371/53691/F4444/8/61, Minute by J. Wilson, 28 March 1946.
5   WO 203/6419, Killearn to FO, no.422, 31 March 1946.
6   Short, *op. cit.*, p. 51.
7   Irving, *op. cit.*
8   Tarling, *op. cit.*, p. 86.
9   Bills, *op. cit.*, p. 168.
10   Byrnes to Bonnet, 12 April 1946, Porter (ed.), *Vietnam, the Definitive Documentation of Human Decisions. Volume 1, op. cit.*, p. 102.

11 Short, *op. cit.*, p. 50.
12 Irving, *op. cit.*
13 Spector, *op. cit.*
14 Short, *op. cit.*, p. 52.
15 Lampson 6/2, p. 104, 9 April 1946.
16 FO 371/53964/F9041/8/61, Meiklereid to Bevin, no.67, 7 June 1946, Enclosure, Report by Lt.-Commander Simpson-Jones, 27 May 1946.
17 FO 371/53964/F941/8/61, Minutes of the Consul-General's 5th Meeting with Service Representatives, 26 June 1946.
18 Tarling, *op. cit.*, p. 153.
19 FO 371/53965/F9670/8/61, B.B.C monitoring, 11.49, FMM, 25 June 1946.
20 Lampson 6/3, p. 207, 13 August 1946; FO 371/53966/F140255/8/61, Meiklereid to Bevin, no.96, 26 August 1946.
21 FO 371/53966/F13898/8/61, Record of an interview with Narn, 13 September 1946,
22 WO 203/6352, Meiklereid to FO, no.387, 8 October 1946.
23 Hess, *op. cit.*, p. 200.
24 Bills, *op. cit.*, p. 170.
25 FO 800/464/FR46/24, Conversation between Bevin and Bidault, 11 October 1946.
26 Acheson to Moffat, 5 December 1946, Porter (ed.), *Vietnam, the Definitive Documentation of Human Decisions. Volume 1*, *op. cit.*, pp. 128–9.
27 FO 371/53968/F17052/8/61, Allen to Meiklereid, 4 December 1946.
28 FO 371/53969/F18065/8/61, Meiklereid to Killearn, no.520, 17 December 1946.
29 Hess, *op. cit.*, pp. 202–3.
30 Lampson 7/1, pp. 8–12, 16 January 1947.
31 FO 371/53968/F16235/8/61, Saigon to Bevin, no.133, 25 November 1946, Report on Mr Meiklereid's visit to Hanoi from 1–6 October 1946, 23 October 1946.
32 FO 371/53968/F16237/8/61, Minutes of the Consul-General's 21st Meeting with Service Representatives, 30 October 1946.
33 FO 371/53969/F17458/8/61, Meiklereid to Bevin, no.149, 22 November 1946.
34 Tarling, *op. cit.*, p. 158.
35 FO 371/53969/F18076/8/61, Minute by Dening, 16 December 1946.
36 FO 371/53969/F18076/8/61, Minute by Allen, 21 December 1946.
37 FO 371/53969/F18076/8/61, Dening to Harvey, 23 December 1946.
38 FO 371/63451/F5/5/86, Inverchapel to FO, no.7372, 31 December 1946.
39 Chen, *op. cit.*, p. 155; FO 371/63456/F13421/5/86, Appendix C.
40 FO 959/10, Saigon to FO, no.405, 27 December 1946.
41 Hess, *op. cit.*, p. 205.
42 Spector, *op. cit.*, p. 83.
43 Memorandum by Vincent to Acheson 8 January 1947, *FRUS: 1947: Volume 6: The Far East*, Washington D.C., 1972, pp. 58–9.
44 Gibbons, *op. cit.*, p. 26.
45 Siracusa, *op. cit.*, p. 96.
46 A.J. Rotter, *The Path to Vietnam*, Cornell, 1987, p. 71.

47   FO 371/53970/F18207/8/61, Minute by Dening, 31 January 1947.

48   FO 371/63452/F1127/5/86, Minute by Lambert, 1 February 1947.

49   FO 371/63452/F1127/5/86, Killearn to FO, no.208, from Allen, 27 January 1947.

50   FO 371/63452/F1551/5/86, Meiklereid to FO, no.56, 30 January 1946.

51   FO 371/63452/F1663/5/86, Meiklereid to FO, no.64, 6 February 1946.

52   Gardner, *op. cit.*, p. 79.

53   Telegram 335, 20 January 1947, *FRUS: 1947: Volume 6*, *op. cit.*, p. 64.

54   G.R. Hess, 'The First American Commitment in Indo-China: The Acceptance of the "Bao Dai Solution 1950"', *Diplomatic History*, vol.2, Fall 1978, p. 331.

55   R. Blum, *Drawing the line*, New York, 1979, p. 125.

56   Rotter, *op. cit.*, p. 14; Gibbons, *op. cit.*, p. 27.

57   Rotter, *op. cit.*, p. 52; J.L Gaddis, *The United States and the Origins of the Cold War 1941–47*, New York, 1972, p. 351.

58   Tarling, *op. cit.*, p. 267.

59   FO 371/63452/F1981/5/86, Killearn to Sargent, 3 February 1947.

60   FO 371/63454/F4149/5/86, Minutes of the Consul-General's 34th Meeting with Service Representatives, 12 March 1947.

61   FO 371/63454/F4469/5/86, Minutes of the Consul-General's 35th Meeting with Service Representatives, 19 March 1947.

62   FO 371/63454/F5281/5/86, Minutes of the Consul-General's 36th Meeting with Service Representatives, 26 March 1947.

63   Spector, *op. cit.*, p. 87, citing J. Buttinger, *Vietnam a Political History*, pp. 316–17.

64   Spector, *op. cit.*

65   FO 371/63455/F7229/5/86, Saigon to FO, 14 May 1947.

66   Department of State to US diplomats in Paris, Saigon and Hanoi, 13 May 1947, *The Pentagon Papers*, *op. cit.*, p. 31.

67   L. Gelb, 'Vietnam: The System Worked', *Foreign Policy*, Summer 1971, p. 142.

68   Adamthwaite, *op. cit.*, p. 227.

69   Spector, *op. cit.*, p. 84.

70   Hess, *The United States' Emergence as a Southeast Asian Power, 1940–1950*, *op. cit.*, p. 315.

71   Lampson 7/1, p. 100, 25 June 1947.

72   CAB 21/1956, Killearn to Bevin, no.163, 15 July 1947.

73   FO 371/63456/F13421/5/86, Appendix C; FO 371/63456/F10461/5/86, Gibbs to FO, no.204, 1 August 1947; J. Lacouture, *Ho Chi Minh*, Translated by Peter Wiles, London, 1968, p. 140.

74   FO 371/63456/F10461/5/86, Minute by J. Street (undated).

75   FO 371/63457/F14438/5/86, Unidentified Minute, 7 November 1947.

76   FO 800/462/FE47/21, Conversation between McNeil and Kennan, 11 August 1947.

77   FO 371/63456/F1114/5/86, Minute by Street, 14 August 1947.

78   C.B. McLane, *Soviet Strategies in South-East Asia*, Princeton, 1966, pp. 256, 350.

79   Speech by A. Zhdanov, 22 September 1947, Cameron (ed.), *Viet-Nam Crisis: A Documentary History. Volume 1*, *op. cit.*, p. 114; R.B. Smith, *An*

International History of the Vietnam War Volume 1: Revolution Versus Containment 1955–61, London, 1983, p. 14.

80   Spector, *op. cit.*, p. 85.
81   Chen, *op. cit.*, p. 189.
82   Smith, *op. cit.*, p. 72.
83   Spector, *op. cit.*, p. 91.
84   Hess, *op. cit.*, pp. 316–17.
85   FO 371/63457/F14930/5/86, G. Whitteridge to Falla, 17 December 1947.
86   The Secretary of State to Diplomatic and Consular Officers, 29 January 1948, *FRUS: 1948: Volume 6: The Far East, and Australia*, Washington D.C., 1974, p. 19.
87   CAB 129/33, CP(48)7, Memorandum by Bevin, 5 January 1948, Hyam (ed.), *BDEE, Series A. Volume 2: The Labour Government and the End of Empire 1945–1951: Part 2, op. cit.*, pp. 319–26.
88   Blum, *op. cit.*, p. 119.
89   WO 208/4926, Military Liaison Officer to Consul-General, Military Intelligence Report no.5, 16 February 1948; Military Intelligence Report no.7, 8 March 1948.
90   FO 371/6953B/F255/255/86, Dening to H.A. Clarke, 2 January 1948.
91   FO 371/6953B/F475/255/86, Chancery to SEA Dept, 42/2/48, 3 January 1948.
92   FO 371/6953B/F475/255/86, Clarke to Dening, 42/4/48, 14 January 1948.
93   FO 371/6953B/F1048/255/86, Minute by Street, 21 January 1948.
94   Lampson 7/2, pp. 18–19, 2 February 1948.
95   FO 371/69694/F2252/727/61G, Killearn to Bevin, 2 February 1948.
96   Rotter, *op. cit.*, pp. 14, 72; FO 371/69654/F4531/255/86, Graves to FO, Ref.327/4/48, 19 March 1948.
97   FO 371/69654/F4531/255/86, Minute by Mackworth Young, 1 April 1948.
98   FO 371/69654/F4210/255/86, Minute by Whitteridge, 26 March 1948.
99   Chen, *op. cit.*, p. 196.
100 FO 371/69689/F5922/286/61, Scrivener to Dening, 2:G:64:48, 14 April 1948.
101 Lampson 6/2, p. 97, 26 March 1946.
102 Lampson 6/2, p. 125, 1 May 1946.
103 CAB 21/1951, DO to Canada, Australia, New Zealand, South Africa, no.544, 28 May 1946.
104 Lampson 6/2, pp. 146–7, 30 May 1946.
105 CAB 21/1951, DO to Canada, Australia, New Zealand, South Africa, no.544, 28 May 1946.
106 CAB 21/1951, DO to Canada, Australia, New Zealand, South Africa, no. 630, 5 June 1946.
107 CAB 21/1951, DO to Canada, Australia, New Zealand, South Africa, no.631, 5 June 1946.
108 CAB 21/1951, DO to Canada, Australia, New Zealand, South Africa, no. 632, 5 June 1946.
109 CAB 21/1951, DO to Canada, Australia, New Zealand, South Africa, no.757, 9 August 1946.
110 Lampson 6/3, p. 207, 12 August 1946.

111 Lampson 6/3, pp. 211–12, 15 August 1946.
112 CAB 21/1951, DO to Canada, Australia, New Zealand, South Africa, no.850, 13 September 1946.
113 CAB 21/1951, DO to Canada, Australia, New Zealand, South Africa, no.362, 17 August 1946.
114 CAB 21/1951, DO to Canada, Australia, New Zealand, South Africa, no.850, 13 September 1946; CAB 21/1951, DO to Canada, Australia, New Zealand, South Africa, no.362, 17 August 1946.
115 CAB 21/1951, DO to Canada, Australia, New Zealand, South Africa, no.850, 13 September 1946.
116 CAB 21/1951, Meiklereid to Bangkok, no.100, 26 August 1946.
117 CAB 21/1951, Thompson to FO, no.1209, 29 August 1946.
118 CAB 21/1951, Meiklereid to FO, no.254, 2 September 1946.
119 CAB 21/1951, Report of H.J.K. Toms, Straits Steamship Co. Ltd. visit to Siam 15–26 August 1946, circulated at Cabinet 3 October 1946.
120 CAB 119/201, FO to COS, COS 1356/6, 3 November 1946.
121 CAB 119/201, COS to SACSEA, COSSEA 586, 9 November 1946.
122 CAB 119/201, Stopford to COS, SEACOS 784, 12 November 1946.
123 CAB 119/201, COS 14 14/6, 15 December 1946.
124 CAB 119/201, COS 14 63/6, 22 December 1946, Annex 1, letter from FO F16703/10/40, 21 November 1946; Annex 2, FO to COS, 22 November 1946.
125 CAB 119/201, COS 14 63/6, 22 December 1946, Annex 3, Draft to SACSEA (undated), agreed COS(46)171, 25 November 1946; Stopford to COS, SEACOS 793, 25 November 1946.
126 Draft by the India Office (undated), L/P&S/12/4662:ff4–5, 'Views of the Government of India', Mansergh (ed.), *Constitutional Relations Between Britain and India: The Transfer of Power 1942–7: Volume 6, op. cit.*, pp. 1035–7.
127 Rotter, *op. cit.*, p. 43.
128 *Hansard*, Volume 433, 12 February 1947, p. 361.
129 CAB 21/1954, Killearn to FO, 17.6.46, Stockwell (ed.), *BDEE, Series B Volume 3: Malaya Part 1, op. cit.*, pp. 246–52.
130 CAB 122/1069, Mountbatten to COS, SEACOS 682, 12 April 1946.
131 WO 203/6276, 'Directive on food' for Killearn, 23 March 1946.
132 WO 203/6276, 'World Food Situation', 23 March 1946.
133 PREM 8/211, part 3, WFS(46)6th Meeting, 12 March 1946.
134 PREM 8/211, part 3, WFS(46)75, 21 March 1946, Minute by the Cabinet Secretary.
135 PREM 8/211, part 3, WFS(46)83, 25 March 1946, Memorandum by the Minister of Food; WO 203/6276, PAO(SEA), 2946/Q2, 'Food Situation in Southeast Asia and Action Required Immediately to Increase Exports of Rice', 20 March 1946.
136 WO 203/6276, Special Commissioner's Conference on Food, Minutes, 26 March 1946.
137 WO 203/6276, Special Commissioner's Conference on Food, Minutes, Item 5, 26 March 1946.
138 WO 203/6276, Special Commissioner's Conference on Food, Minutes, Item 2, 26 March 1946.

139 WO 203/6276, Special Commissioner's Conference on Food, Report by Kirkwood, 22 March 1946.
140 WO 203/6276, Special Commissioner's Conference on Food, Minutes, p. 193, 26 March 1946.
141 WO 203/6276, Special Commissioner's Conference on Food, Minutes, Item 11, 28 March 1946.
142 WO 203/6276, Special Commissioner's Conference on Food, Minutes of Sub-Committee no.1, 27 March 1946, PAO(SEA), 145/39, 30 March 1946.
143 FO 371/53963/F6337/8/61, Report by Meiklereid on northern French Indo-China, 11 April 1946.
144 FO 371/53962/F5874/8/61, Forester to McEuen, 5 April 1946.
145 FO 371/53964/F8576/8/61, James to Whitteridge, 1 June 1946.
146 FO 800/461/FE46/72, Killearn to FO, no.285, 21 April 1946.
147 WO 203/6276, Killearn to FO, SAC 11769, 25 April 1946.
148 WO 203/6276, Killearn to Governor Burma, Ceylon, Malaya Union, Singapore, CinC Hong Kong, BMA British Borneo, SAC 108111, 9 April 1946.
149 PREM 8/211, part 3, WFS(46)119, 31 May 1946, Cabinet Report by the Chair of the 'Official Committee on Food Supplies from Southeast Asia and Certain Other Territories'.
150 WO 203/6276, Special Commissioner's Conference on Food, Minutes, p. 14, 15 April 1946.
151 PREM 8/211, part 3, WFS(46)123, 9 July 1946, Cabinet Report by the Chair of the 'Official Committee on Food Supplies from Southeast Asia and Certain Other Territories'.
152 The UN IEFC replaced the interallied Combined Food Board. R.J. Hammond, *Food and Agriculture in Britain 1939–1945*, London, 1954, p. 183; PREM 8/211, part 3, WFS(46)123, 9 July 1946, Cabinet Report by the Chair of the 'Official Committee on Food Supplies from Southeast Asia and Certain Other Territories'.
153 Lampson 6/3, p. 186, 7 July 1946.
154 CAB 21/1956, Killearn to FO, no.1189, 4 July 1946.
155 FO 371/53965/F10994/8/61, Minutes of the Consul-General's 7th Meeting with Service Representatives, 10 July 1946.
156 FO 371/53966/F11987/8/61, Minutes of the Consul-General's 9th Meeting with Service Representatives, 24 July 1946.
157 CAB 21/1956, Killearn to FO, no.1418, 25 July 1946.
158 Lampson 6/3, pp. 190–1, 18 July 1946.
159 FO 371/53966/F12556/8/61, Minutes of the Consul-General's 11th Meeting with Service Representatives, 7 August 1946.
160 WO 203/6352, Killearn to FO, no.1703, 19 August 1946; CAB 21/1956, Killearn to FO, no.1664, part 2, 15 August 1946.
161 CAB 21/1956, Killearn to FO, no.1664, part 1, 15 August 1946.
162 CAB 21/1956, Killearn to FO, Despatch 32, 24 August 1946.
163 WO 203/6325, Killearn to FO, no.1705, 19 August 1946; Lampson 6/3, pp. 210–2, 15 August 1946.
164 Lampson 6/3, p. 236, 2 September 1946.
165 FO 800/461/FE46/90, Killearn to FO, no.1511, 1 August 1946.
166 CAB 21/1956, Killearn to FO, Despatch 32, 24 August 1946.

167 Lampson 6/3, p. 248, 17 September 1946.
168 PREM 8/211, part 4, Nathan to Attlee, 9 September 1946.
169 WO 208/4923, Killearn to FO, no.2026, 8 September 1946.
170 FO 643/56, Saigon to FO, no.105, 10 September 1946.
171 CAB 21/1956, Killearn to FO, no.2176, 19 September 1946.
172 CAB 21/1956, Killearn to FO, no.2266, 26 September 1946.
173 CAB 21/1956, Killearn to FO, no.2416, 10 October 1946.
174 CAB 21/1956, Empson to FO, no.2557, 24 October 1946.
175 FO 371/53967/F16071/8/61, Meiklereid to FO, no.326, 4 November 1946.
176 FO 371/53969/F17458/8/61, Meiklereid to Bevin, no.149, 22 November 1946.
177 CAB 21/1956, Empson to FO, no.2769, 14 November 1946.
178 CAB 121/742, Meiklereid to FO, no.16, 8 January 1947.
179 FO 800/462/FE47/3, Bevin to Attlee, PM/47/19, 23 January 1947; Attachment 'Rice January–June 1947'.
180 CAB 21/1956, Monthly Economic Bulletin, Volume 2, no.2, February 1947, Killearn, 11 March 1947.
181 CAB 21/1956, Monthly Economic Bulletin, Volume 4, no.9, September 1949, MacDonald, 30 September 1949.
182 MAF 97/2837, Gibbs to FO, no.5, 13 September 1948.
183 CAB 21/1956, Monthly Economic Bulletin, Volume 2, no.2, February 1947, Killearn, 11 March 1947.
184 Lampson 7/1, pp. 8–12, 16 January 1947.
185 CAB 21/1956, Monthly Economic Bulletin, Volume 2, no.2, February 1947, Killearn, 11 March 1947; Volume 4, no.9, September 1949, MacDonald, 30 September 1949.
186 FO 371/63460/F3711/6/86, Meiklereid to FO, no.32, 7 March 1947.
187 Lampson 7/1, pp. 19–20, 27 January 1947.
188 FO 371/63545/F10010/1147/10, Killearn to Bevin, 15 July 1947.
189 FO 371/63545/F15073/1147/61, '3rd Quarter Report 1947', Killearn to Bevin, 5 November 1947.
190 CAOM, INDO/NF/1340, British Vice-Consul for India to Consulate-General Saigon, 20 January 1947; Sarojini Naidu to Sihanouk, 20 January 1947; Minute by Ministry for France Overseas, 30 July 1947.
191 Lampson 7/1, pp. 61–2, 11 April 1947.
192 FO 371/63518/F7103/56/61, Wright to Dening, 14 May 1947.
193 FO 371/63544/F8918/1147/61, 1st Quarter 1947 Report, Killearn to Bevin, no.150, 17 June 1947.
194 FO 371/63518/F16507/56/61, Minute by Dening, 10 December 1947.
195 FO 371/63455/F9591/5/86, Whitteridge to Bourdillon, 17 July 1947.
196 Lampson 7/1, p. 178, 3 October 1947.
197 WO 203/4933, Sir Keith Park, SAC 325th Meeting, 22 March 1946.
198 CAB 121/742, COS to Mountbatten, COSSEA 506, 29 March 1946.
199 WO 203/6276, 'Movements and transportation considerations affecting the export of rice', 22 March 1946; WO 203/6209, HQSACSEA to HQ Air Command SEA, 101/SD, 20 May 1946; FO 371/53964/F9106/8/61, Meiklereid to Bevin, no.60, 24 May 1946.
200 FO 371/53965/F10384/8/61, Minutes of the Consul-General's 5th Meeting with Service Representatives, 26 June 1946; FO 371/53965/F10994/8/61,

Minutes of the Consul-General's 7th Meeting with Service Representatives, 10 July 1946.
201   WO 2036352, Killearn to D'Argenlieu, no.327, 27 October 1946.
202   WO 208/4923, Meiklereid to FO, no.195, 8 July 1946.
203   FO 371/53970/F18413/8/61, Minute by Anderson, 31 December 1946.
204   FO 371/53970/F18418/8/61, Inverchapel to FO, no.7339, 28 December 1946.
205   FO 371/63459/F132/6/86, FO to Paris, no.19, 3 January 1947.
206   FO 371/63459/F132/6/86, Air Ministry to Air HQ Burma, MSX 479, 6 January 1947.
207   FO 371/63460/F1905/6/86, Gibson to Anderson, 12 February 1947.
208   CAB 121/742, Killearn to FO, no.202, 26 January 1947.
209   CAB 121/742, Cooper to FO, no.96A, 29 January 1947.
210   CAB 121/742, Cooper to FO, no.121, 6 February 1947.
211   CO 533/2194, Clarke to Dening, 3 January 1947.
212   CO 533/2194, Governor of Hong Kong to CO, no.8, 28 January 1947; FO 371/63455/F8114/5/86, Minute by Street, 12 June 1947.
213   FO 371/63547/F1969/1969/61, Paper by Dening, 7 February 1947.
214   FO 371/63547/F1969/1969/61, Minutes of meeting held by Bevin to discuss Southeast Asia, 10 February 1947.
215   CAB 121/742, Cabinet Session 170/1, 1st Meeting, 11 February 1947.
216   Hansard, Volume 433, 19 February 1947, pp. 174–5.
217   FO 371/63453/F2431/5/86, Minute by Whitteridge, 20 February 1947.
218   CAB 121/742, Thompson to FO, no.225, 10 March 1947.
219   CAB 121/742, Cooper to FO, no.231, 22 March 1947.
220   Hansard, Volume 435, 24 March 1947, p. 827.
221   DEFE 6/2, JP(47)68(Final), 26 July 1947.
222   FO 371/63455/F7371/5/86, India Office to WO, no.3942, 22 May 1947.
223   FO 371/63455/F7371/5/86, Minute by Allen, 8 June 1947.
224   FO 371/63455/F8541/5/86, Allen to Massigli, 11 July 1947.
225   FO 371/63455/F8114/5/86, Minute by Street, 12 June 1947.
226   Chen, op. cit., p. 189.
227   FO 371/63458/F16960/5/86, Crowther to Bevin, no.168, 15 December 1947.
228   FO 371/63543/F7265/1147/61G, Dening to Bevin, 7 May 1947.
229   FO 371/63544/F7572/1147/61G, Minute by K. Christofas, 17 April 1947.
230   FO 371/63544/F7728/1147/61G, Minute by Attlee to Foreign and Colonial Secretaries, 31 May 1947; Bevin to Killearn, 6 June 1947.
231   FO 800/462/FE48/8, Sargent to Attlee, 7 January 1948.

Chapter 4   The Winds of Change, May 1948–January 1950

1   FO 371/69689/F5858/286/61, P.F. Grey to Dening, 15 April 1948.
2   Hess, 'The First American Commitment in Indo-China: The Acceptance of the "Bao Dai Solution 1950"', Diplomatic History, op. cit., p. 338; The Pentagon Papers, op. cit., p. 78.
3   Hess, op. cit., p. 349.
4   Holland, op. cit., p. 183.

5   A. Bullock, *Ernest Bevin Foreign Secretary 1945–51*, London, 1983, p. 32.
6   J. Darwin, 'British Decolonisation since 1945: A pattern or a puzzle?', *Journal of Imperial and Commonwealth History*, vol.12, January 1984, p. 194.
7   W.J. Duiker, *US Containment Policy and the Conflict in Indochina*, Stanford, 1994, p. 76.
8   Rotter, *op. cit.*, p. 14.
9   C. Fenn, *Ho Chi Minh: A Biographical Introduction*, New York, 1973, p. 84.
10 FO 371/69655/F7187/256/86, Minute by Mackworth Young, 26 May 1948.
11 CO 537/3334, Harvey to FO, no.694, 21 May 1948.
12 FO 371/69655/F7472/255/86, Gibbs to FO, no.59, 24 May 1948.
13 CO 537/3334, Vietnam-US Friendship Association INC, 15 May 1948.
14 CO 537/3334, Gibbs to FO, no.65, 7 June 1948.
15 CO 537/3334, Gibbs to FO, no.66, 8 June 1948; FO 371/69656/F7866/255/86, Minute by Mackworth Young, 10 June 1948.
16 FO 371/69656/F8706/255/86, Gibbs to Grey, 3 June 1948.
17 CO 537/3334, Vietnam-US Friendship Association INC, 4 July 1948.
18 Hess, *The United States' Emergence as a Southeast Asian Power, 1940–1950*, *op. cit.*, p. 321.
19 FO 371/69657/F10042/255/86, Clarke to Dening, 42/86/48, 14 July 1948.
20 FO 371/69657/F10042/255/86, Minute by Mackworth Young, 23 July 1948.
21 FO 371/69657/F10613/255/61, Lloyd to Bevin, 26 July 1948.
22 CO 537/3334, Gibbs to Bevin, 17 August 1948; FO 371/69657/F11803/255/86, Harvey to FO, no.162, 21 August 1948.
23 A. Marie 'Declaration to the National Assembly', 19 August 1948, Cameron (ed.), *Viet-Nam Crisis: A Documentary History. Volume 1*, *op. cit.*, pp. 118–20.
24 FO 371/69657/F11803/255/86, Harvey to FO, no.162, 21 August 1948.
25 FO 371/69657/F11899/255/86, British Embassy Paris to FO, 42/101/48, 24 August 1948.
26 Vickery, *op. cit.*, p. 10; Smith, *op. cit.*, p. 73.
27 FO 371/69658/F12842/255/86, Gibbs to FO, 7 September 1948.
28 FO 371/69658/F12842/255/86, Minute by Lloyd, 7 October 1948.
29 CO 537/3334, Consul-General Saigon to British Embassy Paris, 18 September 1948.
30 FO 371/69658/F13855/255/86, Gibbs to FO, no.8, 29 September 1948.
31 FO 371/69658/F14890/255/86, Clarke to Dening, 42/138/48, 20 October 1948.
32 Department of State Policy Statement, 27 September 1948. Porter (ed.), *Vietnam, the Definitive Documentation of Human Decisions. Volume 1*, *op. cit.*, pp. 178–81.
33 FO 371/69658/F15982/255/86, Graves to Grey, no.5189, 12 November 1948.
34 CO 537/3334, Harvey to FO, no.1699, 23 November 1948.
35 CO 537/3334, Hopson to FO, no.154, 29 November 1948.
36 Tarling, *op. cit.*, p. 308.
37 FO 371/69659/F18068/255/86, Graves to Dening, 327/38/48, 7 December 1948.

38 CO 537/3334, Gibbs to FO, no.165, 13 December 1948.
39 FO 959/20, Gibbs to Grey, 13 December 1948; CO 537/3334, Gibbs to FO, no.165, 13 December 1948.
40 CAB 134/285, FE(0)(48)9th Meeting 8 December 1948.
41 FO 371/69659/F18067/255/82, Dening to Bevin, 16 December 1948.
42 FO 800/462/FE49/1, Bevin to Attlee, PM/49/3, 5 January 1949, Attachment 'Report by Dening'.
43 FO 800/462/FE49/1, Bevin to Attlee, PM/49/3, 5 January 1949.
44 DEFE 4/18, COS(48)180th Meeting, 16 December 1948, JIC(48)110 Final, 1 December 1948, Annex.
45 Chandler, *op. cit.*, p. 41.
46 FO 371/75960/F720/1015/86, Clarke to Dening, 7 January 1949; Minute by Bevin (undated).
47 Tarling, *op. cit.*, p. 374.
48 FO 800/465/FR49/4, Conversation between Bevin and Schuman, Item 17, 14 January 1949.
49 Kiernan, *op. cit.*, p. 66.
50 FO 371/75960/F1125/1015/86, Harvey to FO, no.85, 20 January 1949.
51 Spector, *op. cit.*, p. 95.
52 Kiernan, *op. cit.*
53 Tarling, *op. cit.*
54 FO 371/75960/F1540/1015/86, Minute by Mackworth Young, 2 February 1949; Minute by Scott, 5 February 1949; Dening to Clarke, 8 February 1949.
55 Gibbons, *op. cit.*, p. 49.
56 Hess, *op. cit.*, p. 322.
57 FO 371/75960/F3420/1015/86, FO to High Commissioners, Qno.7, 5 March 1949.
58 Rotter, *op. cit.*, p. 91.
59 FO 371/75961/F3519/1015/86, Memorandum by R. Blackham, 9 March 1949.
60 Rotter, *op. cit.*, pp. 91–2.
61 FO 371/75961/F4159/1015/86, Gibbs to Bevin, no.28, 15 March 1949.
62 FO 371/75961/F4159/1015/86, Minute by Dening, 28 March 1949.
63 FO 371/75961/F4599/1015/86, Scrivener to Saigon, 160/44/49, 22 March 1949.
64 Blum, *op. cit.*, p. 107.
65 FO 371/75961/F4341/1015/86, Minute by Christofas, 25 March 1949.
66 FO 371/75961/F4667/1015/86, Clarke to FO, no.352, 30 March 1949.
67 Spector, *op. cit.*
68 FO 371/75962/F5512/1015/86, Minute by Lloyd, 22 April 1949.
69 FO 371/75962/F5512/1015/86, Scott to Gibbs, 5 May 1949.
70 FO 371/75962/F6378/1015/86, Gibbs to Bevin, no.40, 19 April 1949.
71 Kiernan, *op. cit.*, p. 65.
72 MJM 27/5/56, MacDonald to Roux, 7 May 1949.
73 MJM 27/8/4–17, Broadcast by MacDonald, 15 May 1949.
74 FO 371/75963/F6721/1015/86, Minute by Blackham, 12 May 1949.
75 FO 371/75963/F6721/1015/86, Minute by Dening, 17 May 1949.
76 Blum, *op. cit.*, pp. 111, 115.

77   Gibbons, *op. cit.*, p. 50.
78   Blum, *op. cit.*
79   FO 371/75963/F7634/1015/86, Hopson to FO, 18 May 1949; Minute by Blackham, 27 May 1949.
80   FO 371/75963/F7490/1015/86, British Embassy Paris to FO, 20 May 1949.
81   Gibbons, *op. cit.*
82   Spector, *op. cit.*
83   *The Pentagon Papers, op. cit.*, p. 51.
84   FO 371/75963/F8308/1015/86, Gibbs to Scott, 24 May 1949.
85   FO 371/75963/F8308/1015/86, Minute by Blackham, 13 June 1949.
86   Blum, *op. cit.*, pp. 116, 122–3; Hess, *op. cit.*, pp. 322–4.
87   Spector, *op. cit.*
88   FO 371/75965/F9644/1015/86, Minute by Graves, 10 June 1949.
89   Hess, *op. cit.*; FO 371/75964/F9052/1015/86, Minute by Scott, 18 June 1949.
90   FO 371/75964/F9257/1015/86, FO to Saigon, no.89, 27 June 1949; FO 371/75964/F9051/1015/86, Minute by Lloyd, 15 June 1949.
91   FO 959/30, Bevin to MacDonald, no.89, 27 June 1949; FO 371/75965 /F9601/1015/86, Hopson to FO, no.106, 29 June 1949.
92   FO 371/75964/F9051/1015/86, State Department Memorandum, 15 June 1949; Minute by Lloyd, 15 June 1949.
93   FO 371/75964/F9264/1015/86, High Commissioner India to CRO, no. X1155, 23 June 1949.
94   FO 371/75964/F9051/1015/86, Minute by Lloyd, 15 June 1949.
95   FO 371/F75966/F11110/1015/86, Hopson to Scott, 12 July 1949; FO 371/F75967/F12798/1015/86, Thompson to FO, no.625, 25 August 1949.
96   FO 371/75966/F11793/1015/86, Hopson to Scott, 19 July 1949.
97   FO 371/75965/F10846/1015/86, Hopson to Scott, Saigon, 5 July 1949; FO 371/75965/F10829/1015/86, Minute by Blackham, 22 July 1949.
98   MJM 28/3/28–32, Speech by MacDonald, 12 August 1949.
99   Smith, *op. cit.*
100   Kiernan, *op. cit.*, p. 60.
101   FO 371/75967/F13255/1015/86, Scott to Dening, 3 September 1949.
102   FO 371/75968/F14716/1015/86, Scott to Ford, 25 October 1949.
103   FO 371/75969/F15704/1015/86, Dening to Bevin, 12 September 1949.
104   FO 800/462/FE49/25, Meeting at the State Department, 18 September 1949.
105   Short, *op. cit.*, p. 78.
106   FO 800/462, Franks to FO, from Bevin, no.4532, 19 September 1949.
107   FO 371/75568/F13946/1015/86, Scott to Hood, 23 September 1949.
108   Kiernan, *op. cit.*, p. 74.
109   FO 371/75980/F15658/10340/86, Bangkok to FO, no.25, 10 October 1949.
110   Blum, *op. cit.*, p. 147.
111   FO 371/75969/F155441/1015/86, Minute by Scott, 13 October 1949.
112   FO 371/75969/F15960/1015/86, Clarke to Dening, 20 October 1949.
113   PREM 8/964, Attlee to Bevin, M193/49, 22 October 1949.

114 FO 371/75969/F15960/1015/86, Dening to Clarke, 28 October 1949.
115 Smith, *op. cit.*
116 Ambassador E. Stanton to Acheson, Bangkok, 3 November 1949, Porter (ed.), *Vietnam, the Definitive Documentation of Human Decisions. Volume 1, op. cit.*, p. 213.
117 MAF 97/2837, FO to Washington, no.Intel 395, 31 October 1949.
118 FO 371/75967/F13711/1015/86, High Commissioner Australia to CRO, no.627, 22 September 1949; Acting High Commissioner Ceylon to CRO, no.746, 5 October 1949; CRO to High Commissioners, no.331, 11 September 1949.
119 PREM 8/1221, Memorandum by Bevin, SAC(49)17, 14 December 1949.
120 PREM 8/964, MacDonald to FO, no.919, 4 November 1949.
121 PREM 8/1221, Memorandum by Bevin, SAC(49)17, 14 December 1949.
122 CAB 134/288, FE(0)(49)82 Final, 8 December 1949, Report on Bukit Serene.
123 PREM 8/964, Minute by Attlee, 6 November 1949.
124 PREM 8/964, Bevin to Attlee, 6 November 1949.
125 PREM 8/964, Attlee to Creech Jones, 18 November 1949.
126 Smith, *op. cit.*
127 FO 371/75969/F16497/1015/86, Scott to Hood, 9 November 1949.
128 FO 800/465/FR49/24, Harvey to FO, no.278, from Bevin, 9 November 1949.
129 FO 800/448/CONF49/19, Meeting of the Foreign Ministers of Western Powers, Item 6C, 10 November 1949; FO 371/76004/F17167/1017/6, FO brief for Bevin to Attlee, 10 November 1949.
130 MJM 20/9/5, MacDonald to FO, no.1018, 28 November 1949; MJM 28/8/76–8, Minute by MacDonald, 29 November 1949.
131 FO 371/75970/F16640/1015/86, Scott to Bevin, 10 November 1949.
132 MJM 20/9/3–4, MacDonald to FO, no.1017, 28 November 1949.
133 MJM 28/8/76–8, Minute by MacDonald, 29 November 1949.
134 MJM 20/9/6–8, MacDonald to FO, no.1019, 28 November 1949.
135 MJM 28/8/81, Minute by MacDonald, 29 November 1949.
136 MJM 20/9/6–8, MacDonald to FO, no.1019, 28 November 1949.
137 MJM 20/9/12–13, MacDonald to FO, no.1020, 29 November 1949.
138 PREM 8/1221, Memorandum by Bevin, SAC(49)17, 14 December 1949.
139 Rotter, *op. cit.*, p. 179.
140 MJM 28/9/16–17, MacDonald to Lockhead, 2 December 1949.
141 MJM 28/9/61–2, MacDonald to Dening, 9 December 1949.
142 DEFE 5/18, COS(49)436, Memorandum by COS Committee, 12 December 1949, copy of a memorandum (Ref:JIC(FE)(49)56), Head of Far East Defence Secretariat Singapore to Secretary COS Committee, 2 December 1949; Appendix 2, JIC(FE)(49)56(Final) 10 November 1949.
143 CAB 134/286, FE(0)(49)18th Meeting, Cabinet Far Eastern Committee, 8 December 1949.
144 FO 371/75893/F18687/1055/86, Minute by Scott, 15 December 1949.
145 PREM 8/1221, Memorandum by Bevin, SAC(49)17, 14 December 1949.
146 CAB 134/288, FE(0)(49)79(Final), 15 December 1949, 'Indo-China: Brief for the United Kingdom Delegation to the Colombo Conference', 14 December 1949.

147 PREM 8/1221, SAC(49)8th Meeting, 16 December 1949.
148 PREM 8/1221, Bevin to Schuman, no.3391, 16 December 1949.
149 FO 800/462/FE49/40, Franks to FO, no.5855, 17 December 1949.
150 FO 371/75983/F19106/1055/86, P. Murray to FO, no.1098, 19 December 1949; Murray to FO, no.1128, 29 December 1949.
151 PREM 8/1221, Schuman to Bevin, 22 December 1949.
152 FO 371/75983/F19627/1055/86, Dening to Harvey, 29 December 1949.
153 FO 371/75983/F19625/1055/86, Hayter to Dening, 23 December 1949.
154 FO 800/462/FE49/42, Bevin to Attlee, PM49/160, 23 December 1949.
155 PREM 8/1221, Massigli to Strang, 27 December 1949.
156 PREM 8/1221, McNeil to Massigli, 29 December 1949.
157 FO 800/462/FE49/46, McNeil to Attlee, 29 December 1949.
158 PREM 8/1221, McNeil to Attlee, PM/HM/49/161, 29 December 1949.
159 PREM 8/1221, Minute by Attlee, 30 December 1949.
160 DEFE 5/10, COS(48)74(0), Memorandum by COS Committee, 6 April 1948, WO brief part 1.
161 FO 371/69694/F6644/727/61, Grey for Bevin to H.M. Representatives, 10 May 1948.
162 FO 371/69694/F10350/727/61, Revised brief by Lloyd for Bevin, 17 July 1948.
163 MJM 22/2/36–7, MacDonald to Sir Ralph Hone, 2 June 1948.
164 FO 371/69694/F12630/727/61, Graves to FO, 7 September 1948.
165 FO 371/69694/F10265/727/61, Franks to FO, no.3587, 21 July 1948.
166 FO 371/69694/F9634/727/61, Whitington to Grey, 2G/48, 2 July 1948.
167 FO 371/69694/F10265/727/61, Franks to FO, no.3587, 21 July 1948.
168 FO 959/20, Grey to Gibbs, 24 June 1948.
169 MJM 22/2/71–3, Sir R.S. Stevenson to MacDonald, 12 July 1948, Enclosure, Minute by Lamb, 8 July 1948.
170 FO 371/69657/F9145/255/86, Minute by Mackworth Young, 3 July 1948.
171 FO 371/69657/F9461/255/86, Gibbs to Grey, 29 June 1948.
172 FO 371/69657/F9145/255/86, Minute by Dening, 14 July 1948.
173 Tarling, *op. cit.*, p. 304.
174 FO 371/69657/F10613/255/61, Lloyd to Bevin, 26 July 1948.
175 FO 371/69657/F11028/255/61, Minute by Mackworth Young, 11 August 1948.
176 Blum, *op. cit.*, p. 109.
177 Rotter, *op. cit.*, p. 43.
178 MAF 97/2837, Gibbs to FO, no.5, 13 September 1948.
179 FO 371/69653A/F13174/72/86, Gibbs to FO, 14 September 1948.
180 FO 371/69657/F12048/255/86, Lloyd to Battye, 10 September 1948.
181 FO 371/69658/F14021/255/86, Battye to Lloyd, 4 October 1948.
182 FO 371/69658/F14343/255/86, FO to Saigon, no.104, 18 October 1948; FO 371/69658/F14798/255/86, Minute by Mackworth Young, 23 October 1948.
183 Department of State Policy Statement on Indo-China, 27 September 1948, *FRUS: 1948: Volume 6, op. cit.*, pp. 43–9.
184 Blum, *op. cit.*
185 FO 959/23, Gibbs to Scrivener, no.82, 19 October 1948.
186 McLane, *op. cit.*, p. 364.

187 FO 371/69658/F15982/255/86, Graves to Grey, no.5189, 12 November 1948.
188 FO 371/69690/F15948/286/61/G, Minute by Christofas, 15 November 1948.
189 FO 371/69658/F15982/255/86, FO to Singapore, no.1284, 17 November 1948.
190 J.L. Gaddis, *Strategies of Containment, op. cit.*, p. 57.
191 Application of the DRVN for membership in the UN, 22 November 1948, Cole (ed.), *Conflict In Indochina and International Repercussions: A Documentary History, 1945–1955, op. cit.*, p. 70.
192 FO 371/69659/F18239/255/86, Minute by Mackworth Young, 18 January 1949.
193 Blum, *op. cit.*, p. 127.
194 CAOM, INDO/NF/1395, British Embassy in Paris, Aide Memoire, 29 December 1948.
195 R. Aldrich, *British Intelligence, Strategy and the Cold War 1945–51*, London, 1992, p. 323.
196 CAB 134/285, FE(0)(48)8th Meeting, Cabinet Far Eastern Committee, 4 December 1948.
197 CAB 21/1947, FE(0)(48)34(Revise), 10 December 1948, The Situation in China.
198 Blum, *op. cit.*, p. 109.
199 FO 371/69659/F18067/255/82, Dening to Bevin, 16 December 1948.
200 MJM, 22/4/43, MacDonald to Mackay, 14 December 1948.
201 FO 800/462/FE49/1, Bevin to Attlee, PM/49/3, 5 January 1949, Attachment 'Report by Dening'.
202 MAF 97/2837, Hopson to FO, no.6, 10 May 1949.
203 MAF 83/2307, Ferguson to Pratt, 15 December 1948.
204 FO 800/465/FR49/4, Conversation between Bevin and Schuman, Item 14, 14 January 1949.
205 FO 800/465/FR49/4, Conversation between Bevin and Schuman, Item 16, 14 January 1949.
206 FO 800/465/FR49/4, Conversation between Bevin and Schuman, Item 17, 14 January 1949.
207 E. Colbert, *Southeast Asia in International Politics 1941–1956*, London 1977, p. 141.
208 CAB 21/1947, COS(49)29, 20 January 1949.
209 MAF 83/2307, Haig to Christofas, 25 February 1949.
210 CO 537/4832, FE(0)(49)9, Cabinet Far Eastern Committee, 24 February 1949.
211 MJM 22/6/80-1, MacDonald to Killearn, 26 February 1949.
212 Rotter, *op. cit.*, p. 61.
213 FO 371/75961/F3519/1015/86, Memorandum by Blackham, 9 March 1949.
214 FO 371/76013/F4286/10119/61G, Dening to Bevin, 16 March 1949; Minute by Barcley, 17 March 1949.
215 MJM 27/5/84-7, Speech by MacDonald, 24 March 1949.
216 FO 371/75961/F3620/1015/86, Note by FO, 24 March 1949.
217 FO 371/75962/F4920/1015/86, MacDonald to Dening, 160/49/49, 29 March 1949.

218 Blum, *op. cit.*, p. 112.
219 FO 371/75961/F4667/1015/86, Clarke to FO, no.352, 30 March 1949; FO 371/75962/F4949/1015/86, Minute by A.M. Palliser, 7 April 1949.
220 FO 371/75962/F5164/1015/86, British Embassy Paris to FO, 102/8/4/49, 7 April 1949.
221 FO 800/483/NA49/10, Memorandum by Bevin to Acheson, 2 April 1949.
222 FO 371/76023/F5743/1023/61G, Graves to Dening, 16 April 1949.
223 MJM 22/8/88-90, MacDonald to Strang, 3 April 1949.
224 Bullock, *op. cit.*, pp. 744–5.
225 Aldrich, *op. cit.*, p. 324.
226 Gibbons, *op. cit.*
227 MJM 27/7/32-3, MacDonald to Thompson, 4 May 1949.
228 CAB 21/1956, Quarterly Report of the Commissioner-General January–March 1949, 24 May 1949.
229 Darwin, *op. cit.*, p. 197.
230 FO 371/76049/F5704/1114/61, Economic Intelligence Department FO Report, 13 April 1949.
231 *Hansard*, Volume 467, London, 18 July 1949, p. 1099.
232 Rotter, *op. cit.*, p. 21.
233 McLane, *op. cit.*
234 Blum, *op. cit.*, p. 123.
235 Spector, *op. cit.*
236 Hess, *op. cit.*, p. 345; Blum, *op. cit.*
237 CAB 134/288, FE(0)(49)57, 16 August 1949, Meade to FO, 18 July 1949.
238 FO 371/76384/W4468/3/500G, PUSC(31) Final, 'British Policy towards Soviet Communism', 28 July 1949.
239 Hess, *op. cit.*, p. 338; Rotter, *op. cit.*, p. 29.
240 CO 537/5013, COS(49)256, 3 August 1949.
241 CO 537/5013, Harris to Briggs, 13 September 1949.
242 Rotter, *op. cit.*, p. 104.
243 DEFE 5/15, COS(49)281, Memorandum by COS Committee, 1 September 1949, Commanders-in-Chief Far East Memorandum, CIC(FE)(49)2(P), 12 August 1949.
244 Gibbons, *op. cit.*, p. 58.
245 Memorandum of Conversation by the Assistant Secretary of State for Far Eastern Affairs, Butterworth, 9 September 1949, *FRUS: 1949: Volume 7: Part 1: The Far East, and Australia*, Washington D.C., 1975, pp. 76–9.
246 FO 800/462/FE49/25, Record of a meeting held in the State Department, 18 September 1949.
247 CO 537/5013, JP(49)87(Final), 22 September 1949.
248 AIR 8/1584, GHQ Far East Land Forces to COS, SEACOS 974, 3 October 1949; VCOS Meeting, 10 October 1949.
249 CAB 134/288, FE(0)(49)71, 18 October 1949, Brief for the UK Representative to Conference on Rice Singapore.
250 CAB 134/288, FE(0)(49)81 Final, 15 December 1949, 'Southeast Asia: General, Brief for the United Kingdom Delegation to the Colombo Conference', 14 December 1949.
251 FO 800/445/COM49/42, Bevin to Attlee, PM49/143, 18 October 1949.
252 FO 800/465/FR49/15, Attlee to Bevin, M193/49, 22 October 1949.

253   CAB 129/37, CP(49)209, Memorandum by Bevin, 19 October 1949, R. Hyam (ed.), *BDEE, Series A, Volume 2: The Labour Government and the End of Empire 1945–1951: Part 3: Strategy, Policies and Constitutional Change*, London, 1991, pp. 382–6.
254   Aldrich, *op. cit.*
255   MJM 28/6/94, MacDonald to Commanders-in-Chief Far East, 25 October 1949; FO 371/75991/F16253/1201/86, MacDonald to FO, no.889, 28 October 1949.
256   Short, *op. cit.*; Blum, *op. cit.*, p. 142.
257   FO 800/462/FE49/32, FO to Saigon, no.194, 1 November 1949.
258   Aldrich, *op. cit.*, p. 325.
259   CAB 134/288, FE(0)(49)81 Final, 15 December 1949, 'Southeast Asia: General, Brief for the United Kingdom Delegation to the Colombo Conference', 14 December 1949.
260   PREM 8/964, MacDonald to FO, no.928, 6 November 1949.
261   CAB 134/288, FE(0)(49)82 Final, 8 December 1949, Report on Bukit Serene.
262   FO 371/76047/F7189/1105/61, Minute by Christofas, 20 May 1949.
263   MAF 97/2837, Hopson to FO, no.10A, 8 November 1949; PREM 8/964, MacDonald to FO, no.929, 6 November 1949.
264   CAB 134/288, FE(0)(49)72(Final) 10 November 1949, 'Report on Economic and Social Development in South and South East Asia and Far East', Annex A.
265   FO 371/76004/F17167/1017/6, FO brief for Bevin to Attlee, 10 November 1949; Tomkins to Pumphrey, 10 November 1949.
266   CAOM, INDO/NF/1338, French Ambassador New Delhi to French Foreign Minister, 16 November 1949.
267   MJM 20/9/9-10, MacDonald to FO, no.1021, 29 November 1949.
268   MJM 20/9/11, MacDonald to FO, no.1022, 29 November 1949.
269   FO 371/75977/F18202/1026/86, Minute by Scott, 1 December 1949.
270   FO 371/75981/F18832/10345/86, Minute by Lloyd, 19 December 1949; Minute by Strang, 22 November 1949.
271   FO 371/75991/F17742/1201/86, Harvey to FO, no.717, 23 November 1949.
272   DEFE 4/27, COS(49)179th Meeting, 30 November 1949.
273   FO 371/75972/F18013/1017/86, Hopson to FO, no.223, 30 November 1949.
274   FO 371/75972/F18013/1017/86, Minute by Blackham, 2 December 1949.
275   *The Pentagon Papers, op. cit.*, pp. 37–8, 82; Notes on NSC 48/1 by Ralph Smith, London University, 1996–7.
276   Gaddis, *op. cit.*, p. 70.
277   PREM 8/1407/Part1, EPC(49)152, 1 December 1949, 'Economic Development in the Far East'.
278   PREM 8/1407/Part1, EPC(49)152, 1 December 1949, 'Economic Development in the Far East', Appendix A.
279   AIR 8/1584, COS(49)180th Meeting, 2 December 1949.
280   Short, *op. cit.*, p. 76.
281   DEFE 4/27, COS(49)183rd Meeting, 9 December 1949.
282   DEFE 4/27, COS(49)184th Meeting, 12 December 1949.

283 DEFE 6/11, JP(49)162(0)(TofR), 14 December 1949, Minute by the Secretary T. de F. Jago.

284 DEFE 5/18, COS(49)458, 29 December 1949, 'Anglo-French Staff Talks on External Defence in the Far East', FO to Secretary COS, 23 December 1949.

285 Short, *op. cit.*, p. 77.

286 FO 800/462/FE49/40, Franks to FO, no.5855, 17 December 1949.

287 Aldrich, *op. cit.*, p. 324.

288 CO 537/6278, H. Lamb to J.C. Morgan, ref:52/B/Def/16/14, 7 January 1950.

289 Fenn, *op. cit.*, p. 40, citing Tran Ngoc Danh, *Historie du President Ho*, Hanoi, 1949, p. 33.

290 Gardner, *op. cit.*, p. 100.

291 Duiker, *op. cit.*, pp. 89, 187.

292 Short, *op. cit.*, pp. 69, 79.

293 D. McLean, 'American Nationalism, the China Myth, and the Truman Doctrine: The Question of Accommodation with Peking, 1949–1950', *Diplomatic History*, vol.10, no.1, Winter 1986, p. 25.

294 Hess, 'The First American Commitment in Indo-China: The Acceptance of the "Bao Dai Solution 1950"', *Diplomatic History*, *op. cit.*, p. 344.

295 McLean, *op. cit.*, p. 27.

296 Ambassador L. Henderson in India to the Secretary of State, 7 January 1950, Porter (ed.), *Vietnam, the Definitive Documentation of Human Decisions. Volume 1*, *op. cit.*, pp. 223–4.

297 Rotter, *op. cit.*, p. 160.

Chapter 5   Consequences, January–June 1950

1 FO 371/83598/F1016/17, Minute by Blackham, 11 January 1950.

2 Messages Establishing Diplomatic Relations between the DRVN and PRC 15–18 January 1950, Cole (ed.), *Conflict In Indochina and International Repercussions: A Documentary History, 1945–1955*, *op. cit.*, p. 121.

3 Recognition of the DRVN by the U.S.S.R. 30 January 1950, *Ibid.*, p. 122.

4 M. Furuta, 'The Indochina Communist Party's Division into Three Parties: Vietnamese Communist Policy Toward Cambodia and Laos, 1948–1951', T. Shiraishi and M. Furuta (eds), *Indochina in the 1940s and 1950s*, New York, 1992, pp. 151–2.

5 CAOM, GGI/65498, 'Etudes sur les movements rebelles au Cambodge 1942–1952', pp. 85–90.

6 Rotter, *op. cit.*, pp. 187–8.

7 FO 371/83399/FC1193/1, Franks to FO, no.530, 16 December 1949.

8 Rotter, *op. cit.*, pp. 177–8.

9 FO 371/83013/F1022/4, Franks to FO, no.33, 13 January 1950.

10 FO 371/83595/F1015/4, CRO to Canada, Australia, New Zealand, South Africa, India, Pakistan, Ceylon, no.5, 11 January 1950.

11 FO 371/83595/F1015/4, Gibbs to FO, no.17, 13 January 1950.

12 FO 371/83595/F1015/13, Minute by H.B.C Keeble, 26 January 1950.

13 FO 371/83593/F1013/1, Gibbs to Bevin, no.11, 3 February 1950, Enclosure: Political Summary, no.1, January 1950.

14 FO 800/445/COM50/1, Conversation between Bevin and the US Ambassador to Ceylon, 13 January 1950, UK delegation, no.44, 13 January 1950.

15 FO 371/83613/F10317/15, Harvey to FO, no.38, 20 January 1950.

16 FO 371/83595/F1015/16, Minute by Dening, 25 January 1950.

17 CO 537/7136, Franks to FO, no.32, 14 January 1950.

18 FO 371/83598/F1016/8, Franks to FO, no.64, 7 January 1950.

19 FO 371/83598/F1016/25, High Commissioner India to CRO, no.203, 17 January 1950.

20 FO 371/83601/F1017/2, FO to Paris, no.47, 6 January 1950.

21 FO 371/83599/F1016/49, Hoyer-Millar to FO, no.76, 3 February 1950. Department of State Press Release, no.102, 30 January 1950.

22 MJM 20/9/14, MacDonald to FO, no.66, 23 January 1950.

23 MJM 20/9/15-16, MacDonald to FO, no.65, 23 January 1950.

24 MJM 20/9/18, MacDonald to FO, no.68, 23 January 1950.

25 FO 371/83599/F1016/33, Paris to FO, no.35, 24 January 1950; Editorial Note, Statement by Acheson, 1 February 1950, *FRUS: 1950: Volume 6: East Asia and The Pacific*, Washington D.C., 1976, p. 711.

26 FO 371/83604/F10110/8, Sir D. Kelly to FO, no.103, 31 January 1950.

27 French Government Protest against Soviet Recognition of the DRVN, Cameron (ed.), *Viet-Nam Crisis: A Documentary History. Volume 1, op. cit.*, p. 144.

28 Short, *op. cit.*, p. 79.

29 MJM 20/9/20, MacDonald to FO, no.98, 1 February 1950.

30 MJM 27/3/108-10, MacDonald to A.D.P Heeney, 1 February 1950.

31 DEFE 4/28, COS(50)3rd Meeting, 6 January 1950; COS(50)10th Meeting, 16 January 1950; COS(50)16th Meeting, 27 January 1950.

32 FO 371/83656/F1202/1, MLO Saigon to Consul-General, 31 January 1950.

33 FO 371/83593/F1013/1, Gibbs to Bevin, no.11, 3 February 1950, Enclosure: Political Summary, no.1, 1 January 1950.

34 FO 371/83595/F1015/21, Minute by Keeble, 21 February 1950.

35 MJM 29/4/42-3, MacDonald to Sir P. McKerron, 28 February 1950.

36 PREM 8/1407 PT1, C.P.(50)18, 22 February 1950, Memorandum by Bevin, Annex A, Recommendations on Economic Policy in South and Southeast Asia.

37 PREM 8/1221, McNeil to Attlee, PM/HM/50/7, 30 January 1950; Minute by Attlee, 30 January 1950.

38 PREM 8/1221, FO to Attlee, 1 February 1950.

39 PREM 8/1221, Minute by Attlee, 1 February 1950.

40 PREM 8/1221, CRO to Canada, Australia, New Zealand, South Africa, India, Pakistan, Ceylon, A.no.20, 2 February 1950.

41 MJM 29/2/80-1, MacDonald to Scrivener, 3 February 1950.

42 FO 800/449/CONF50/2, Conversation between Bevin and Schneider, 3 February 1950.

43 FO 800/462/FE50/7, Conversation between Bevin and Schneiter, 3 February 1950.

44 FO 800/449/CONF50/2, Conversation between Bevin and Schneiter, 3 February 1950.
45 FO 371/83599/F1016/65, Soviet Monitor issued by TASS, no.11287, to Hope-Jones, 6 February 1950.
46 PREM 8/1221, CM(50)4th, Conclusions, 7 February 1950.
47 PREM 8/1221, CRO to Australia, Canada, New Zealand, South Africa, India, Pakistan, Ceylon, A.no.23, 7 February 1950; A.no.24, 7 February 1950.
48 CAB 128/7, CM(50)4th, Conclusions, 7 February 1950.
49 MAF 97/2837, FO to Washington, no.29, 7 February 1950.
50 FO 371/83627/F1051/45, Brief by Scott for Bevin, 7 February 1950.
51 FO 371/83627/F1051/31, Scott to Ringwalt, 2 February 1950.
52 FO 371/83604/F10110/30, CRO to Canada, Australia, New Zealand, South Africa, India, Pakistan and Ceylon, no.25, 9 February 1950.
53 FO 371/83628/F1051/47, Bevin to Hayter, no.165, 8 February 1950.
54 MJM 20/13/5, Guibant to MacDonald, 8 February 1950.
55 MJM 20/13/8-9, MacDonald to Guibant, 24 February 1950.
56 MJM 19/1/4, MacDonald to Strang, no.145, 14 February 1950.
57 MJM 19/1/3, MacDonald to Dening, no.237, 14 March 1950.
58 Halifax to Bevin, 6 April 1946, Enclosure, R.D. Crockatt (ed.), *British Documents on Foreign Affairs: Reports and Papers from the Foreign Office Confidential Print: Series C, North America, Part 4: Volume 1: January–December 1946*, University Publications of America, 1999, pp. 97–9; Rotter, *op. cit.*, pp. 178, 189.
59 FO 371/83655/F1201/6, Franks to FO, no.632, 21 February 1950.
60 FO 371/83655/F1201/5, Graves to Scott, 14 February 1950.
61 FO 371/83644/F1103/1, MacDonald to Dening, 7 February 1950.
62 Rotter, *op. cit.*, p. 175.
63 FO 371/83655/F1201/7, Paris to FO, no.76, 21 February 1950
64 FO 371/83655/F1201/8, Paris to FO, no.80, 23 February 1950.
65 Harvey to Bevin, no.129, Paris, 22 February 1950, R.D. Crockatt (ed.), *British Documents on Foreign Affairs: Reports and Papers from the Foreign Office Confidential Print: Series C, North America, Part 4: Volume 4: January 1950–December 1950*, University Publications of America, 2003, pp. 40–4.
66 PREM 8/1202, Minutes of an Informal Meeting of Ministers, 15 May 1950, R. Bullen, and M. Pelly (eds), *Documents on British Policy Overseas Series 2: Volume 2: The London Conferences: Anglo-American Relations and Cold War Strategy January–June 1950*, London, 1987, pp. 352–4.
67 FO 371/83655/F1201/7, FO to Paris, no.624, 23 February 1950.
68 FO 371/83644/F1103, Dening to MacDonald, 3 March 1950.
69 Spector, *op. cit.*, p. 102.
70 Acheson to the embassy in the UK, 30 January 1950, Porter (ed.), *Vietnam, the Definitive Documentation of Human Decisions. Volume 1, op. cit.*, pp. 224–5; *The Pentagon Papers, op. cit.*, pp. 75–81.
71 MJM 19/1/1, MacDonald to FO, no.157, 21 February 1950.
72 CAB 134/290, FE(O)(50)6, Minute by the Chair, 23 February 1950.
73 CAB 134/290, FE(O)(50)6, Minute by the Chair, 23 February 1950, Appendix A, MacDonald to FO, no.23, 10 February 1950.

74 CAB 134/290, FE(0)(50)7, 23 February 1950, 'Economic Development in South and Southeast Asia'; MJM 19/9/5–7, MacDonald to FO, no.213, 4 March 1950.

75 MJM 29/3/83, MacDonald to General Harding, 16 February 1950.

76 MJM 19/11/12, MacDonald to FO, no.137, 12 February 1950.

77 DEFE 4/29, COS(50)28th Meeting, 17 February 1950, Annex, JIC(50)1/4(Final), 15 February 1950.

78 MJM 18/9/1-11, Statement by Pearson, 22 February 1950.

79 Rotter, *op. cit.*, p. 107.

80 Irving, *op. cit.*, p. 80.

81 FO 371/83600/F1016/77, Minute by Dening, 23 February 1950.

82 FO 371/83600/F1016/79, Bevin to Strang and Dening, 22 February 1950; FO 371/83625/F10385/10, High Commissioner India to CRO, no.538, 14 February 1950.

83 FO 371/83600/F1016/79, Dening to Harvey, 2 March 1950.

84 FO 371/83620/F10340/9, Sterndale Bennett to FO, no.202, 1 March 1950.

85 FO 371/83600/F1016/80, Harvey to FO, no.93, 3 March 1950.

86 FO 371/83600/F1016/82, Hood to Dening, 4 March 1950.

87 FO 959/68, CRO to High Commissioner Ceylon, no.270, 6 March 1950.

88 FO 800/465/FR50/1, Conversation between Bevin and Massigli, 2 March 1950, Bevin to Harvey, no.266.

89 DEFE 5/20, COS(50)81, Memorandum by COS Committee, 2 March 1950, copy of letter from FO to Secretary COS Committee, 28 February 1950.

90 DEFE 4/29, COS(50)35th Meeting, 6 March 1950.

91 FO 800/465/FR50/5, Conversation between Bevin and Schuman, 7 March 1950.

92 FO 800/462/FE50/10, Conversation between Bevin and Schuman, 7 March 1950.

93 FO 800/462/FE50/13, Conversation between Bevin and Schuman, 7 March 1950.

94 FO 371/83600/F1017/88, Paris to FO, no.108, 14 March 1950.

95 Blum, *op. cit.*, p. 203.

96 FO 371/83607/F1023/3, Scott on behalf of Bevin to Paris, no.819, 18 March 1950.

97 FO 115/4480/F1022/75/50G, Franks to FO, no.944, 22 March 1950.

98 FO 115/4480/F1022/221/50G, FO to Washington, no.1782, 25 April 1950.

99 FO 371/83595/F1015/27, Gibbs to FO, no.65, 13 March 1950.

100 DEFE 5/20, COS(50)89, 9 March 1950.

101 CO 537/6264, COS(50)89, 9 March 1950, COS Committee minute by the secretary, Appendix, Memorandum by the Commissioner-General and the CinC FE, BDCC(FE)(50)1/1, 11 February 1950.

102 CAB 134/225, EPC(50)40, 22 March 1950, Joint Memorandum by the Working Parties on the Sterling Area and on Development in South and Southeast Asia, 18 March 1950, Annexes: A and B.R. Hyam (ed.), *BDEE, Series A. Volume 2: The Labour Government and the End of Empire 1945–1951: Part 2, op. cit.*, pp. 142–52.

103 MJM 29/5/35, MacDonald to Jessup, 18 March 1950.

104 DEFE 4/30, COS(50)49th Meeting, 24 March 1950, Annex 1, JP(49)162(Final), 17 March 1950.
105 CO 537/6264, Annex to JP(49)108(0), Draft, 2nd Revise, 'Strategy and Defence Policy in Southeast Asia and the Far East', 22 March 1950, Part 3.
106 DEFE 4/30, COS(50)49th Meeting, 24 March 1950.
107 MJM 19/7/6, MacDonald to FO, no.265, 24 March 1950.
108 MJM 19/7/7, MacDonald to FO, no.264, 24 March 1950.
109 MJM 19/7/8, MacDonald to FO, no.275, 27 March 1950.
110 FO 371/83593/F1013/4, Gibbs to Bevin, no.32, 3 April 1950, Enclosure: Political Summary, no.3, March 1950.
111 FO 371/83595/F1015/27, Gibbs to FO, no.65, 13 March 1950.
112 MJM 19/7/8, MacDonald to FO, no.275, 27 March 1950.
113 FO 371/83593/F1013/4, Gibbs to Bevin, no.32, 3 April 1950, Enclosure: Political Summary, no.3, March 1950; FO 371/83593/F1013/6, Gibbs to Bevin, no.38, 1 May 1950, Enclosure: Political Summary, no.4, April 1950.
114 FO 628/70, Sterndale Bennett to Thompson, 23 March 1950.
115 FO 371/83638/F1081/1, Selby to Maclennan, 28 March 1950.
116 FO 371/83642/F1101/5, Gibbs to FO, no.10, 29 May 1950.
117 PREM 8/1221, MOD to Attlee, 29 March 1950, Annex II to JP(49)162.
118 PREM 8/1221, MOD to Attlee, 29 March 1950.
119 PREM 8/1221, Minute by Attlee, 30 March 1950; MOD to Attlee, 29 March 1950; PREM 8/1221, SAC(50)3, 31 March 1950.
120 PREM 8/1221, Cabinet China and Southeast Asia Committee note, 5 April 1950.
121 CAB 21/3280, Garner to Luke, 5 April 1950.
122 PREM 8/1221, Cabinet China and Southeast Asia Committee note, 5 April 1950; CAB 21/3280, Dening to Garner, 19 April 1950.
123 MAF 97/2837, FO to Washington, no.67, 3 April 1950.
124 FO 371/83593/F1013/6, Gibbs to Bevin, no.38, 1 May 1950, Enclosure: Political Summary, no.4, April 1950.
125 Irving, *op. cit.*, p. 101.
126 Gaddis, *op. cit.*, p. 91.
127 Rotter, *op. cit.*, pp. 182–4.
128 *The Pentagon Papers*, *op. cit.*, p. 83.
129 McLane, *op. cit.*, p. 441.
130 DEFE 5/20, COS(50)120, Memorandum by COS Committee, 12 April 1950; DTC(EA)(50)1(Final Revise), 29 March 1950.
131 DEFE 4/30, COS(50)61st Meeting, 19 April 1950.
132 DEFE 4/31, COS(50)70th Meeting, 2 May 1950, Annex, JP(50)47(Final), 6 April 1950.
133 MJM 19/1/8, MacDonald to Saigon, no.12, 20 April 1950.
134 MJM 19/1/11, MacDonald to FO, no.486, 5 June 1950.
135 FO 371/83646/F11381/1, Gibbs to Bevin, no.39, 25 April 1950.
136 MJM 20/9/22-3, MacDonald to FO, no.400, 2 May 1950.
137 MJM 20/9/24, MacDonald to FO, no.401, 2 May 1950.
138 MJM 20/9/25, MacDonald to FO, no.402, 2 May 1950.
139 MJM 20/9/26-7, MacDonald to FO, no.427, 8 May 1950.
140 FO 371/83596/F1015/49, Harvey to Bevin, no.297, 9 May 1950.

141 FO 371/83609/F1025/2, United Kingdom Brief, no.9, Indo-China, 24 April 1950.

142 Spector, *op. cit.*, p. 103.

143 FO 371/83013/F1022/15, Dening to Bevin, 6 May 1950, Brief, Annex 1–MIN/TRI/P/9.

144 FO 371/83021/F1051/1, Panikaar to Stevenson, 5 May 1950.

145 FO 371/83634/F1062/1, Starkey to Keeble, 9 May 1950; FO 371/83634/F1062/2, Montague-Brown to Keeble, 12 May 1950.

146 FO 371/83634/F1062/1, FO to Paris, 9 May 1950; Keeble to Montague-Brown, 6 June 1950.

147 Chandler, *A History of Cambodia, op. cit.*, p. 181; FO 959/49, Major Lunn-Rockcliffe to WO, Weekly Intelligence Summary, no.3, 6 May 1950.

148 Short, *op. cit.*, p. 81; FO 800/462/FE50/22, Conversation between Bevin and the Indian High Commissioner, 26 May 1950, Enclosure Nehru to Bevin, 24 May 1950.

149 CAB 128/17, CM29(50)3, 8 May 1950, Hyam (ed.), *BDEE, Series A. Volume 2: The Labour Government and the End of Empire 1945–1951: Part 2, op. cit.*, pp. 357–60.

150 FO 800/449/CONF50/25, Conclusions of the 5th Tripartite Ministerial Meeting, 13 May 1950.

151 FO 371/83610/F1026/1, FO to Saigon, no.115, 16 May 1950.

152 Gibbons, *op. cit.*, p. 80.

153 FO 800/462/FE50/22, Conversation between Bevin and the Indian High Commissioner, 26 May 1950, Enclosure Nehru to Bevin, 24 May 1950.

154 FO 800/462/FE50/22, Conversation between Bevin and the Indian High Commissioner, 26 May 1950.

155 DEFE 4/31, COS(50)80th Meeting, 22 May 1950.

156 FO 371/83647/F1192/9, Consul-General Saigon to Southeast Asia Department, 13 June 1950.

157 FO 371/83593/F1013/7, Gibbs to Bevin, no.45, 8 June 1950, Enclosure: Political Summary, no.5, May 1950.

158 CAOM, INDO/NF/1403, Massigli to Ministry for France Overseas, 1 June 1950.

159 PREM 8/1407 PT2, British Commonwealth Consultative Committee, Colombo, July 1950, Report of the Standing Committee, August 1950.

160 CAOM, INDO/NF/1403, Massigli to Ministry for France Overseas, 25 May 1950.

161 MJM 29/7/52, MacDonald to F.S. Madden, 9 May 1950.

162 CO 537/5970, Minutes of the 15th Conference held by the Commissioner-General for the United Kingdom in Southeast Asia, 7 June 1950.

163 MAF 83/2307, High Commissioner Australia to CRO, no.544, 6 June 1950.

164 PREM 8/1407 PT1, CP(50)127, 19 June 1950, Memorandum by the Chancellor of the Exchequer, the Secretary of State for Commonwealth Relations and the Minister of State; CM(50)38th, Conclusions, 22 June 1950.

165 CO 537/6262, CinC FES Afloat to CinC FES Ashore, 8 June 1950.

166 CO 537/6277, CO to Higham, 21 June 1950.

167 CO 537/6277, Draft Morgan to Captain Butler-Bowden, June 1950.

210 *Notes*

168   CO 537/6277, Marnham to Murray, 23 June 1950.
169   DEFE 5/22, COS(50)225, Memorandum by the COS Committee, Services Public Relations Policy Committee, 29 June 1950, Appendix, Copy of (Q.no.19) from CRO to High Commissioner Canada, Australia, New Zealand, South Africa, 22 June 1950.
170   CO 537/6277, BDCC to COS, SEACOS 67, 23 June 1950.
171   DEFE 4/32, COS(50)95th Meeting, 26 June 1950.
172   CO 537/6277, COS(50)95th Meeting, 26 June 1950.
173   DEFE 4/32, COS(50)98th Meeting, 28 June 1950.
174   Minutes of a Meeting of the Cabinet Defence Committee, 28 June 1950, H.J. Yasamee, and K.A. Hamilton (eds), *Documents on British Policy Overseas Series 2: Volume 4: Korea June 1950–April 1951*, London, 1991, pp. 7–10.
175   CO 537/6277, COS(50)100th Meeting, 30 June 1950.
176   FO 371/83593/F1013/8, Gibbs to Bevin, no.51, 1 July 1950, Enclosure: Political Summary, no.6, June 1950.
177   Gibbons, *op. cit.*, p. 69.
178   Spector, *op. cit.*, p. 125.
179   FO 371/83593/F1013/8, Gibbs to Bevin, no.51, 1 July 1950, Enclosure: Political Summary, no.6, 6 June 1950; FO 371/83596/F1015/57, Consul-General Saigon to FO (10A/50), 12 June 1950.
180   FO 371/83593/F1013/8, Gibbs to Bevin, no.51, 1 July 1950, Enclosure: Political Summary, no.6, 6 June 1950.
181   FO 371/83613/F10317/6, Gibbs to FO, no.5, 1 May 1950.
182   FO 371/83593/F1013/8, Gibbs to Bevin, no.51, 1 July 1950, Enclosure: Political Summary, no.6, 6 June 1950.
183   FO 371/84604/FZ1193/7, E.D.(S.A.)(50)(61), Cabinet Committee on Economic Working Party on Economic Development in South and Southeast Asia, Memorandum by the Foreign Office, 26 June 1950, Attachment, Franks to Younger, no.464, 9 June 1950.
184   FO 371/83593/F1013/8, Gibbs to Bevin, no.51, 1 July 1950, Enclosure: Political Summary, no.6, 6 June 1950; FO 371/83642/F1101/6, Gibbs to FO, no.19, 4 August 1950.
185   FO 371/83613/F10317/16, Younger to Harvey, no.666, 21 June 1950.
186   FO 371/83613/F10317/19, Minute by Keeble, 5 July 1950.
187   FO 371/83613/F10317/12, British Embassy Paris to FO, 2 June 1950.
188   FO 959/73, Gibbs to Singapore, no.110, 31 May 1950; Saigon to Singapore, 12 June 1950; FO 371/83636/F1071/4, Younger to Harvey, no.584, 26 May 1950.
189   FO 371/83642/F1101/6, Gibbs to FO, no.19, 4 August 1950; FO 371/83636/F1071/2, Harvey to Younger, no.354, 15 June 1950.
190   FO 371/83647/F1192/12, Consul-General Saigon to FO, Military Intelligence Report no.7, 30 June 1950.
191   FO 959/68, FO to Djakarta, no.40, 23 June 1950.
192   Statement by the President, 27 June 1950, *The Pentagon Papers, op. cit.*, pp. 372–3.
193   Statement by PRC Foreign Minister Chou En-Lai, 28 June 1950, Cameron (ed.), *Viet-Nam Crisis: A Documentary History. Volume 1, op. cit.*, pp. 150–1.
194   Kissinger, *op. cit.*, p. 626.

195 Minutes of a Meeting Held to discuss Korea, 30 June 1950, Yasamee, and Hamilton (eds), *Documents on British Policy Overseas Series 2: Volume 4, op. cit.*, pp. 21–4.

196 Appendix 1, Report by the COS, DO(50)45 [CAB 131/9] Ministry of Defence, 7 June 1950, Defence Policy and Global Strategy, Yasamee, and. Hamilton (eds), *Documents on British Policy Overseas Series 2: Volume 4, op. cit.*, pp. 411–31.

197 *Hansard*, Volume 475, 24 May 1950, pp. 2089–90.

198 MJM 29/8/22-5, MacDonald to Gibbs, 3 June 1950.

199 MJM 29/9/13-14, MacDonald to Sir Feroze Khan Noon, 19 July 1950.

200 MJM 79/8/183, Diary, 4 July 1950.

Conclusion

1 Smith, *Viet-Nam and the West, op. cit.*, p. 5.

Bibliography

Archival sources

Britain

The National Archives, Public Record Office, London:

Admiralty:
ADM 119 Accountant General's Department
ADM 199 War History Cases and Papers
ADM 223 Naval Intelligence Papers

Air Ministry:
AIR 8 Department of the Chief of Air Staff
AIR 23 Overseas Commands
AIR 40 Directorate of Intelligence and other Intelligence Papers

Board of Trade:
BT 64 Industries and Manufacturers Department

Cabinet Office:
CAB 21 Registered Files 1916–65
CAB 65 War Cabinet Minutes
CAB 66 War Cabinet Memoranda
CAB 69 War Cabinet Defence Committee (Operations)
CAB 79 War Cabinet Chiefs of Staff Committee Minutes
CAB 80 War Cabinet Chiefs of Staff Committee Memoranda
CAB 81 War Cabinet Chiefs of Staff Committee and Sub-Committees
CAB 84 War Cabinet Joint Planning Committees
CAB 99 War Cabinet Commonwealth and International Conferences
CAB 119 Joint Planning Staff Files
CAB 120 Minister of Defence: Secretariat Files
CAB 121 Special Secret Information Centre
CAB 122 British Joint Staff Mission: Washington Office Files
CAB 128 Cabinet Minutes 1945–72
CAB 129 Cabinet Memoranda 1945–72
CAB 134 Cabinet Miscellaneous Committees: Minutes and Papers

Colonial Office:
CO 323 Colonies: General Original Correspondence
CO 537 Confidential General and Confidential Original Correspondence
CO 825 Eastern Original Correspondence
CO 968 Defence Department and Successors: Original Correspondence

Defence:
DEFE 4 Chiefs of Staff Committee Minutes 1946–onwards
DEFE 5 Chiefs of Staff Committee Memoranda 1946–onwards
DEFE 6 Chiefs of Staff Committee: Joint Planning Staff and Defence Planning
Staff Reports

Foreign Office:
FO 115 Embassy and Consulates, United States of America: General
Correspondence
FO 371 Political Departments: General Correspondence
FO 628 Embassy and Consulates, Thailand: General Correspondence
FO 643 Burma Office, Burma Secretariat and Foreign Office, Rangoon, Burma:
General Correspondence
FO 660 Offices of Various Political Representatives, Second World War: Papers
FO 800 Private Offices: Various Ministers and Officials Papers (Ernest Bevin)
FO 930 Foreign Publicity Files
FO 950 Claims Department: Correspondence and Claims
FO 953 Information Policy Department and Regional Information Departments
FO 954 Private Office Papers of Sir A. Eden
FO 959 Consulates, French Indochina: Various Papers 1945–59

Special Operations Executive:
HS 1 Far East: Registered Files
HS 7 Histories and War Diaries

Government Communications Headquarters:
HW 1 Government Code and Cipher School: Signals Intelligence Passed to
The Prime Minister, Messages and Correspondence

Ministry of Agriculture and Food:
MAF 83 Supply Department
MAF 97 Establishment Department: British Food Mission, Washington

Prime Minister:
PREM 3 Prime Minister's Papers 1940–45
PREM 4 Prime Minister's Papers 1940–45
PREM 8 Prime Minister's Papers 1945–51

War Office:
WO 32 Registered Papers General Series
WO 106 Directorate of Military Operations and Intelligence
WO 162 Adjutant General
WO 172 SEAC War Diaries
WO 193 Directorate of Military Operations
WO 203 Far East Forces
WO 208 Directorate of Military Intelligence
WO 220 Directorate of Civil Affairs
WO 252 Surveys, Maps and Reports
WO 311 War Crimes Files

Birmingham University Library:

Papers of Anthony Eden, Lord Avon (AP)

Durham University Library:

Papers of Sir Malcolm MacDonald (MJM)

King's College, University of London, Liddell Hart Centre for Military Archives:

Papers of Major-General Sir Douglas David Gracey (Gracey)

Southampton University Library:

Papers of Admiral Lord Louis Mountbatten Earl of Burma (MB)

St Anthony's College, Middle East Centre Archive, Oxford:

Papers of Sir Miles Lampson, Lord Killearn (Lampson)

University of East Anglia Library, Norwich:

Papers of Sir Winston Spencer Churchill, the Chartwell Papers, microfilm (CHAR)

France

Centre des Archives d'Outre-Mer, Aix-en-Provence (CAOM):

Gouvernement General de l'Indochine (GGI)

Indochine Nouveau Fonds (INDO/NF)

Papers of Emile Bollaert

Papers of Leon Pignon

Printed primary sources

British Documents on the End of Empire, Series A, Volume 1: Ashton, S.R. and Stockwell, S.E. (eds),
   Imperial Policy and Colonial Practice 1925–1945: Part 1: Metropolitan Reorganisation, Defence and International Relations, Political Change and Constitutional Reform, London, 1996.
   Imperial Policy and Colonial Practice 1925–1945: Part 2: Economic Policy, Social Policies and Colonial Research, London, 1996.

British Documents on the End of Empire, Series A, Volume 2: Hyam, R. (ed.),
   The Labour Government and the End of Empire 1945–1951: Part 1: High Policy, London, 1991.
   The Labour Government and the End of Empire 1945–1951: Part 2: Economics and International Relations, London, 1991.

The Labour Government and the End of Empire 1945–1951: Part 3: Strategy, Policies and Constitutional Change, London, 1991.

The Labour Government and the End of Empire 1945–1951: Part 4: Race Relations and the Commonwealth, London, 1991.

British Documents on the End of Empire, Series B, Volume 3: Stockwell, A.J. (ed.),
    Malaya: Part 1: The Malayan Union Experiment 1942–1948, London, 1995.
    Malaya: Part 2: The Communist Insurrection 1948–1953, London, 1995.

British Documents on Foreign Affairs: Reports and Papers from the Foreign Office Confidential Print: Series C, North America, Part 3: Crockatt, R.D. (ed.),
    Volume 2: January 1942–March 1943, University Publications of America, 1999.
    Volume 3: April 1943–December 1943, University Publications of America, 1999.
    Volume 4: January 1944–December 1944, University Publications of America, 1999.
    Volume 5: January 1945–December 1945, University Publications of America, 1999.

British Documents on Foreign Affairs: Reports and Papers from the Foreign Office Confidential Print: Series C, North America, Part 4: Crockatt, R.D. (ed.),
    Volume 1: January–December 1946, University Publications of America, 1999.
    Volume 2: January–December 1947, University Publications of America, 1999.
    Volume 3: January 1948–December 1949, University Publications of America, 1999.
    Volume 4: January 1950–December 1950, University Publications of America, 2003.

Burma: The Struggle For Independence 1944–1948: Documents From Official And Private Sources: Tinker, H. (ed.),
    Volume 1: From Military Occupation to Civil Government 1 January 1944 to 31 August 1946, London, 1983.
    Volume 2: From General Strike to Independence 31 August 1946–4 January 1948, London, 1984.

Constitutional Relations Between Britain and India: The Transfer of Power 1942–7: Mansergh, N. (ed.),
    Volume 3: Reassertion of Authority, Gandhi's Fast and the Succession of the Viceroyalty 21 September 1942–12 June 1943, London, 1971.
    Volume 4: The Bengal Famine and the New Viceroyalty 15 June 1943–31 August 1944, London, 1973.
    Volume 5: The Simla Conference: Background and Proceedings 1 September 1944–28 July 1945, London, 1974.
    Volume 6: The Post War Phase: New Moves by the Labour Government 1 August 1945–22 March 1946, London, 1976.
    Volume 7: The Cabinet Mission 23 March–29 June 1946, London, 1977.
    Volume 8: The Interim Government 31 July–1 November 1946, London, 1979.
    Volume 9: The Fixing of a Time Limit 4 November 1946–22 March 1947, London, 1980.

Volume 10: The Mountbatten Viceroyalty: Formulation of a Plan 22 March–30 May 1947, London, 1981.

Volume 11: The Mountbatten Viceroyalty: Announcement and Reception of the 3 June Plan 31 May–7 July 1947, London, 1982.

Volume 12: The Mountbatten Viceroyalty: Princes, Partition and Independence 8 July–15 August 1947, London, 1984.

Documents on British Policy Overseas Series 1:

Butler, R. and Pelly, M. (eds), *Volume 1: The Conference at Potsdam, 1945*, London, 1984.

Bullen, R. and Pelly, M. (eds), *Volume 2: Conferences in London, Washington and Moscow, 1945*, London, 1985.

Bullen, R. and Pelly, M. (eds), *Volume 3: Britain and America: Negotiation of the United States Loan, 3 August–7 December 1945*, London, 1986.

Bullen, R. and Pelly, M. (eds), *Volume 4: Britain and America: Atomic Energy, Bases and Food, 12 December 1945–31 July 1946*, London, 1987.

Pelly, M. and Yasamee, H.J. (eds), *Volume 5: Germany and Western Europe, 11 August–31 December 1945*, London, 1990.

Pelly, M. and Yasamee, H.J. (eds), *Volume 6: Eastern Europe 1945–1946*, London, 1991.

Yasamee, H.J. and Hamilton, K.A. (eds), *Volume 7: United Nations: Iran, Cold War and World Organisation, 2 January 1946–13 January 1947*, London, 1995.

Documents on British Policy Overseas Series 2:

Bullen, R. and Pelly, M. (eds), *Volume 1: The Schuman Plan, the Council of Europe and Western European Integration 1950–1952*, London, 1986.

Bullen, R. and Pelly, M. (eds), *Volume 2: The London Conferences: Anglo-American Relations and Cold War Strategy January–June 1950*, London, 1987.

Yasamee, H.J. and Hamilton, K.A. (eds), *Volume 4: Korea June 1950–April 1951*, London, 1991.

Foreign Relations of the United States: Diplomatic Papers: Department of State Publication:

The Conferences at Washington 1941–2, and Casablanca 1943, Washington D.C., 1968.

The Conferences at Washington and Quebec 1943, Washington D.C., 1970.

The Conferences at Cairo and Tehran 1943, Washington D.C., 1961.

1943: Volume 3: The British Commonwealth, Eastern Europe, The Far East, Washington D.C., 1963.

The Conference at Quebec 1944, Washington D.C., 1972.

The Conferences at Malta and Yalta 1945, Washington D.C., 1955.

The Conference at Berlin 1945 (The Potsdam Conference) Volume 1, Washington D.C., 1960.

The Conference at Berlin 1945 (The Potsdam Conference) Volume 2, Washington D.C., 1960.

1945: Volume 6: The British Commonwealth, The Far East, Washington D.C., 1969.

1946: Volume 1: General, The United Nations, Washington D.C., 1972.
1946: Volume 8: The Far East, Washington D.C., 1971.
1947: Volume 6: The Far East, Washington D.C., 1972.
1948: Volume 6: The Far East, and Australia, Washington D.C., 1974.
1949: Volume 7: Part 1: The Far East, and Australia, Washington D.C., 1975.
1949: Volume 7: Part 2: The Far East, and Australia, Washington D.C., 1976.
1950: Volume 6: East Asia and The Pacific, Washington D.C., 1976.

Bordinier, G. (ed.), *La Guerre D'Indochine 1945–54: Textes et Documents, Volume 1, Le Retour de la France en Indochine 1945–1946*, Vincennes, 1987.
Cameron, A.W. (ed.), *Viet-Nam Crisis: A Documentary History. Volume 1, 1940–1956*, New York, 1971.
Cole, A.B. (ed.), *Conflict In Indochina and International Repercussions: A Documentary History, 1945–1955*, New York, 1956.
Danchev, A. and Todman, D. (eds), *War Diaries 1939–1945: Field Marshal Lord Alan Brooke*, London, 2001.
Documents Relating to British Involvement in the Indochina Conflict 1945–65, London, 1965.
Hansard House of Commons Parliamentary Debates, 1943–1950, Volumes 386–476, London, 1943–1950.
Kimball, W., *Churchill and Roosevelt: The Complete Correspondence: Alliance Forged, 1942–1944*, Princeton, 1984.
Kimball, W., *Churchill and Roosevelt: The Complete Correspondence: Alliance Declining, 1944–1945*, Princeton, 1984.
The Pentagon Papers, The Defense Department History of United States Decision Making on Vietnam, Volume 1, Gravel Edition, Boston, 1971.
Porter, A.N. and Stockwell, A.J. (eds), *British Imperial Policy and Decolonization, Volume 1, 1938–1951*, London, 1987.
Porter, G. (ed.), *Vietnam, the Definitive Documentation of Human Decisions. Volume 1*, Philadelphia, 1979.
Smith, R.B. and Stockwell, A.J. (eds), *British Policy and the Transfer of Power in Asia. Documentary Perspectives*, London, 1988.
Ziegler, P. (ed.), *The Personal Diaries of Admiral, the Lord Louis Mountbatten, Supreme Commander Southeast Asia 1943–1946*, London, 1988.

Secondary sources

Articles

Adamthwaite, A., 'Britain and the World 1945–9: The View from the Foreign Office', *International Affairs*, vol.61, no.2, Spring 1985, pp. 223–35.
Aldrich, R., 'Imperial Rivalry: British and American Intelligence in Asia 1942–6', *Intelligence and National Security*, vol.3, no.1, January 1988, pp. 5–55.
Brown, K.E., 'The Interplay of Information and Mind in Decision making: Signals Intelligence and Franklin D. Roosevelt's Policy Shift on Indochina', *Intelligence and National Security*, vol.13, no.1, 1998, pp. 109–31.
Chandler, D.P., 'The Kingdom of Kampuchea, March–October 1945: Japanese Sponsored Independence in Cambodia in World War Two', *Journal of Southeast Asian Studies*, vol.17, no.1, March 1986, pp. 80–93.

Colbert, E., 'The Road Not Taken: Decolonization and Independence in Indonesia and Indochina', *Foreign Affairs*, April 1973, pp. 608–28.

Darwin, J., 'British Decolonisation since 1945: A pattern or a puzzle?', *Journal of Imperial and Commonwealth History*, vol.12, January 1984, pp. 187–209.

Day, D., 'Promise and Performance: Britain's Pacific Pledge 1943–5', *War and Society*, vol.4, no.2, September 1988, pp. 71–93.

Dulles, F.R. and Ridinger, G., 'The Anti-colonial policies of Roosevelt', *Political Science Quarterly*, 1955, pp. 1–18.

Duncanson, D., 'General Gracey and the Vietminh', *Journal of the Royal Central Asian Society*, vol.55, part 3, October 1968, pp. 288–97.

Duncanson, D., 'Ho Chi Minh And The August Revolution Of 1945 In Indochina', *Lugano Review*, May 1975.

Garrett, C.W., 'In Search of Grandeur: France in Vietnam 1940–1946', *The Review of Politics*, vol.29, no.3, July 1967, pp. 303–23.

Gelb, L., 'Vietnam: The System Worked', *Foreign Policy*, Summer 1971, pp. 140–67.

Habibuddin, S.M., 'Franklin D. Roosevelt's Anti-colonial Policy Towards Asia. Its Implications for India, Indo–china and Indonesia 1941–5', *Journal of Indian History*, vol.53, 1975, pp. 497–522.

Herring, G.C., 'The Truman Administration and the Restoration of French Sovereignty in Indochina', *Diplomatic History*, vol.1, no.2, Spring 1977, pp. 97–117.

Hess, G.R., 'The First American Commitment in Indo-China: The Acceptance of the "Bao Dai Solution 1950"', *Diplomatic History*, vol.2, Fall 1978, pp. 331–50.

Hess, G.R., 'Franklin D. Roosevelt and French Indochina', *Journal of American History*, vol.59, no.2, September 1972, pp. 353–68.

Hess, G.R., 'United States Policy and the Origins of the Vietminh War 1945–1946', *Peace and Change*, 3, Summer and Fall, 1975, pp. 24–33.

Holland, R.F., 'The Imperial Factor in British Strategies From Attlee to Macmillan 1945–63', *Journal of Imperial and Commonwealth History*, vol.12, January 1984, pp. 165–85.

Huynh Kim Kanh., 'The Vietnamese August Revolution Reinterpreted', *Journal of Asian Studies*, vol.30, no.4, August 1971, pp. 761–82.

Jacobson, M., 'Winston Churchill and the Third Front', *Journal of Strategic Studies*, vol.14, no.3, September 1991, pp. 337–62.

Kennan, G. ('X' Pseudo), 'The Sources of Soviet Conduct', *Foreign Affairs*, vol.25, no.4, 1946–7, pp. 566–82.

Kent, J., 'Anglo-French Co-operation 1939–49', *Journal of Imperial and Commonwealth History*, vol.17, no. 1, 1988, pp. 55–82.

La Feber, W., 'Roosevelt, Churchill and Indochina 1942–5', *American Historical Review*, vol.80, 1975, pp. 1277–95.

Lawrence, M., 'Transnational Coalition Building The Making of the Cold War in Indochina', *Diplomatic History*, vol. 26, no. 3, Summer 2002, pp. 453–80.

Marr, D.G., 'Vietnam 1945: Some Questions', *Vietnam Forum*, vol.6, Summer 1985, pp. 155–93.

Marsot, A., 'The Crucial Year: Indochina 1945', *Journal of Contemporary History*, vol.19, no.2, April 1984, pp. 337–54.

McLean, D., 'American Nationalism, the China Myth, and the Truman Doctrine: The Question of Accommodation with Peking, 1949–1950', *Diplomatic History*, vol.10, no.1, Winter 1986, pp. 25–42.

Melby, J.F., 'Vietnam 1950', *Diplomatic History*, vol.6, no.1, Winter 1982, pp. 97–109.

Nitz, K., 'Independence without Nationalists? The Japanese and Vietnamese Nationalism during the Japanese period 1940–5', *Journal of Southeast Asian Studies*, vol.15, no.1, March 1984, pp. 108–33.

Robinson, R., 'Imperial Theory as a Question of Imperialism after Empire', *Journal of Imperial and Commonwealth History*, vol.12, January 1984, pp. 42–54.

Rotter, A.J., 'The Triangular Route to Vietnam: The United States, Great Britain and Southeast Asia', *International History Review*, 1984, pp. 404–23.

Sbrega, J., 'First Catch Your Hare: Anglo-American Perspectives on Indochina during the Second World War', *Journal of Southeast Asian Studies*, vol.14, no.1, August 1984, pp. 63–78.

Sbrega, J., 'Determination Versus Drift: The Anglo-American Debate over the Trusteeship Issue 1941–5', *Pacific Historical Review*, vol.55, no.2, May 1986, pp. 256–80.

Sbrega, J., 'The Anti-Colonial Policies of Franklin D. Roosevelt: A Re-appraisal', *Political Science Quarterly*, vol.101, no.1, 1986, pp. 65–84.

Siracusa, J.M., 'The United States, Viet-Nam and the Cold War: A Re-appraisal', *Journal of Southeast Asian Studies*, 1974, pp. 82–101.

Smith, R.B., 'The Japanese Period in Indochina and the Coup of 9 March 1945', *Journal of Southeast Asian Studies*, September 1978, pp. 268–301.

Smith, T.O., 'Britain and Cambodia, September 1945–November 1946: A Reappraisal', *Diplomacy and Statecraft*, vol.17, no.1, 2006, pp. 73–91.

Smith, T.O., 'Europe, Americanization and Globalization', review article, *European History Quarterly*, vol.37, no.2, 2007, pp. 301–9.

Smith, T.O., 'Resurrecting the French Empire: British Military Aid to Vietnam 1945–7', *University of Sussex Journal of Contemporary History*, issue 11, 2007.

Soustelle, J., 'Indochina and Korea: One Front', *Foreign Affairs*, vol.29, 1950, pp. 56–66.

Spector, R., 'Allied Intelligence and Indochina 1943–45', *Pacific Historical Review*, vol.51, 1982, pp. 23–50.

Tarling, N., 'Some Rather Nebulous Capacity: Lord Killearn's Appointment in Southeast Asia', *Modern Asian Studies*, vol.20, no.3, 1986, pp. 559–600.

Tarling, N., 'The United Kingdom and the Origins of the Colombo Plan', *Journal of Commonwealth and Comparative Politics*, vol.24, part 1, 1986, pp. 3–34.

Thomas, M., 'Free France, the British Government and the Future of French Indo-China 1940–45', *Journal of Southeast Asian Studies*, vol.28, no.1, 1997, pp. 137–60.

Thompson, V., 'Regional Unity in Southeast Asia', *Pacific Affairs*, vol.21, no.2, June 1948, pp. 170–6.

Thorne, C., 'Indochina and Anglo-American Relations 1942–5', *Pacific Historical Review*, 1976, pp. 73–96.

Tinker, H., 'The Contradiction of Empire in Asia 1945–48: The Military Dimension', *Journal of Imperial and Commonwealth History*, vol.16, January 1988, pp. 218–33.

Ton That Thien., 'The Influence of Indo-China On The Evolution Of The French Union', *India Quarterly*, vol.10, part 4, 1954, pp. 295–313.

Tonnesson, S., 'The Longest Wars: Indochina 1945–75', *Journal of Peace Research*, vol.22, no.1, 1985, pp. 9–29.
Turnball, M., 'Britain and Vietnam 1948–1955', *War and Society*, vol.6, no. 2, September 1988, pp. 104–24.
Vo Nguyen Giap., 'Unforgettable Months And Years', Translated by Mai Van Elliot, data paper no.99, *Southeast Asia Program*, Department of Asian Studies, Cornell University, New York, May 1975.
Warner, G., 'The United States and Vietnam Part 1 1945–54', *International Affairs*, vol.48, no.3, July 1972, pp. 379–94.

Books

Aldrich, R., *British Intelligence, Strategy and the Cold War 1945–51*, London, 1992.
Argenlieu, G.T., d'., *Chronique D'Indochine 1945–1947*, Paris, 1985.
Bills, S., *Empire and the Cold War: The Roots of United States–Third World Antagonism*, London, 1990.
Blum, R., *Drawing the line*, New York, 1979.
Boucher De Crevecoeur, J., *La Liberation Du Laos 1945–46*, Vincennes, 1985.
Bourdain, A., *A Cook's Tour: In Search of the Perfect Meal*, London, 2001.
Bullock, A., *Ernest Bevin Foreign Secretary 1945–51*, London, 1983.
Buttinger, J., *Vietnam: A Dragon Embattled Volume 1*, London, 1967.
Buttinger, J., *Vietnam: A Dragon Embattled Volume 2*, London, 1967.
Chandler, D.P., *The Tragedy of Cambodian History: Politics, War and Revolution since 1945*, Yale, 1991.
Chandler, D.P., *A History of Cambodia*, Washington D.C., 1999.
Charlton, M. and Moncrieff, A., *Many Reasons Why: The American Involvement in Vietnam*, London, 1978.
Charmley, J., *Churchill's Grand Alliance: The Anglo-American Special Relationship 1940–57*, London, 1995.
Charmley, J., *Duff Cooper*, London, 1986.
Chen, K.C., *Vietnam and China 1938–54*, Princeton, 1969.
Colbert, E., *Southeast Asia in International Politics 1941–1956*, London, 1977.
Cruickshank, C., *SOE in the Far East*, Oxford, 1983.
Dennis, P., *Troubled Days of Peace: Mountbatten and South-East Asia Command, 1945–46*, Manchester, 1987.
Donnison, F.S.V., *British Military Administration in the Far East 1943–1946*, London, 1956.
Drachman, E.R., *United States Policy towards Vietnam 1940–45*, New Jersey, 1970.
Duiker, W.J., *China and Vietnam: The Roots of Conflict*, Berkley, 1986.
Duiker, W.J., *US Containment Policy and the Conflict in Indochina*, Stanford, 1994.
Duiker, W.J., *Vietnam: Revolution in Transition*, Boulder, 1995.
Duncanson, D., *Government and Revolution in Vietnam*, London, 1968.
Dunn, P.M., *The First Vietnam War*, London, 1985.
Eden, A., *The Memoirs of Anthony Eden, Earl of Avon: The Reckoning*, Boston, 1965, (second printing).
Epstein, L.D., *Britain: An Uneasy Ally*, Chicago, 1954.
Fall, B., *Last Reflections on a War*, New York, 1967.

Fall, B., *The Two Vietnams*, London, 1963.

Fenn, C., *Ho Chi Minh: A Biographical Introduction*, New York, 1973.

Furuta, M., 'The Indochina Communist Party's Division into Three Parties: Vietnamese Communist Policy toward Cambodia and Laos, 1948–1951', in T. Shiraishi and M. Furuta (eds), *Indochina in the 1940s and 1950s*, New York, 1992.

Gaddis, J.L., *Strategies of Containment*, New York, 1982.

Gaddis, J.L., *The United States and the Origins of the Cold War 1941–47*, New York, 1972.

Gardner, L.C., *Approaching Vietnam: From World War Two through Dienbienphu*, London, 1988.

Gardner, L.C., 'How We Lost Vietnam 1940–54', in D. Ryan and V. Pungong (eds), *The United States and Decolonization, Power and Freedom*, Basingstoke, 2000.

Gibbons, W.C., *The U.S. Government and the Vietnam War, Part 1: 1945–1960*, Princeton, 1986.

Gilbert, M., *Winston Spencer Churchill, Volume 7: The Road to Victory 1941–1945*, London, 1986.

Gilbert, M., *Winston Spencer Churchill, Volume 8: Never Despair 1945–1965*, London, 1988.

Gormly, J.L., *From Potsdam to the Cold War; Big Three Diplomacy 1945–7*, Delaware, 1990.

Gupta, P.S., *Imperialism and the British Labour Movement 1914–1965*, London, 1975.

Halifax, Lord, *Fulness of Days*, London, 1957.

Hammond, R.J., *Food and Agriculture in Britain 1939–1945*, London, 1954.

Hess, G.R., *The United States' Emergence as a Southeast Asian Power, 1940–1950*, New York, 1987.

Hesse-D'Alzon, C., *Presence Militaire Francaise En Indochine 1940–1945*, Vincennes, 1985.

Ho Chi Minh, *The Prison Diary of Ho Chi Minh*, Translated By A. Palmer, New York, 1971.

Hull, C., *The Memoirs of Cordell Hull Volume 2*, London, 1948.

Irving, R.E.M., *The First Indochina War, French and American Policy 1945–1954*, London, 1975.

Kiernan, B., *How Pol Pot Came to Power: A History of Communism in Kampuchea, 1930–75*, London, 2004.

Kimball, J., *To Reason Why: The Debate about the Causes of United States Involvement in the Vietnam War*, London, 1990.

Kissinger, H., *Diplomacy*, London, 1994.

Lacouture, J., *De Gaulle: The Rebel: 1890–1944*, London, 1993.

Lacouture, J., *De Gaulle: The Ruler: 1945–1970*, London, 1993.

Lacouture, J., *Ho Chi Minh*, Translated by Peter Wiles, London, 1968.

Lancaster, D., *The Emancipation of French Indochina*, London, 1961.

Lin Hua., 'The Chinese Occupation of Northern Vietnam 1945–1946: A reappraisal', pp. 144–169, in H. Antlov and S. Tonnesson (eds), *Imperial Policy and Southeast Asian Nationalism 1930–1957*, Surrey, 1995.

Louis, W.R., *Imperialism at Bay: The United States and the Decolonisation of the British Empire 1941–5*, New York, 1978.

Machiavelli, N., *The Prince*, London, 2003.

Marr, D.G., *Vietnam 1945: The Quest for Power*, Berkley, 1995.

McLane, C.B., *Soviet Strategies in South-East Asia*, Princeton, 1966.

Morgan, D.J., *The Official History of Colonial Development Volume 2, Developing British Colonial Resources 1945–1951*, London, 1980.

Munro, D., *The Four Horsemen: The Flames of War in the Third World*, New Jersey, 1987.

Ovendale, R., *The English Speaking Alliance*, London, 1985.

Patti, A., *Why Vietnam?* Berkley, 1980.

Reddi, V.M., *A History of the Cambodian Independence Movement 1863–1955*, Triupati, 1973.

Remme, T., *Britain and Regional Co-operation in South East Asia 1945–9*, London, 1995.

Rosie, G., *The British in Vietnam*, London, 1970.

Rotter, A.J., *The Path to Vietnam*, Cornell, 1987.

Sainsbury, K., *Churchill and Roosevelt at War: The War They Fought and the Peace They Hoped to Make*, London, 1994.

Sainteny, J., *Histoire d'une Paix Manquee: Indochine 1945–1947*, Paris, 1967.

Sainteny, J., *Ho Chi Minh and His Vietnam: A Personal Memoir*, Translated By H. Briffault, Chicago, 1972.

Saville, J., *The Politics of Continuity: British Foreign Policy and the Labour Government 1945–1946*, London, 1993.

Sbrega, J., *Anglo American Relations and Colonialism in East Asia 1941–5*, London, 1983.

Short, A., *The Origins of the Vietnam War*, London, 1989.

Sihanouk, N., *Souvenirs Doux et Amers*, Paris, 1981.

Singh, A.I., *The Limits of British Influence: South Asia and the Anglo-American Relationship 1947–56*, London 1993.

Smith, G., *American Diplomacy During the Second World War 1941–1945*, New York, 1965.

Smith, R.B., *Viet-Nam and the West*, London, 1968.

Smith, R.B., *An International History of the Vietnam War Volume 1: Revolution Versus Containment 1955–61*, London, 1983.

Sockeel-Richarte, P., 'Le Probleme De La Soverainte Francaise Sur L'Indochine', in Institut Charle De Gaulle, *General De Gaulle Et L'Indochine 1940–61*, Actes Etablis par G. Pilleul, Paris, 1982.

Spector, R.H., *The U.S. Army in Vietnam: Advice and Support: The Early Years*, Washington D.C., 1983.

Tarling, N., *Britain, Southeast Asia and the onset of the Cold War 1945–1950*, Cambridge, 1998.

Thorne, C., *Allies of a Kind: The United States, Britain and the War Against Japan, 1941–1945*, London, 1979.

Tonnesson, S., 'Filling the Vacuum: 1945 in French Indochina, the Netherlands East Indies and British Malaya', pp. 110–43, in H. Antlov and S. Tonnesson (eds), *Imperial Policy and Southeast Asian Nationalism 1930–1957*, Surrey, 1995.

Tonnesson, S., *The Vietnamese Revolution of 1945: Roosevelt, Ho Chi Minh and De Gaulle in a World at War*, London, 1991.

Vickery, M., *Kampuchea: Politics, Economics and Society*, London, 1986.

Viorst, M., *Hostile Allies: FDR and Charles De Gaulle*, New York, 1965.

Watt, D.C., *Succeeding John Bull, America in Britain's Place, 1900–1975*, Cambridge, 1984.

Windrow, M., *The Last Valley: Dien Bien Phu and the French Defeat in Vietnam*, London, 2004.

Ziegler, P., *Mountbatten*, Glasgow, 1985.

Theses

Griffiths, A.D., *Britain, the United States and French Indochina 1946–54*, MPhil Thesis, University of Manchester, 1984.

Hack, C.A., *British Strategy and Southeast Asia*, DPhil Thesis, Oxford, 1995.

Hutton, C., *A Policy of Neglect: British Diplomacy towards French Indochina 1943–45*, PhD Thesis, UEA, 1995.

Palleson, E.S., *United States Policy toward Decolonization in Asia 1945–50*, DPhil Thesis, Oxford, 1995.

Smith, T.O., *British Foreign Policy towards Vietnam 1943–1950*, PhD Thesis, UEA, 2005.

Index

CPSIA information can be obtained at www.ICGtesting.com
Printed in the USA
LVOW01*0223060114

368227LV00007B/43/P